THE JEWISH WOMAN 1900-1985
A BIBLIOGRAPHY

⊄ *Partially annotated by* AVIVA CANTOR *with 1983-1986 citations compiled by* ORA HAMELSDORF, *M.L.S. Editorial coordinator:* DORIS B. GOLD. *Editorial assistant:* JUDITH PEARL.

BIBLIO PRESS

Fresh Meadows, New York: Mcmlxxxvii

(c) Copyright 1987 by Biblio Press
(c) Copyright Aviva Cantor 1979
All Rights Reserved
LC Card 87-70090
Library of Congress Cataloging In Publication Data
Cantor, Aviva.
    The Jewish woman, 1900-1985.

    Citations to 1986 compiled by Ora Hamelsdorf.
    Bibliography: p.
    Includes index.
    1. Women, Jewish -- Bibliography. I. Hamelsdorf, Ora.
II. Title.
Z7963.J4C36   1987 [HQ1172] 016.3054'089'924 87-6627
ISBN 0-930395-04-2

Manufactured in the United States of America

Acknowledgements:
Jewish Theological Seminary Library, NYC
Blaustein Library, American Jewish Committee
Zionist Library, NYC
Jewish Women's Resource Center, NY
Lilith Magazine
Response Magazine
Thanks to Sherri L. Rice, Salome Cory, Esther Fuchs, Yael Feldman, Marcia Cohn Spiegel.

We thank the many Jewish women's organizations who responded to our call for citations from their publications, and especially to compilers to the Index to Jewish Periodicals, for the first edition of 1979 in Part I and subsequent supplements of 1981 and 1982.

THE JEWISH WOMAN: 1900-1985

BIBLIOGRAPHY
Second Edition

CONTENTS

	Part I 1st edition 1979 page	Part II 2nd edition page
Introduction .... i.		
A Note on Bibliographical Criteria/Selection .... ix.		
Corrections and Additions to Part I .... pp. 85-92		
I. JEWISH WOMEN IN HISTORY/HERSTORY		
A. Non-Fiction Books	1	94
B. Periodicals and Book Chapters	4	96
C. Fiction	8	98
II. JEWISH WOMEN IN RELIGIOUS LIFE AND LAW		
A. Non-Fiction Books	10	101
B. Periodicals and Book Chapters	12	108
III. JEWISH WOMEN IN THE UNITED STATES AND CANADA		
A. Non-Fiction Books	23	119
B. Periodicals and Book Chapters	29	127
C. Fiction	46	138
IV. JEWISH WOMEN IN ISRAEL		
A. Non-Fiction Books	53	145
B. Periodicals and Book Chapters	55	147
C. Fiction	62	153
V. JEWISH WOMEN IN OTHER COUNTRIES		
A. Non-Fiction Books	63	
B. Periodicals and Book Chapters	63	161
C. Fiction		161
VI. JEWISH WOMEN IN THE HOLOCAUST AND RESISTANCE		
A. Non-Fiction Books	65	155
B. Periodicals and Book Chapters	68	
C. Fiction	70	159

	Part I 1st edition 1979 page	Part II 2nd edition page
VII. JEWISH WOMEN IN POETRY		
A. Anthologies	72	162
B. Jewish Women Poets	73	163
VIII. Special Issues and Pamphlets	78	165*
IX. ADDENDA		
A. Unpublished Papers	80	
B. Recent Women's Conferences	81	168**
X. Studies and Surveys	83	172***
XI. Bibliographies	84	177****
Reference for Part I and II.		183
Index to Authors		188

      * Diss. Papers
    ** Bibliography Guides
  *** 1986 Books
**** 1986 Articles

Dedication

This second edition of the BIBLIOGRAPHY ON THE JEWISH WOMAN, 1900-1985, is dedicated to my two grandmothers: my mother's mother, Esther Eisengardt Freedman, who saved her husband from military induction after World War I by wrapping him head-to-foot in bandages, but who later died in her twenties in a typhoid epidemic in Dubno; and my father's mother, Malka Waxman Cantor, who helped support her melamed (teacher) husband and four sons by selling pins and needles in a corner of their one-room home. She was murdered in her 80's by the Nazis in Vizneh (Slutzk region), during World War II. Both grandmothers, whom I never met, epitomize the strong, courageous and resourceful East European Jewish woman of legend and reality.

Aviva Cantor

Introduction

THE NEED FOR A NEW EDITION of this Bibliography to encompass the abundance of materials appearing since the publication of the 1979 edition and subsequent supplements of 1981 and 1982, attests to the burgeoning growth of interest in the subject, to its increasing acceptance as a legitimate object of study and discussion, and to the phenomenal strides made by Jewish women in North America in most areas of Jewish life in the past decade and a half.

The popularity, history and demand for this Bibliography over the years also demonstrates the advance made in the study of this subject.

The Bibliography had its origin in a one-page mimeographed summer reading list requested by women for a course given by this writer at the Jewish Free High School in New York City in early 1972. The list expanded into five successive formats in response to requests by various groups, many now defunct, and by inquirers at *Lilith* magazine. When the first edition of this Bibliography was published by Biblio Press in 1979, it included more than twice as many citations for 1975-1979 as for the preceding 75 years. This second edition, which updates the first edition by including materials published between 1980 and 1985 (with "Selections of 1986"), reflects widespread discussion of the subject of the Jewish woman, and its expansion into the realm of books and mainstream publications, as well as in Jewish periodicals.

This growth of interest in and acceptance of the subject results from, and at the same time, influences the progress of Jewish feminism in North America. Within a mere 15 years, the status of Jewish feminism has evolved from being considered an alien threat or an oddball joke, to a serious controversial issue, or even a *fait accompli*. While a mosaic of progress (actually more like a crazy quilt) prevails, nowhere in North America is Jewish feminism considered a joke. This is progress, and much of the credit for it must go to the printed word, a phenomenon that Jews apparently cannot resist, no matter how they feel about a particular issue.

In point of fact, the most popular activity of Jewish feminists thus far has been that of the written word, as contrasted with meetings, conferences or speak-outs, or creating alternative institutions such as day-care centers, or engaging in street theater, or '60's style confrontations with the power structure -- all of which in my opinion are necessary, but such is not the view of the majority of Jewish women. The movement, if it is indeed such, has been characterized by its lack of fire and ire, as well as by an absence of strategy, organizing and direction. Its successes, therefore, are all the more amazing and remarkable.

Despite the lack of a stated agenda and strategy, there is slowly emerging a kind of consensus on priorities among Jewish feminists via the written exchange of views by the movement's recognized leaders, all of them writers, scholars and/or rabbis. It is a small group and everyone is known on a first-name basis, though contact is sporadic and discussions few and far between. This, in an era in which high-tech communication and cross-country travel have become commonplace, is also remarkable. It attests once again to the Jewish belief in the power of the written word.

This belief is a Jewish cultural characteristic, and Jewish history is replete with illustrations of the respect for this power: the story of the Torah accepted at Sinai and the scrolls carried by the people during their dispersions; the rededication of the Temple during Josiah's reign because of the scroll of Deuteronomy "discovered" there; the acrimonious battles over the works of Maimonides whose feverish temperature made the medieval Jewish-Christian disputations seem cool by comparison; the Kabbalistic (Jewish mystical) concept that the very letters of the Torah contained the secret of redemption if they could only be rescrambled into the right combinations.

It is perhaps no wonder, then, that Jewish feminists turned to words rather than to action, to persuade, convince and recruit others to their cause. This is not to say that non-Jewish feminists did and do not also use words for these purposes; they did and do -- discussions concerning sexist language are proof. But non-Jewish feminists also engage in physical activity such as political lobbying and staffing rape-crisis centers. Many Jewish women within the general feminist movement participate in these actions; Jewish women who consider themselves "Jewish feminists" do not; they write.

Thus, Jewish feminists have relied almost exclusively on the power of words as their surrogate, their champion, their advocate. They send out their writing like Noah sent forth the dove from the Ark, hoping it will bring back a conciliatory olive branch. The reliance on and belief in the power of the word -- that if words cannot do it in Jewish life, nothing can -- the assumption that those who read words will respect them, reflects a deep faith and a fear of rejection at one and the same time.

In terms of achieving what were widely regarded as goals in the early stages of Jewish feminism, words were indeed a powerful tool. These goals were mainly in the area of religion -- and the section on Religious Life and Law in this bibliography correspondingly contains the largest number of citations. This is the area which has been addressed most by Jewish feminists in the early period, 1970 to 1979, which stimulated in 1980 the publication of a companion bibliography, "Jewish Women and Jewish Law," by Biblio Press; and also within the period of 1980-1985 represented by the Second Edition of this work in Part II.

The issues, however, have changed over the course of the past 16 years, from what Paula Hyman terms "equal access" (full participation in all areas of religious life) to the "feminization of culture" (new ways of behavior and expression emphasizing gender differences and their celebration). The works listed in the first and second editions reflect this evolution.

The majority of writings by Jewish feminists in the early period deal with the justice of different aspects of equal access -- women in the minyan (quorum of worshippers), being called to an aliyah of the Torah, women's ordination -- both in terms of feminist ethics and of Jewish survival.

The content and number of counter-arguments of the early period indicate how threatening was equal access. The venomously anti-female pseudo-psychological arguments posed by Mortimer Ostow and Richard Yellin served as excellent consciousness-raising tools for women who had thought their case so convincing as to engender instant agreement. Gradually, a body of apologetica by Orthodox scholars has emerged in the current period, replacing the diatribes by Orthodox rabbis, and encomiums by Orthodox women (some newly hatched) on the wonders of their lifestyle, arguments which were common in the earlier period.

Such writings expressed the fear that if women were to have equal access in religious life they would overwhelm the men and cause them to flee, a view propounded by such neo-conservatives as Ruth Wisse and Lucy Davidowicz. This argument was a recycling of the anti-Semitic myth of the powerful aggressive Jew "taking over." It demonstrated the persistence of such myths, their internalization by self-hating Jews, and their projection onto the female gender, a phenomenon which occurs in many individual Jewish male-female relationships and is described in the ethnotherapy works of Judith Klein and Esther Perel listed in the citations.

As Reform, and to a lesser degree Conservative synagogues were integrated (the Reform and Reconstructionist movements were always theoretically in favor of equality), it became clear that women were not "taking over" and propelling men away. Thus the great fear abated and with it the writings promoting such paranoia. At the same time many Jewish feminists began to claim that feminism actually draws more people into religious life, as indeed it has.

Another issue which launched many articles, was that of the struggle for women's ordination in the Conservative movement, with its many pro and con arguments covered in the press. When, after much soul-searching and political maneuvering, the Jewish Theological Seminary finally decided to ordain women, there were few cries of jubilation or triumph, perhaps because Jewish feminists, aside from writing on the subject, had done little else to midwife the decision.

Parallel to the growth of Jewish feminism after 1967 -- the watershed dating the onset of the Jewish cultural renaissance -- was the growth of the "Bal Teshuvah" (returnees to the faith) movement, the embracing of Orthodoxy by young, assimilated and often Yuppie types who "had it all" and who had found their materialistic existence alienating. These neo-Orthodox, however, have not tended to bring any egalitarian views they may have harbored into their reconstituted lives. On the contrary, they accepted the tenet that Orthodoxy in all its aspects is the only authentic Judaism.

Still, Orthodox women have been much influenced by feminism. In the past five to six years, they have begun to organize *tefillah* (prayer) groups, encountering hostility from some rabbis and support from others. The issue of get (Jewish legal divorce) has become the main issue which Orthodox women are confronting. While male rabbis continue to write about the need for reform, little has been accomplished in either American or Israeli halachic circles.

The only equal access issue which Orthodox women were and continue to be concerned with is education, and during this period, opportunities for religious education of women expanded. For example, Yeshiva University's Stern College for Women has finally permitted its students to study Gemara (commentary on the Mishnah, which, together with it, constitutes the Talmud). Private schools, such as Drisha in New York, have featured it in their curriculum.

Discussion of equal access seemed to peak with the publication of Cynthia Ozick's germinal "A Vindication of the Rights of Jewish Women" in *Lilith* in 1979. That equal access has ceased to be a burning issue among Jewish feminists can be seen from the paucity of writings on this subject in the later period. With the equality of access issue moving toward resolution (and implementation slowly following) and with only the Orthodox remaining obdurately opposed, Jewish feminists turned their attention to discussing "what have we gotten equal access to?" A series of groundbreaking pieces on this subject appeared one after another; Rachel Adler (1983) and Judith Plaskow (1986) who questioned whether women are included in the Covenant. Plaskow and Annette Daum, in a 1980 interview in *Lilith* asked how far is "too far" in reforming Judaism, and whether "going too far" will propel Jewish feminists out of their religion -- as has happened with some Christian feminists.

As in the general women's movement, the questions among Jewish feminists now pertain to the "feminization of culture," i.e., as women enter religious life, should they, rather than adopt or emulate pre-existing male substance and styles of expression, create their own? Should women fit into Jewish religious life and behave as Jews have always done (a question which occasioned the debate among women rabbinical students at the Jewish Theological Seminary as to whether or not to wear a *kipa*, (traditional male head covering?) Or should women consider their gender differences to be positive and celebrate rather than minimize them? If yes, is this authentic Judaism? Could this be achieved within patriarchal Judaism? What does viewing God as patriarchal mean? Could Judaism be non-patriarchal?

The tendency to celebrate difference rather than deny it, indicates a level of confidence and sense of strength among Jewish feminists. As Albert Memmi once observed, the oppressed tend to deny difference because the oppressor argues that difference means inferiority and justifies oppression. As Rabbi Amy Eilberg stated in a 1985 interview in *Lilith*, it was only after equal access was a fact that women could begin to explore and celebrate their gender differences.

Many Jewish feminists, in search of spiritual expression hitherto denied them, have occupied themselves with creating new rituals and non-sexist liturgies; this has, in fact, become a Jewish feminist "cottage industry." The trend began in the early 1970's with the writing of alternative feminist *haggadot* (Passover seders) and birth ceremonies to mark a baby girl's entry into the Covenant -- long before the issue of whether women are Covenanted arose. These writings were greatly encouraged by the rise of the Havurah (small self-led prayer and study group) movement; Jewish feminists, in turn, had an important influence on this evolving movement, although some conflicts remain to be resolved.

The birth ceremonies were first collected and published by Toby Reifman of Ezrat Nashim (the first Jewish feminist group) in 1978. Writing them has become so popular that Shalom Bat ceremonies are even accepted in modern Orthodox circles. The next phase was the writing of new Bar and Bat Mitzvah and wedding ceremonies, rituals for Rosh Hodesh (the new moon; which some Jewish women see as a quintessentially female expression) and marking women's life cycles with rituals at the time of menarche and menopause. Nina Cardin collected some of these ceremonies for the Jewish Women's Resource Center of NY in 1978, while others were published earlier by Arlene Agus in *Response* and other sources. Later, more were written and published by the Women's Institute for Continuing Jewish Education in San Diego; in 1986 a collection by Penina V. Adelman, *Miriam's Well: Rituals for Jewish Women Around the Year* came from Biblio Press. This went hand in hand with the reappropriation of mikvah (post-menstrual ritual immersion). At first rejected by many Jewish feminists as degrading and insulting (a view still held by Israeli feminists), *mikvah* has now become, in Rabbi Elyse Goldstein's words, a "taking back of the waters." It is now non-Orthodox women who evince ecstasy and exhilaration over mikvah, while Orthodox women accept this obligation without being carried away by the experience.

Another "cottage industry" has been the writing of *midrashim* -- often fanciful stories about Biblical characters and events that have been written in every period of history, linking present experiences with a past point of view. Possibly in response to the interest in midrash, *Tsena-Urena*, the collection of legends in Yiddish compiled for the use of women in Eastern Europe, is now available in a three-volume English translation.

What is interesting to observe about books and articles on Jewish religion and law in both the early and later periods of Jewish feminism, is the increase in serious scholarly and popular books about *halacha* -- the body of Jewish law which has served as the "constitution" of the Jewish people's "government in exile" for over 2000 years, and the decrease in the number of writings about how to reform it.

In the earlier period, there were Jewish feminists who believed that equality of access to religious education would enable Jewish feminists to become religious arbiters (scholars who make decisions on Jewish law which become part of *halacha*) and that their assumption of such roles would lead to necessary reforms. While 130 women have become rabbis, their interest in religious arbitration is nil, as is their interest in *halachic* reform -- which is signalled by a decrease in such writings. Dr. Trude Weiss-Rosmarin, one of the pioneer Jewish feminists whose *Jewish Spectator* stood squarely for halachic reform long before most present-day Jewish feminists were born, still believes this is the key issue. But with the exception of Weiss-Rosmarin and Orthodox feminist Blu Greenberg, few Jewish feminists seem to be interested in the issue. Greenberg's article on how to change *halacha*, published in Lilith's premiere issue in 1976 stands alone. Meanwhile, the Orthodox establishment in North America and even more so in Israel, has become more intransigent and opposed to change -- any change.

Still, the area of religion and law is the only one in which the promise of the works of the earlier period has borne fruit in the later period. Earlier, the publication of Christian feminist Leonard Swidler's *Women in Judaism* (1976) as well as in the same year, Elizabeth Koltun's *The Jewish Woman: New Perspectives* (expanded from the 1973 Response Magazine anthology which she edited and which included essays on history, Israel and women in North America) appeared. The later period saw the publication of Rosalyn Lacks' *Women and Judaism, Myth History and Struggle* (1980), Blu Greenberg's *Women and Judaism: A View from Tradition* (1982), Rachel Biale's *Women and Jewish Law* (1984), and in the realm of spirituality, Susannah Heschel's anthology *On Being a Jewish Feminist* (1983).

Unfortunately, in most other areas covered by this Bibliography -- History, U.S. and Canada, Holocaust and Resistance -- the few pioneering works of an earlier period have not, with one exception, spawned, inspired or been followed by major works since 1980.

Jewish women's history remains a weak area, and much of what has been included in this section, as well as in that on U.S. and Canada, is in the form of biography and autobiography, many of them reprints. Mark Wischnitzer's Jewish Crafts and Guilds (1967), an important source of information on Jewish working women in pre-modern Europe, has not been followed up with any important book on this subject. Much work remains to be done on the role of Jewish women in pre-modern European domestic economy. Unlike the non-Jewish peasant and noblewoman, Jewish women in Western medieval Europe were primarily urban. Did they weave cloth, make candles and soap and heal the sick (as did Rebecca in *Ivanhoe*)? Nor has Shlomo Noble's fascinating monograph on "The Jewish Woman in Medieval Martyrology" (1971) stimulated works on Jewish women's communal roles in various historical eras, nor is there any study of Sephardic women in this connection. (Sephardic and Yemenite women in Israel today, however, have been the subject of doctoral theses soon to be published; one to appear in England in 1987.)

Marion Kaplan's excellent study of "The Jewish Feminist Movement in Germany (1979) stands alone in scholarship on European Jewish women. (Edward Bristow's *Prostitution and Prejudice: The Fight Against White Slavery*, 1983, which covers some of the same ground, is marred by Bristow's sexist point of view and shows a critical need for Jewish feminist scholarship generally.)

The publication of *The Jewish Woman in America* by Charlotte Baum, Paula Hyman and Sonya Michel (1975) was a milestone -- the first Jewish feminist history on the subject -- but one which did not trigger an explosion of scholarship on the lives of Jewish women in the USA. The only "follow-up" of this work, which dealt with portraits of women in literature of the post-immigrant period, is contained in two critical essays cited on the portrayal of Jewish women in America literature -- Marc Lee Raphael's in 1981 and Evelyn Avery's in 1986 -- and Norma Fain Pratt's excellent article on Yiddish women writers (1980).

While it is true that women's history is largely oral, and documentation of Jewish history is not as plentiful as general history -- many primary sources disappeared or were destroyed during Jewish wanderings and persecutions -- there seems to be an insufficient attempt to explore sources that do exist.

Primary among them is the *halacha* itself, including the vast body of Responsa literature (questions submitted to the religious arbiters and their subsequent legal decisions). The role of *halacha* in shaping both the character and the culture of the Jewish people until modern times cannot be underestimated and remains to be explored by feminists. It is also a primary source on attitudes, behavior, customs, and daily life. No body of Jewish feminist scholarship has arisen to explore Jewish law from this perspective, and it remains virgin territory. I. Epstein's study, *Women in the Responsa Literature* (1934), reprinted in the 1973 *Response* anthology, which demonstrates how *halachic* changes were made as women's economic power arose, stands alone. With *Responsa* literature now computerized and accessible at Bar Ilan University and via libraries linked to it, this mother lode appears fairly easy to mine.

Israeli feminists are only now beginning to research the history of women in pre-State Israel and their contemporary sociology, but little is available in English translation. The main sources in this area are Ada Maimon's classic *Women Build a Land* translated into English in 1962, and *The Plough Woman*, published in 1932 with a paper edition in 1975. Several monographs have appeared on women in pre-state Israel, including that of Shulamit Reinharz, a sociologist who has researched Manya Shochat, a pioneer and activist in the Hashomer (defense) movement credited with co-founding the first collective settlement at Sejera. (Biblio Press will publish next year an English translation of the Shochat biography by Rahel Yanait Ben Zvi.) Nor has there been any book since 1980 comparable to Lesley Hazleton's *Israel Women: The Reality Behind the Myth* (1978), now out of print.

In most sections except Religious Life and Law, biographies have been included, in the belief that women's lives constitute a prime source of material and are part of our as yet unwritten history.

In only one area has there been a veritable explosion of autobiography -- Holocaust and Resistance. Literally dozens of testimonies have emerged during recent years, joining those earlier published, including Ruth Kluger's inspiring work *The Last Escape* (1973) -- which should be made into a film as was the moving novel *Angry Harvest*. Memoirs of the ghetto resistance penned by the late Zivia Lubetkin have also been published here recently in English, and those of Chaika Grossman are expected in 1987. Several local Jewish communities are engaged in collecting oral histories from Holocaust survivors, and many have already been taped at Yale, the University of Wisconsin and the American Jewish Committee. Still, there are few biographies -- notable for its absence is that of Regina Jonas, ordained in 1935, who perished after deportation from Theresienstadt.

Two important recent works in this area are *Vera Laska's Women in the Resistance and the Holocaust* (1983) and the proceedings of the conference on women in the Holocaust organized by Joan Ringelheim issued by the Institute for Research on History in 1984. The conference raised questions about women's experiences in the ghettos, concentration camps and forest partisan units which need answers through serious research and interviews with survivors before this generation disappears.

In other sections, biographical gleanings are somewhat skimpy. Recent ones of note include Ellen Umansky's on Lily Montagu, two interesting works on Emma Goldman, and one on Rose Schneiderman. Biographies by relatives, hopefully inaugurating a trend, include Kim Chernin's deeply moving story of her Communist mother, *In My Mother's House* (1985) and Lawrence Bush's equally affecting fictionalized biography of his Communist grandmother, *Bessie* (1984). These join earlier biographical works: Taitz and Henry's *Written Out of History* (1978 and 1980) and Joan Dash's excellent Henrietta Szold biography *Summoned to Jerusalem* (1979). The autobiographies of Elizabeth Stern (pseud. Leah Morton), Harriet Levy, Maud Nathan and Mary Antin, among others, have now been reprinted, but the late Yuri Suhl's biography of Ernestine Rose (1959) is still out of print. And while Anzia Yezierska's novels and stories are being reissued, there is still no book-length biography of the immigrant author, though she is a favorite subject for scholarly dissertations.

Three interesting collections of autobiographical materials have appeared since 1980; Julia Wolf Mazow's *The Woman Who Lost Her Names* also includes fiction, is currently out of print and needs to be reissued. Evelyn Torton Beck's *Nice Jewish Girls: A Lesbian Anthology* was reissued in 1985 by Crossing Press. In this collection, of note are the many essays that concern anti-Semitism in the women's and lesbian movement -- an issue addressed elsewhere by one of the landmark articles of this period, Letty Cottin Pogrebin's essay in *Ms.* magazine in 1982. Another fine anthology, *The Tribe of Dina*, edited by Kaye/Kantrowitz and Klepfisz, was published in 1986.

While in an earlier period the novel form was more favored as the vehicle for portraying the lives of women now increasingly conveyed through biography and memoir; since 1980, more Jewish women novelists and short fiction writers have appeared on the scene to challenge the male monopoly in depicting American Jewish life. The works of Schaeffer, Jong, Ozick, Broner, Paley, Greenberg, Markus, Rosen, Epstein, Rapoport, Goldstein and Tax, among others, are now exploring this territory, especially in the short story. Themes now emerging in fiction are mother-daughter relations, sibling rivalry, the influence of fathers on daughter's aspirations, and lesbian awakenings. Women's writing of fiction, however, is still largely fixated either on the family epic of immigrant struggle, its success and angst, or on the post-divorce search for self.

The Jewish family saga, found in recent popular fiction by Belva Plain and others, lacks Jewish feminist viewpoint. A remarkable exception is Rivington Street by *Meredith Tax* (1982), which is permeated with strong radical and Jewish feminist consciousness. One yearns for good historical fiction about Jewish women; its paucity points to the general lack of sufficient historical material available, or of willingness by authors to engage in research, despite the increase in serious scholarship by Jewish women in the universities. On the plus side, writers Marge Piercy (author of the feminist blockbuster, *Small Changes*, 1973), and Rosellen Brown, are both reported working on novels about Jews set in the past.

The post-divorce search-for-fulfillment type of novel, a feminist *bildungsroman* (the 19th century saga of a young man's coming of age), tends to feature women whose Jewishness is even more marginal than that of the "fourth child" at the Passover seder. None of the recent works of fiction by Jewish women seem to have the dramatic quality and intense Jewish identity struggle of Herman Wouk's anti-feminist *Marjorie Morningstar* (1955) which influenced a generation of women. As the subject of the Jewish woman becomes more "mainstreamed" into Jewish and general periodicals, one hopes that the ferment generated may one day be channeled into a Great American Jewish Feminist Novel.

By far the greatest lack is of studies -- social, political or analytical -- concerning the communal lives of Jewish women in North America (and for that matter, Israel, Europe and Latin America). There is little serious reportage or scholarship on this aspect of Jewish women's lives, an absence which is shocking and incomprehensible.

Little of a sociological nature has been written on North American Jewish women since the first edition of this work, on the germinal level of "Portnoy's Mother's Complaint," i.e., a study by Pauline Bart of middle-aged Jewish women facing the empty nest (1970), Mary Cahn Schwartz's "The High Price of Failure" in low-income families (1976), and the late Barbara Myerhoff's classic on the elderly, *Number Our Days* (1978). And while the Jewish mother (and the Jewish American Princess) continues to be exploited by stand-up comics and greeting card companies, no serious feminist work has been expounded on these myths since Ruth Adler's analysis of "The Real Jewish Mother" (1977). While there have been some studies by Jewish organizations and social work professionals on various aspects of the Jewish family, as yet there is no book-length sociological or anthropological composite portrait of Jewish women in the work force, their family relationships, the changes they have made in their lives because of the women's movement. Nor have there been book-length studies on women in the Havurah or Sephardic communities, elderly women, lesbians, women rabbis and their congregations' response to them. The only exception is the pilot study, *The Political Life of American Jewish Women* (1980) from Biblio Press, and Judith Klein's pioneering work on ethnotherapy, published in 1982 as a pamphlet by the America Jewish Committee.

Even fewer are essays on the position of women in the Jewish communal power structure: three -- by Doris Gold, Paula Hyman and this writer -- have appeared since 1976, three in the pages of *Lilith* and one each in *Present Tense* and *Congress Monthly*. But there has been no serious book-length investigative report, let alone, sociological analysis of the major coed or women-only groups in the community and the volunteer phenomenon as a whole. While a few studies of advances made in local communities and by Federations have been published as pamphlets, there is no serious work about women's roles in the major fundraising/disbursing structures which dominate the Jewish community. Even critiques on the lack of democracy in it are few and far between. Why, one might ask, was it so much easier to demand equal access to religious life but not to the communal power structure? Is it because the secular community, and especially its philanthropic apparatus, is where the real power lies? Is it because equal access to positions of power in the communal structure means little as long as the structure itself, in the words of Ann Wolfe, is "etched in stone"?

The one bright spot here was the publication of Susan Weidman Schneider's *Jewish and Female: Choices and Changes in Our Lives Today*, published in 1984. This 640-page work covers every area of Jewish women's lives and struggles. The book outlines the problems in each area and reports on solutions and resolutions offered, providing a huge resource "yellow pages" section at the end.

It is instructive and distressing to juxtapose that compendium, with its wealth of information on virtually every activity in which Jewish women are involved, with Charles Silberman's widely reviewed *A Certain People* (1986) which allocates only 5 1/2 pages out of 366 of text to Jewish feminism. While that book's research is generally sloppy and its approach anecdotal, there is simply no excuse for sloughing over what the author himself calls "the most important source of Jewish renewal."

This points to the question of timing, of what educator Irene Fine, in an essay in *Lilith* (1979) called for: the "mainstreaming" of Jewish women's experiences and history into general works. In some instances "mainstreaming" has worked well, i.e., Harriet and Fred Rochlin's *Pioneer Jews: A New Life in the Far West*

(1984). But it must be remembered that a prerequisite for this process is unearthing the data later to be "mainstreamed."

While much has been accomplished by the Jewish feminist movement in creating interest in Jewish women's lives and history and expanding their choices, serious work remains to be done to provide the information and social thought that is necessary for the consolidation of fundamental change. If there are huge gaps in subjects that call for research, there is a virtual chasm in theoretical formulation, which seems practically non-existent. By citing these specific gaps we hope to stimulate further research and new publication on Jewish women. Oral history with mothers, grandmothers, aunts, neighbors and the elderly at home and in custodial care should certainly continue to go forward as well. It is not inconceivable that with the increase in serious scholarship, a Jewish Women Studies discipline will be created, which, will in turn further enhance this field. We do not consider it utopian to envision a Chair and a central archive in Jewish Women Studies at a major university!

We can draw inspiration and strength from our achievement of the past fifteen years. In a little more than a decade and a half, Jewish feminists have created out of almost nothing what is perhaps the most important challenge to Jewish life since the Zionist movement. Jewish feminism has within it the possibility of transforming all of Jewish life and of releasing into it creativity dormant for hundreds of years. The very existence of this Bibliography and the works cited in it demonstrate the change that has already occurred. The next stage will appear more difficult; issues that will need to be confronted are more fundamental. But the foundation is now laid for building a new house, brick by brick, in which the Jewish people can live and flourish.

A Note on Bibliographical Criteria and Selection

MY AIM IN COMPILING THIS BIBLIOGRAPHY was to provide as complete a listing as was possible, of citations both useful and accessible to scholars, students, members of informal study groups, and those in search of information on the subject of Jewish women.

By useful I mean works that offer information about Jewish women -- their past and present history; also the views of the educated and the ignorant opposition to growing Jewish woman consciousness. (There comments are marked: "know the enemy.") By "accessible" I refer to works in English available in a good public or university library or specialized collection, of books from trade publishers, Judaica presses, organizations, as well as alternative or small presses.

The ideological problems faced in compiling the Bibliography's second edition continued from the first edition published in 1979, reprinted here. For example, there is still the age-old question: What constitutes Jewish writing and especially "Jewish women's writing": should works by Jewish women be included if they do not focus primarily on women? This choice arose in confronting the "family epic" form in fiction. There we decided to err on the side of inclusion rather than exclusion if a main character was a Jewish woman. We also asked: should a work by a Jewish woman be cited if it contained little or no Jewish or Jewish women's content? The decision was no in regard to non-fiction (i.e., general feminist essays) but yes when a specific work was biography or fiction, since the absence of Jewish content or its marginality revealed something important about the life of the subject portrayed (in the case of biography) or the author (in the case of fiction). I acknowledge that some selections or omissions may appear arbitrary and welcome reader response.

A second and thornier question concerned selection of categories in which to place various works, both because of natural overlap (immigrant chronicles, for example, stretch from Eastern Europe to North America), and because many issues impinge in Jewish women's lives and problems. Six categories were therefore designed, four of which combine history and geography with the sixth, Religion and Law. The section on History includes all citations except where such history involves North America, Israel, or the Holocaust and Resistance, which are separate. That of Women in Other Countries does not include history; only modern description or narration. I placed biographies and autobiographies in the appropriate six categories, because it seemed to me that such accounts are related to our unwritten history and sociology.

The Religion and Law section includes theoretical writings as well as pro and con arguments on various aspects of that topic. Reports of action in combatting inequity were included there if a given essay dealt with issues rather than action. If the opposite was true, it is listed under North America (where most activity has occurred). When issues or activity primarily pertains to Israel, it will be found in that section.

Attention is called to a change in placement of chapters in books in the second edition. In the first edition, chapters were listed in periodicals sub-sections, as if they were short articles. In the second edition they are grouped with Books. This makes it easier to retrieve when working in a library.

The user should definitely note "Corrections and Additions to the First Edition" which later came to light, mainly via readers, and because citations of 1980 (formerly in various supplements issued after 1979) are now part of the 1980-1985 Bibliography in Part II of this work.

To Miriam Hipsh (M.H. in annotations) and Shebar Windstone (S.W.) and others who assisted in updating the first edition, and those contributing to the preparation of the second edition, as well as to my patient and farsighted coordinating editor, Doris B. Gold of Biblio Press, I extend appreciation and thanks.

Aviva Cantor

I. <u>HISTORY/HERSTORY</u>*

A. <u>Books: Non-fiction</u>**

Adler, Ruth Pomerance: <u>Women of the Shtetl: Through the Eyes of Y.L. Peretz</u>. New Jersey: Fairleigh Dickinson University Press, 1980.

> A socio-psychological and socio-historical study of Jewish women of the East European Shtetl as they were perceived by Yiddish author Isaac Leib Peretz.

Antin, Mary: <u>The Promised Land</u>. Boston: Houghton-Mifflin. Sentry paperback, 1969 (Rept.).

> Autobiography of Russian woman immigrant from Plotsk, Poland, originally published in 1912.

Arendt, Hannah: <u>Rahel Varnhagen</u>. Harcourt, 1974.

> Biography of German-Jewish 19th-century intellectual "Salon Jewess." (See Rivlin review.)

Bakan, David: <u>And They Took Themselves Wives: The Emergence of Patriarchy in Western Civilization</u>. Harper & Row, 1979.

Chagall, Bella: <u>Burning Lights</u>. Schocken, 1946. Also paper.

> Autobiography.

Chesler, Phyllis: <u>About Men</u>. Morrow, 1978.

> Includes material on the Bible and Judaism. Powerful work showing how patriarchy perpetuates itself.

Davis, Elizabeth Gould: <u>The First Sex</u>. Putnam, 1971.

> Interesting thesis, but sloppy research and bias in relation to Torah make its authenticity questionable.

Edinger, Dora: <u>Bertha Pappenheim, Freud's Anna O</u>. Highland Park, Ill.: Cong. Solel, 1968.

> Mostly letters of this founder of German-Jewish women's organization in 1920.

---

*For historical works on the Jewish Woman in America, in Israel and in the Holocaust and Resistance, see those sections.

**Includes biography and autobiography.

Fink, Greta: *Great Jewish Women: Profiles of Courageous Women from the Maccabean Period to the Present.* Menorah Publishing, 1978.

Freeman, Lucy: *The Story of Anna O.* Walker, 1972.
> Biography of Bertha Pappenheim, especially important for information on condition of Jewish women in the late 19th century. Last section where Freeman "analyzes" Pappenheim is gratuitously insulting and extremely sexist.

Gary, Romain: *Promise at Dawn.* Harper & Row, 1961. Also paperback.
> Devoted, offbeat but self-sacrificing Russian mother raises him to be famous.

Gittelman, Sol: *From Shtetl to Suburbia: The Family in Jewish Literature and Imagination.* Boston: Beacon Press, 1978.
> Good on attitudes to women.

Gluckl of Hameln, Life of, Written by Herself. Th. Yoseloff, 1962, Schocken, pap. 1977.
> Diary of 44-year-old German-Jewish widow and businesswoman, begun in 1690.

Gray, Bettyanne: *Marya's Story.* Lerner/Bobbs Merrill, 1978.

Gross, David C.: *Pride of Our People: Stories of 100 Outstanding Jewish Men and Women.* Doubleday, 1979.
> Out of 100 sketches, only 14 are of women. Many errors, indicating poor editing and/or research.

Guggenheim, Peggy: *Out of This Century: Confessions of an Art Addict.* London: Andre Deutsch, 1980.

Heller, Celia S.: *On the Edge of Destruction: Jews of Poland Between the Two World Wars.* Columbia University Press, 1977.
> Some material on women.

Henry, Sondra and Taitz, Emily: *Written Out of History.* Bloch, 1978.
> Accounts of unknown (to us) women from ancient times through 19th century. Based on secondary sources.

Kaminska, Ida: *My Life, My Theatre.* Macmillan, 1973.

Kaminska, Ruth Turkow: *I Don't Want To Be Brave Anymore.* New Republic Books, 1978.

Kaplan, Marian A.: The Jewish Feminist Movement in Germany: The Campaigns of the Judischer Frauenbund, 1904-38. Westport, Ct.: Greenwood Press, 1979.

An important contribution to Jewish women's literature.

Kapp, Yvonne: Eleanor Marx, 2 volumes, International 1973 and 1977.

Klein, Carole: Aline. Warner, 1980.

Biographical account of Aline Bernstein, Jewish stage designer, who was the lover of Thomas Wolfe, American writer.

Kobler, Franz: Her Children Call Her Blessed. Stephen Daye Press, 1955.

Sentimentalized biographies of Jewish mothers of famous men.

LaZebnik, Edith: Such a Life. Morrow, 1978.

Author's autobiography of her youth in a Czarist Shtetl and cities of the Jewish Pale. Reveals the terror of everyday life; and the raw courage of women and men in those circumstances.

Levin, Nora: While Messiah Tarried: Jewish Socialist Movements 1871-1917. Schocken Books, 1977.

Lowenthal, Marvin: Henrietta Szold, Life and Letters. Westport, Ct.: Greenwood Press. (Rept.)

Pesotta, Rose: Days of Our Lives. Boston: Excelsior, 1958.

Description of author's childhood in the Pale of Czarist Russia.

Remy, Nahida: The Jewish Woman. Bloch Publishing Co., 1915.

This out of print work is an indispensable source book. [S.W.]

Richardson, Joanna: Sarah Bernhardt and Her World. London: Weidenfeld and Nicolson, 1977.

Rosmarin, Trude: Jewish Women Through the Ages. Pamphlet, 1940.

A publication of the Jewish Spectator, edited by the author.

Roth, Cecil. Dona Gracia of the House of Nasi. Phila.: Jewish Publication Society, 1974.

Rubin, Ruth: Voices of a People: The Story of Yiddish Folksong. McGraw-Hill, 1973.

The book on Yiddish folksong; contains much material on lives of women around the world from the 14th through the 20th centuries. Rubin has argued elsewhere that folksong is primarily a vehicle of women's expression and this text strongly supports that argument. (Also see her Treasury of Jewish Folksongs, Schocken, pap. 1976.) [S.W.]

Shcharansky, Avital with Ben-Josef, Ilana: <u>Next Year in Jerusalem</u>. Translated from the Russian by Stefani Hoffman. William Morrow, 1979.

Scheppes, David: <u>Remarkable Women of Scriptures</u>. Phila.: Dorrance & Company, 1976.

> Biblical women, from Eve to Judith, and their relationship to Hebrew culture.

Wischnitzer, Mark: <u>A History of Jewish Crafts</u>. Jonathan David, 1967.

> Tantalizing references to trades and professions of Jewish women from Second Temple period through 19th century. Inadequate index.

Yezierska, Anzia: <u>Red Ribbon on a White Horse</u>. Persea Books, 1981 (Rept.).

> Anzia Yezierska's autobiography—originally published in 1950 and long out of print.

Zbrowski, Karl and Herzog, Elizabeth: <u>Life Is with People, The Culture of the Shtetl</u>. University Press, 1952, also Schocken pap.

> Sentimentalized anthropology of Eastern Europe on Shtetl, 50 years after the fact. Should not be regarded as holy writ.

Zunser, Miriam Shomer: <u>Yesterday</u>. Harper & Row, 1978.

> Reprint of 1939 edition, Leider, Emily, ed. Perceptive and informed portrait of three generations of an Orthodox family in Pinsk during Czarist times.

B. <u>Periodicals and Book Chapters</u>

Adler, Ruth: "The Real Jewish Mother," <u>Midstream</u>, October 1977.

> Theorizes that American Jewish mother stereotype is not the derivative of the Shtetl "Yiddish Mameh" but rather its antithesis.

Axelrod, Albert S.: "Remembering Shifra and Purah," <u>Sh'ma</u>, October 13, 1978.

Brownmiller, Susan: <u>Against Our Will</u>. Simon & Schuster, 1975. Also pap.

> In this pioneering study of rape, a portion of chapter four (riots, pogroms and Nazism) reveals part of our history that has been ignored until now. [M.H.]

Cantor, Aviva: "The Lilith Question," <u>Lilith</u>, vol. I, no. 3.

> Analyzes condition of Jewish women throughout history and reasons behind Lilith story.

Cantor, Aviva: "The Oppression of the Jewish Woman," JSP feature in
ORT Reporter, September/October 1972.

Analysis of historic role of Jewish women.

_____: "The Real Story of Esther," Off Our Backs, March, 1972.

Analysis of role Jewish women have played in exile.

David, Jay, ed.: Growing Up Jewish. Pocket Books/Simon & Schuster, 1970.

Includes autobiographical essays by Rebekah Kohut, Anne Frank, Edna Ferber, Yael Dayan and others.

Duckat, Walter: "The Jewish Working Woman," Hadassah, September, 1971.

Fascinating account of occupations of Jewish women through the ages. Offprint available from author, c/o Jewish Occupational Council.

Engel, Barbara Alpern and Rosenthal, Clifford N.: Five Sisters—Women Against the Tsar. Schocken, 1977. Also pap.

Some are Jews.

Epstein, I.: "Women in the Responsa Literature." In vol. 3 of Jewish Library, Jewish Library Publishing Co., 1934.

Fascinating clues on connections between economic power of women and rights to observe certain rituals. (See also Responsa Anthology.)

Florence, Ronald: Marx's Daughters. Dial, 1975.

Heartbreaking accounts of life and work of Eleanor Marx, Rosa Luxemburg and Angelica Balabanoff.

Friedman, Joni: "Miriam the Prophetess: A Feminist Perspective." In Philadelphia Jewish Exponent, Friday Forum, April 26, 1974.

Friedman, Mordecai A.: "Termination of the Marriage Upon the Wife's Request: A Palestinian Ketubah Stipulation." Proceedings of the American Academy of Jewish Research, vol. 37, 1969.

Goitein, Solomon: "Jewish Women in the Middle Ages," Hadassah, 1973.

Picture of medieval Jewish life in Islamic countries, gleaned mostly from women's letters.

Grant, Annette: "Bertha Pappenheim Alias Anna O," Ms. magazine, September, 1974.

Complete picture of Pappenheim's productive, charitable life and accomplishments.

Hill, Melvyn A., ed.: <u>Hannah Arendt: The Recovery of the Public World</u>. St. Martin's Press, 1980.

> A dozen essays on the ideas and career of Hannah Arendt (1906-75), one of this century's most original thinkers, plus a symposium in which she participated and a bibliography of her publications, some of relevance to Jewish women. The topics, discussed by specialists who make no attempt at popularization, include the nature of politics, of community, of totalitarianism, of Marxism and of violence and revolution.

Kaplan, Marion A.: "German-Jewish Feminism in the Twentieth Century," <u>Journal of Jewish Social Studies</u>, Winter, 1976.

> Brief biography of Bertha Pappenheim, founder of the Movement, plus the organization's history.

Liptzin, Sol: "Princess Hagar," <u>Dor-Le-Dor</u>, World Bible Society, Jerusalem, vol. VIII, no. 3, Spring 1980, pp. 114-126.

_____: "Abishag the Shu Nammite," <u>Dor-Le-Dor</u>, World Bible Society, Jerusalem, vol. VII, no. 4.

_____: "Rehabilitation of Lilith,: <u>Dor-Le-Dor</u>, World Bible Society, Jerusalem.

Marcus, Jacob Rader: <u>The Jew in the Medieval World</u>. Atheneum, 1974.

> Several sections on the Jewish woman.

May, Antoinette: <u>Different Drummers—They Did What They Wanted</u>. Millbrae, Ca.: Les Femmes.

> Includes a chapter about Sarah Bernhardt.

Meyer, Michael: <u>Origins of the Modern Jew</u>. Wayne State Univ. Press, 1968.

> See chapter on Salon Jewesses.

Noble, Shlomo: "The Jewish Woman in Medieval Martyrology." In <u>Studies in Jewish Bibliography, History and Literature in Honor of I. Edward Kiev</u>. Ktav, 1971.

> Historical research on crucial role played by Jewish women during the era of Crusades and forced conversions in Middle Ages.

Polt, Harriet: "American Girl: A Memoir," <u>Moment</u>, March 1980.

Porter, Jack Nusan: "Rosa Sonneschein and the 'American Jewess' Revisited: New Historical Information on an Early American Zionist/Jewish Feminist," <u>American Jewish Archives</u>, vol. XXXII, no. 2, November 1980, pp. 125-131.

> Fascinating account of a forerunner of modern <u>Lilith</u> magazine.

_____: "The American Jewess," <u>American Jewish History</u>, Waltham, Mass., September 1978.

> Story of Rosa Sonneschein's short-lived 19th-century newspaper. Worth noting.

Rabinowicz, Harry M.: "Lady Rabbis and Rabbinic Daughters." In <u>The World of Hassidim</u>, Hartmore House, 1970, pp. 202-210.

    Fascinating and footnoted.

Rakowski, Puah: "A Mind of My Own," In <u>The Golden Tradition</u>, Davidowicz, Lucy, ed. Holt, Rinehart, 1967.

    Autobiography of Zionist leader.

Riesman, D.: "Exemplary Women Leave Mark on Jewish History." In <u>Israel Digest</u>, August 24, 1979.

Ribalow, Harold U.: "Susan Fromberg Schaeffer." In <u>The Tie that Binds: Conversations with Jewish Writers</u>. A.S. Barnes, 1980.

Rivlin, Lily: "The Futility of Assimilation: Hannah Arendt's Rahel Varnhagen," <u>Ms.</u>, February 1975.

    Powerful review of (op cit.) biography of this "Salon Jewess" showing the consequence of "personalizing oppression rather than politicizing it."

Rosen, Norma: "Simone Weil: Saint or Bigot," <u>Ms.</u>, September 1975.

    Thought-provoking and insightful review of <u>Simone Weil: A Life</u> and <u>The Simone Weil Reader</u>. Raises important questions about Weil's self-hatred as a Jew.

Rosenberg, Janet: "From Patriarchy to Partnership—The Evolution of the Jewish Woman," <u>Journal of Jewish Communal Service</u>, vol. 55, Summer 1979.

Ross, Elaine: "The Jewish Woman and Her Heritage," <u>Reconstructionist</u>, June 1975.

    Cites many examples of Biblical and cultural oppression of Jewish women.

Schneier, Sarah: "Mother of the Beth Jacob Schools." In <u>The Golden Tradition</u>, Davidowicz, L., ed., op cit.

Schwartz, Mary Cahn: "Beating Patriarchy at Its Own Game," <u>Lilith</u>, vol. I, no. 2.

    Rebekah as quintessential example of how women function under patriarchy.

Seller, Maxine S.: "Reclaiming Jewish Herstory," <u>Lilith</u>, no. 7, 1981, pp. 23-26.

    How to include material on women in an American Jewish history survey course.

Swidler, Leonard: "Beruriah—Her Word Became Law," <u>Lilith</u>, vol. I, no. 3.
    The only woman taken seriously in/by the Talmud.

_____: "Women and Torah in Judaism," <u>Conservative Judaism</u>.
    Discussion of relationship of women in the Torah during Talmudic period.

Wall, Susan: "The Forgotten Woman in Jewish History," Phila.: <u>Jewish Exponent</u>, May 24, 1974.

C. Fiction

Aguilar, Grace: <u>The Vale of Cedars.</u> Max N. Malsel, N.d.
    Jewish woman in 15th-century Spain.

Andrews, Gini: <u>Esther: The Star and the Sceptre.</u> Zondervan Pub.
    A novel based on the story behind the feast of Purim.

Baron, Dvora: <u>The Thorny Path.</u> Jerusalem: Universities Press, 1969.
    Short stories set in the Shtetl period often feature strong women struggling with the conditions of their lives.

Bedford, Sybille: <u>A Legacy.</u> Meridian, NY, 1960.
    Fictionalized family history of intermarried Germany family with some strong women characters.

Berman, Hannah: <u>Melutouna: A Novel.</u> Arno Press, 1979.
    Jewish life in the 19th century—Poland. Concerns a woodcutter and his daughter Zelda. Reprint, originally published in 1913.

Durrell, Lawrence: <u>The Alexandria Quartet.</u> E.P. Dutton, 1961, pap.
    The ultimate novel about a Jewish woman in pre-war Alexandria.

Goldworth, Bella. <u>Across the Border.</u> YKUF, 1971
    Sentimental, old-fashioned but still moving short stories mostly about pre-Holocaust Europe. See especially "New Days."

Grade, Chaim: <u>The Agunah.</u> Twayne, 1974 (transl. from Yiddish).
    A woman's husband vanished in WWI and her suitor tries to have her released from Agunah status.

Gross, Joel: <u>The Books of Rachel</u>. Seaview Books, 1979.

>A Jewish family in the diamond industry passes an heirloom gem from one Rachel to another Rachel in each generation. Each Rachel suffers at the hands of Anti-Semites from Spanish inquisitors to the Nazis.

Halporn, Louise: "The Dowry," <u>Hadassah</u>, April 1974.

>Young American Jewish woman who marries Viennese in 1920's experiences social pressures of family.

High, Monique: <u>Four Winds of Heaven</u>. Delacorte, 1980.

>A wealthy and prominent Jewish family in Russia copes with the tumult of the 1917 Revolution and its aftermath. Based on the diaries of the author's grandmother.

Powers, Anne: <u>Rachel</u>. Pinnacle, 1973, pap.

>Fictionalized biography of great French-Jewish actress.

Rosenstein, Harriet: "The Fraychie Story," <u>Ms.</u>, March 1974.

>Story of Eastern European family.

Schneider, Nina: <u>The Woman Who Lived in a Prologue</u>. Boston: Houghton-Mifflin, 1980.

>A woman in her seventies recounts her life, beginning as an upper class immigrant early in the century. She regrets having been pushed into traditional female roles without knowing enough to object; now she is ready to live her life for herself.

Segal, Brenda Lesley: <u>The Tenth Measure: An Epic Novel of Love and Heroism in Ancient Judea</u>. St. Martins, 1980.

>An epic novel of love and heroism in Ancient Judea.

Singer, Isaac B.: "Yentl the Yeshiva Boy."

>Young woman disguises herself as boy to study in Yeshiva. In writer's <u>Short Friday</u> collection.

_____: "Zeitel and Rickel." In his collection <u>The Seance</u>, Farrar, Straus, 1968.

>Story of two lesbians; one rich, one poor in the Shtetl.

Wolfenstein, Martha: <u>Idylls of the Gass</u>. Macmillan, 1903.

>While this novel tends to focus on grandson, Maryam is one of the strongest and wisest grandmothers in Jewish fiction. [S.W.]

II. RELIGIOUS LIFE AND LAW*

A. Books: Non-fiction, including biography

Broner, E.M. and Nimrod, Naomi: The Stolen Legacy. Helen Merrill Agency, Reprinted, Ms., April 1977.

A Pesach seder for women.

Christ, Carol P. and Plaskow, Judith: Womanspirit Rising: A Feminist Reader in Religion. Harper & Row, 1980.

A collection of twenty-four essays which includes work of Jewish women.

Falk, Ze'ev: Jewish Matrimonial Law in the Middle Ages. Oxford University Press, 1966.

Feldman, David M.: Marital Relations, Birth Control and Abortion in Jewish Law. NYU Press, 1969; also Schocken, 1974, pap.

The authoritative work on birth control and abortion from Bible through Talmud and Responsa literature.

Goldenberg, Naomi R.: Feminism and the End of Traditional Religions. Boston: Beacon Press, 1979.

Goldin, Grace: Come Under the Wings: A Midrash on Ruth. Phila.: Jewish Publication Society.

Paperbound reprint.

Gruen, Louise M.: The Transformation of a Sophisticate. Privately published, 1960s.

Autobiographical account of how author became religious.

James, Janet Wilson: Women in American Religion. Phila.: Univ. of Pennsylvania Press, 1980.

Essays exploring the elements common to women in both church and temple. One essay surveys women's changing place in Judaism.

Klagsbrun, Francine: Voices of Wisdom: Jewish Ideals and Ethics for Everyday Living. Pantheon, 1980.

This anthology contains some material on Jewish women.

---

*Many of the citations in this section are included, by permission, in Jewish Women and Jewish Law, by Ora Hamelsdorf and Sandra Adelsberg, Biblio Press, 1980.

Latham, Judy: <u>Women in the Bible: Helpful Friends</u>. Broadman, 1979.

<u>Maimonides, Code of: The Book of Women</u>. Klein, Isaac, tr. New Haven and London: Yale University Press, 1972. (Vol. 19 in Yale Judaica series.)

Important source book on law regarding marriage, divorce, halitzah, rape and "adulterous women." Footnoted.

Mann, Denise Berg: The Woman in Judaism. Jonathan Publications,* 1979.

This introductory pamphlet frequently over-simplifies and even ignores problems. Not feminist, but mostly fair and well written.

Meiselman, Moshe: <u>The Jewish Woman in Jewish Law</u>. Ktav, 1979.

Defensive, arrogant, condescending and anti-feminist. Know the enemy.

Moskin, Marietta D.: <u>In the Name of God: Religion in Everyday Life</u>. Atheneum, 1980.

The author explores how religions have affected governments, the arts, attitudes toward sex and women, etc.

Neusner, Jacob: <u>A History of the Mishnaic Law of Women; Part One, Yebamot</u>. Translation and explanation, Brill, 1980.

Patai, Raphael: The Hebrew Goddess. Ktav, 1967. Revised, Avon, 1978, pap.

Traces female component of Godhead from earliest times through the Kabbalah. Germinal.

Priesand, Sally: <u>Judaism and the New Woman</u>. Behrman House, 1975, pap.

By our first rabbi. Introductory work, Reform bias.

Reifman, Toby Fishman: <u>Blessing the Birth of a Daughter—Jewish Naming Ceremonies for Girls</u>. Englewood, NJ: Ezrat Nashim, 1978. (Pamphlet.)

New birth ceremonies to welcome our daughters into the Covenant.

Ross, Bette M. <u>Song of Deborah</u>. Fleming H. Revell, 1981.

Fictionalized reconstruction of events in Judges IV and V celebrating Deborah as a prophet and judge.

Roth, Joel: <u>On the Ordination of Women as Rabbis</u>. Jewish Theological Seminary of America, 1980.

Ruether, Rosemary and McLaughlin, Eleanor, eds.: <u>Women of Spirit: Female Leadership in the Jewish and Christian Traditions</u>. Simon & Schuster, 1979.

Swidler, Leonard: <u>Women in Judaism: The Status of Women in Formative Judaism</u>. Metuchen, NJ: Scarecrow Press, 1976.

> Social status of Jewish women in Talmudic era. Important resource book.

B. Periodicals and Book Chapters

Adler, Rachel: "The Jew Who Wasn't There," <u>Davka</u>,* Summer, 1971.

> Classic and germinal article. (Also see her piece in <u>Lilith</u>, vol. I, no. 2.)

_____: "Full Participation in Jewish Life," <u>Face to Face</u>, Anti-Defamation League, Inter-Religious Bulletin. Spring 1979.

> Excerpt from address to Interfaith National Conference on "Feminism, Religious Tradition and the Future." Denver, Colorado, February 1978.

Bell, Roselyn: "Blessing the New Moon," <u>Network</u>, vol. 10, no. 2, April 1978.

Berkovits, Eliezer: <u>Crisis and Faith</u>. Sanhedrin Press, 1976.

> Essays on contemporary Jewish society, including women.

Berman, Saul: "The Status of Women in Halachic Judaism," <u>Tradition</u>, Fall 1973.

Bernstein, Michal: "Woman Rabbi," <u>Present Tense</u>, Summer 1979.

> Above is reply in response to letter from M.R. Rubin.

Bird, Phyllis: "Images of Women in the Old Testament." In <u>Essays in Religion and Sexism</u>, Reuther, Rosemary R., ed. Simon & Schuster, 1974.

Birnbaum, Martha Rock: "An Affirmative Action Plan for Reconstructionists," <u>Reconstructionist</u>, September 22, 1972.

> Suggestions for implementing equality.

Bleich, David J.: "Women on Synagogue Boards," <u>Tradition</u>, Spring 1976.

> Uses halachic argument to limit women's participation.

Bob, Ellen Sharon: "Women: How Much Has Changed?" Boston: Genesis 21, February 1980.

Brown University: "Judaism Is Not for Men Only." Brown Alumni Monthly, February 1975.

    About Brown University women's minyan. (Also see Lilith, vol. I, no. 4.)

Cantor, Aviva: A Jewish Women's Haggadah. Excerpted in Sister Celebrations. Phila.: Fortress Press, 1974 and in Koltun anthology (op cit.).

Cardin, Nina: "The J.T.S. Women's Hakafah, Symbolic Event," Sh'ma, October 1976.

    Discusses religious ceremonies for women as well as ceremonies which are not gender-linked.

Chernick, Michael: "The Halachic Process—Growth and Change," Sh'ma, April 1976.

    A small section on new women's rituals in which author says that as long as women's rituals and liturgies contribute, and do not violate any Torah or rabbinic prohibition, they will not be opposed but it will take time.

Clamar, Aphrodite: "Torah True and Feminist Too: A Psychotherapist's View of the Conflict between Orthodox Judaism and the Women's Movement," Journal of Jewish Communal Service, no. 4, 1980, pp. 297-300.

Cohen, Ida Selavan: "Women of Valor," and "Women Rabbis, A Short List." In The Jewish Almanac, Siegel Richard and Rheins, Carl, eds. Bantam, 1980, pp. 40-46.

    Useful lists and information. Rabbis named does not include 1980/81. It should be noted that the Almanac does not have a section on Jewish feminism, but under the "Religious Connection" includes "Feminine Imagery in Judaism" and a section on women's devotional prayers.

Corcoran, Martha: Women and Religion. Boston: Beacon Press, 1964.

    Sections II and III deal with women in the Torah. Interesting and provocative, worth reading.

Davidowicz, Lucy: "Women in Shul." In The Jewish Presence: Essays in Identity and History. Holt, Rinehart & Winston, 1977.

    Essay is vehemently anti-feminist. See review by Susannah Heschel, Lilith, no. 5, Spring 1979.

Feldman, David M.: "Women's Role and Jewish Law," Conservative Judaism, Summer 1972.

Freedman, Nina: "When Jewish Women Come of Age," Sh'ma, February, 1976.

    Recommends ceremony of Tevilah for girls to link Jewish identity with the passage to womanhood.

Friedman, Reena Sigman: "How Was This Passover Different from Other Passovers?" Lilith, vol. I, no. 3.

    New Seder ceremonies by and for women.

_____: "The Politics of Ordination," Lilith, no. 6, 1979.

    Major investigatory report on Conservative movement's debate, beginning with establishment of Commission on women's ordination, to summer, 1979.

Furstenberg, Rochelle: "Women Return to Tradition: From Gurus to Gemara," Hadassah, January 1978.

Ganz-Ribner, Mindy: "Observance Despite Reservations," Sh'ma, January 9, 1980.

    One young woman's statement about her observance of "Family Purity."

Geller, Laura: "The Sexism Is Worse than the Metaphors," Sh'ma, March 1975.

_____: "Mikveh Is Not a Viable Mitzvah for Me," Sh'ma, January 9, 1980.

Gellis, Audrey: "The View from the Back of the Shul," Ms., July, 1974.

Gendler, Mary: "Male and Female Created He Them," Jewish Heritage, Winter 1972.

_____: Untitled article in symposium in Response,* vol. 4, no. 4, Winter 1970-71. Also Porter, Jack N. and Dreier, Peter: Jewish Radicalism: A Selected Anthology. Grove Press, 1973, also pap.

Gittelsohn, Roland B.: "Women's Liberation and Judaism," Midstream, October 1971.

    Mostly apologetics, and from a "liberal" rabbi, too.

Gordis, Robert: "Abortion: Major Wrong or Basic Right?" Midstream, March 1978.

    Opposes abortion on demand as "diminishing God's image" but favors therapeutic abortion.

_____: "Women's Rights in Jewish Life and Law," United Synagogue Review, April 1977.

Gordon, Martin L.: "Childbirth, A Covenantal Experience," Sh'ma, April 1976.

>A man writes about birth—his arrogance, ignorance and contempt for women seem boundless. [M.H.]

Gottlieb, Lynn: "It's Called a Calling: An Interview with Rabbi Lynn Gottlieb," Moment, May 1979.

Gould, Shirley: "Woman at the Torah," Reconstructionist, vol. XLV, no. 3, May 1979.

>Social worker asks to be a Gabbai in the synagogue; succeeds on two occasions. This is a report of the first time.

Greenberg, Blu: "Feminism: Is It Good for the Jews?" Hadassah, April 1976.

_____: "Integrating Mikveh and Modernity," Sh'ma, January 9, 1980.

_____: "Jewish Feminism on the Move," Face to Face, Op cit.

_____: "Jewish Divorce Law," Lilith, vol. I, no. 3.

>Authoritative analysis of its direction and development.

_____: "Jewish Women—Perspective in History," JSPS, February 1973.

>Address to 1st Jewish Women's Conference.

_____: "Recent Literature on Jewish Women," Jewish Book Annual, 1977, Jewish Book Council.

_____: "Women's Liberation and Jewish Law," Lilith, vol. I, no. 1.

>Excellent, explains how Halacha (Jewish Law) works and what reforms for women can and should be made.

Greenberg, Blu and Irving: "Equality in Judaism," Hadassah, December 1973.

>Discusses problems forthrightly.

Gross, Rita: "Female God Language in a Jewish Context," Womanspirit Rising, Christ, Carol P. and Plaskow, Judith, eds. Harper & Row, 1979.

Grossman, Roz: "Rebbetzin Reviews Rebbetzin," Moment, May 1978.

Handelman, Shanah Sara: "The Jewish Woman . . . Three Steps Behind?" Nefesh, vol. 2, no. 1, 1978.

> Powerful argument against materialistic life styles of American Jewish woman (she believes feminists only are prone to this) and for Lubavitch approach. But why accept the entire package? Despite her brilliant apologetics, enabling is enabling. When Lubavitch changes its roles for women, let us know. [M.H.]

Hauptman, Judith: "Woman and Change in Jewish Law." Conservative Judaism, Fall 1974.

_____: "Women in the Talmud." In Religion and Sexism, Simon & Schuster, 1974.

_____: "Women's Liberation in the Talmudic Period: An Assessment." Conservative Judaism, Summer 1972.

Haut, Irwin H.: "A Problem in Jewish Divorce Law: An Analysis and Some Suggestions," Tradition, Spring 1977.

Hyman, Paula E.: "Jewish Theology: What's in It For and Against Us," Ms., July 1974.

_____: "The Other Half: Women in the Jewish Tradition," Conservative Judaism, Summer 1972.

Ibn Ezra, Yakkov: "The Mitzvot and the Disciples of Miriam," Ari,* April 1974.

Janowitz, Naomi and Wenig, Maggie: "Selections from a Prayerbook Where God's Image Is Female," Lilith, vol. I, no. 4.

Johnson, George E." Halacha and Women's Liberation," Midstream, January 1974.

Kamen, Marcia: "Wednesday the Rabbi Called at My Divorce," Ms., January 1974.

Kaplan, Arlene M.: "I Never Thought I Could Be a Rabbi," The Feminist Bulletin, October 1978.

> Interview with Hebrew Union College rabbinical student, Helene Ferris.

Kaplan, Joseph C.: Discussing Niddah, Mikveh, Family Purity," Sh'ma, January 9, 1980.

Kaplan, Sharon and Joseph: "Innovation within Halacha for Daughters," Sh'ma, April 1976.

Koehler, Joan: "On the Liberation of Becoming Jewish," Sh'ma, November 5, 1971.

>On her conversion.

Koltun, Elizabeth: "Can I Be a Scholar or a Saint if They Let Me?" Jewish Student Press Service, March 1973.

Laiman, Leah: "Feminism and Judaism: Uneasy Lies the Present," Times of Israel, January 1974.

Leifer, Daniel L.: "Birth Rituals and Jewish Daughters," Sh'ma, February 1976.

Lerner, Anne Lapidus: "In Second Place," Present Tense, Summer 1979.

>A review of Jewish Women in Jewish Law by Moshe Meiselman.

Levinthal, I.H.: "Women as Conservative Rabbis," Jewish Spectator, Summer 1979.

Lipman, Eugene: "Women's Lib and Jewish Tradition," Jewish Heritage, Winter 1971-72.

>Apologetics.

Margolis, Daniel and Patty: "Birth Ceremonies," Second Jewish Catalogue, Strassfeld, Michael and Sharon, eds. Phila.: Jewish Publication Society, 1976.

>Unfortunately, this material contains provisions for preventing the historical Lilith from harming infants. Ignore this, if you can.

Meiselman, Moshe: "Women and Judaism: A Rejoinder," Tradition, Fall 1975.

>A bit of convoluted logic—he would meet feminists' demands—not by changing values or laws, but by educating men and women. [M.H.]

Neudel, Marian: "Being Female, Jewish and Observant," Sh'ma, April 1976.

Neusner, Jacob: "From Scripture to Mishnah: The Origins of Mishnah's Division of Women," Journal of Jewish Studies, vol. 30, Fall 1979, pp. 138-153.

>Debunks some myths about limitations on women.

"Non-Jewish Spouses to Be Welcomed as Full Members in Many Reform Synagogues," The Jewish Week-American Examiner, October 5, 1980.

Ofseyer, Jordan: "Why Not Women as Conservative Rabbis?" United Synagogue Review, Fall, 1976.

Ostow, Mortimer: "Women and Change in Jewish Law," *Conservative Judaism*, Fall, 1974.

> Of all sexist rationalizations for keeping women out of pulpit and off the bima, this one is the most nauseating. Author, who directs the JTS pastoral counseling training program and is psychoanalytically oriented, insults women by saying that if women become active in religious life, men will become impotent—and worse. Great for CR, especially for women who think things are not so bad. Know the super-enemy.

Pfeffer, Leo: "Abortion and Religious Freedom," *Congress Monthly*, June 1976.

> From statement submitted to House Sub-Committee on Civil and Constitutional Rights on how religious attitudes hide under cloak of morality.

_____: "Feminism and Judaism," *Congress Monthly*, June 1975.

Phillips, Melanie: "Blessed Art Thou . . . Who Hath Not Made Me a Woman," *Mosaic*, no. 28.

Plaskow, Judith and Daum, Annette: "Feminists and Faith—A Dialogue at the Brink of the Abyss," *Lilith*, no. 7, 1980.

> Two religious feminists discuss Christian feminist anti-Semitism, pioneering work by Christian feminists and what Jewish and Christian feminists have to learn from each other.

Pogrebin, Letty Cottin: "Barefoot in Shul," *Moment*, September 1976.

> Herstory of non-traditional congregation in Saltaire, Fire Island N.Y. written by the reader of the prayer service.

Porter, Judith R. and Albert, Alexa A.: "Subculture or Assimilation? A Cross-Cultural Analysis of Religion and Women's Role," *Journal for the Scientific Study of Religion*, 16C4, 1977.

Poupko, Chana K. and Wohlgelernter, Devora L.: "Women's Liberation—An Orthodox Response," *Tradition*, Spring 1976.

Prell-Foldes, Riv-Ellen: "Coming of Age in Kelton—The Constraints on Gender Symbolism in Jewish Ritual." In *Women in Ritual and Symbolic Roles*, Hoch-Smith, Judith and Spring, Anita, eds. Plenum Press, 1978.

> Deals with the minyan, planning "redressive ritual," and ritual events.

Rackman, Emanuel: Series of three articles on Jewish women and Jewish Law in *Jewish Week*, November 18, 1971, November 25, 1971 and March 2, 1972.

> First two have interesting data, although apologetic, third is insulting and led to protest letters.

Resnick, Elaine: "Tradition and Society," *Ari*,* April 1974.

Rivlin, Lily: "Lilith," *Ms.*, December 1972.

> Re-write of the story, with happy ending.

Roberts, Hyman J.: "Societal Risks in Sex Preselection with Emphasis upon Jewish Perspectives," *Analysis*, published by Institute for Jewish Policy Planning and Research of the Synagogue Council of America," December 1980.

> Includes study resources from Jewish thought by Rabbi J. David Bleich, with study guide questions by Dr. Jenna Weissman Joselit.

Rotenberg, Mark: "The Buck Stops at the Seminary: Should Women Be Admitted to the Rabbinate?" *Moment*, May 1979.

Routtenberg, Max: "One in a Minyan," *Hadassah*, April 1972.

> Men in a shul at first resist then accept a young woman saying kaddish for her mother.

Rubin, Jane: Letter. In *Sh'ma*, March 5, 1971.

Sacks, Bracha: "Why I Chose Orthodoxy," *Ms.*, July 1974.

> Subtle apologetics, but must be noted.

Sasso, Sandy Eisenberg: Untitled address on women and Judaism using the Book of Ruth as jumping-off point.

> Given at 66th annual meeting of American Jewish Committee. Author is Reconstructionist rabbi.

Schneider, Ilene: "Abortion and Jewish Law," *Reconstructionist*, June 1974.

> A summary of sources from traditional to modern on the subject.

Schnek, F.: "Roundtable Discussion: Women and Jewish Law Today," *Israel Digest*, August 24, 1978.

Schwartz, Helene E.: *Justice by the Book: Aspects of Jewish and American Criminal Law*, Women's League for Conservative Judaism, 1976. (Pamphlet.)

> Comparison of the two legal systems; some material on women.

Selden, Ruth R.: "Women in the Synagogue: A Congregant's View," Conservative Judaism, Winter 1979.

> A discussion of practical issues.

Sh'ma: Debate on Women's Ordination, For: Sarah Lieberman (9/164) and Seymour Siegel (9/166); Against: Pinchas Stolper (9/179) and David Novak (9/166).

_____: Discussions on Women and Halacha, nos. 63, 67, 70 and 76; letters on this subject, March 14, 1971 and November 5, 1971.

_____: Symposium on sex and marriage, by various men. October 8, 1971.

_____: Three pieces on abortion—all written by men. Levy, Richard N., Novak, David, and Leiman, Sid Z. December 9, 1977.

_____: Three more abortion articles—all written by men. Leiman, Sid Z., Borowitz, Eugene, and Siegel, Seymour. December 23, 1977.

Shulman, Gail B.: "View from the Back of the Synagogue: Women in Judaism," paper in Sexism, Religion and Women in the Church: No More Silence. Hageman, Alice L., ed. Association Press, 1974.

Siegel, Rachel: "The Jew as a Woman," The Jewish Spectator, Winter 1977.

Singer, Sholom: "The Jewish Woman and Her Heritage," Reconstructionist, October 1974.

> Generally sympathetic; makes points not made elsewhere.

Smith, Betsy Covington: Breakthrough—Women in Religion, Walker & Co., 1978.

> Chapter on Rabbi Sandy Sasso is a biographical sketch. Heavy on the personal; light on political aspects.

Spero, Moshe Halevi: "Negativism and Feminism," Jewish Life, July 1973.

_____: "Psychiatric Hazard in the Halachic Disposition toward Birth Control and Abortion: The Role of the Caseworker," Journal of Jewish Communal Service, Winter 1976.

> Defines "psychiatric hazard" as it would be applied to dispensation of abortion and birth control decisions for the Orthodox.

_____: "Were Women Created Unequal?" Jewish Life, Winter 1974.

> This must be read to be believed: super-subtle sexist rationalization. Know the enemy.

Stone, Amy: "Gentleman's Agreement at the [Jewish Theological] Seminary," *Lilith*, vol. I, no. 3.

Exhaustively researched expose of JTS's refusal to train female rabbis.

Trible, Phyllis: "Depatriarchalizing in Biblical Interpretation," *Journal of the American Academy of Religion*, XLI (1973), pp. 30-48.

Tucker, G.: "Female Rabbis," *Jewish Spectator*. Fall 1979.

Umansky, Ellen: "From the Reform Movement to Contemporary Religious Feminism." In *Women of Spirit: Female Leadership in the Jewish and Christian Traditions*. Reuther, Rosemary and McLaughlin, Eleanor, eds. Simon & Schuster, 1979.

A general overview of women's ordination through May 1977. Good on unknown women, but strangely omits Regina Jonas.

Weiner, Greta: "The Mourning Minyan," *Lilith*, no. 7, 1980, pp. 27-28.

Two sisters try to say Kaddish for their mother in traditional styles. Essay on omission of women in mourning rituals is followed by one by Cohen, Sybil: "Over My Dead Body," with another view concerning the kind of prayer to be used. The prayer for women at funerals and how it denigrates women [A. Cantor].

Weissman, Deborah: "Towards a Feminist Critique of Judaism," *Congress Bi-weekly* (now called *Congress Monthly*), November 24, 1972.

Weiss-Rosmarin, Trude: "Sexist Language," *Jewish Spectator*, Spring 1975.

Wants "linguistic sexism" abolished but is comfortable with God, the father [M.H.].

_____: "The Plight of the Chained Wife [aguna]," *Jerusalem Post*, October 8, 1971. Offprint available from author.

_____: "The Unfreedom of the Jewish Woman," *Jewish Spectator*, October 1970. Offprint from author.

Excellent on divorce.

Wisse, Ruth R.: "Women as Conservative Rabbis?" *Commentary*, October 1979.

Anti-feminist attack on Rabbinical Assembly Commission recommendation on ordaining women as rabbis. Know the enemy.

Wolpin, Nisson: "Jewish Women in a Torah Society," *Jewish Observer*, Agudath Israel of America. November/December 1974, vol. VX, no. 5-6, pp. 12-18.

The role of Orthodox women and the challenge of women's liberation to Jewish "femininity."

Women's League Outlook: "How Law Changes," Fall 1972.
"Menstrual Taboos and Aliyot for Women," Fall 1973.
"Women in the Minyan," Fall 1974.
"Alternative Services," Summer 1977.
"Position of Women," December 1977.
"Change and the Changeless," December 1978.
"Ordination of Women," Summer 1979.

These articles show the traditional woman's view of the subjects named.

Wyschogrod, Edith: "Shall We Use Masculine Metaphors for God?" Sh'ma, March 1974.

Yaffe, Richard: "Women Under Jewish Law," Council Woman, April 1966.

Excellent; includes interviews with Orthodox rabbis.

Yellen, Richard M.: "A Philosophy of Jewish Masculinity: One Interpretation," Conservative Judaism, Winter 1979.

According to the author, rabbis must be male because they symbolize a Jewish masculine mystique that is family—rather than "success oriented." Pitiful pseudo-psychology showing how threatened some men are. Excellent for c.r.—know the enemy.

III. IN U.S.A. AND CANADA

A. Books: Non-fiction*

Adler, Polly: A House Is Not a Home, Rinehart Co., 1953. Also pap.

Angoff, Charles: Emma Lazarus: Poet, Jewish, Activist, Pioneer Zionist. Jewish Historical Society of New York, 1979.

    American Jewish historian, Morris U. Schappes, in review, October 1979. Jewish Currents, found this pamphlet inaccurate in several respects.

Badt-Strauss, Bertha: White Fire: The Biography of Jessie Sampter, Reconstructionist Press, 1956.

Baum, Charlotte, Hyman, Paula, and Michel, Sonya: The Jewish Woman in America. Dial Press, 1976; also New American Library, 1977, pap.

    Traces and analyzes the historical, socio-cultural background of American Jewish women. Excellent, key resource book. Bibliography.

Beck, Evelyn Torton, ed.: The Jewish Lesbian Anthology. Persephone Press, 1982.

    Forthcoming collection which explores the interconnections of Judaism and lesbianism.

Berkman, Ted: The Lady and the Law: The Remarkable Life of Fanny Holtzman. Boston: Little Brown, 1974.

Bloch, Irvin: Neighbor to the World. World, 1969.

    Biography of Lillian Wald.

Byer, Etta: Transplanted People. Chicago: privately published, 1955.

    Autobiography includes noteworthy description of how women work a double day while men sit around talking about how to improve the world [S.W.].

Cantor, Milton and Laurie, Bruce, eds.: Class, Sex and the Woman Worker. Westport, CT: Greenwood Press, 1977.

    Includes "Organizing the Unorganizable: Three Jewish Women and their Union," about ILGWU organizers Newman, Cohn and Pesotta.

Cohen, Rose: Out of the Shadow. Doran, 1918.

    Author describes her childhood in small Russian village and girlhood in poverty in New York as well as the toll which work in sweatshops took on her health.

---

*Includes biography and autobiography.

Dash, Jean: <u>Summoned to Jerusalem: The Life of Henrietta Szold</u>. Harper & Row, 1979.

> Detailed, documented, honest and moving biography of Szold. Highly recommended.

Davidson, Sara: <u>Loose Change: Three Women of the Sixties</u>. Doubleday, 1977.

> Traces lives of three women from '60s Berkeley into '70s: an artist, a reporter and a political activist, all marginally Jewish.

Drinnon, Richard: <u>Rebel in Paradise: A Biography of Emma Goldman</u>, University of Chicago Press, 1961.

Drinnon, Richard and Drinnon, Anna Maria: <u>Nowhere at Home: Letters from Exile of Emma Goldman and Alexander Berkman</u>. Schocken Books, 1975.

Epstein, Perle: <u>Pilgrimage: Adventures of a Wandering Jew</u>. Boston: Houghton-Mifflin, 1979.

> Journey through Eastern disciplines back to Judaism.

Ferber, Edna: <u>A Peculiar Treasure</u>. Garden City Pub. Co., 1940.

> Includes much discussion of her being Jewish in the predominantly Christian environment where she grew up.

Fineman, Irving: <u>Woman of Valor—Life of Henrietta Szold</u>. Simon & Schuster, 1961.

> Sad, revealing and good for C.R.

Fisher, Florence: <u>The Search for Anna Fisher</u>. Fawcett Crest, 1973, pap.

> Moving story of adoptee who searches for her birth parents.

Ganz, Marie with Ferber, Nat J.: <u>Rebels</u>. Dodd, Mead, 1920.

> Autobiography of young Jewish anarchist who becomes a patriot during WWI; good up to that point.

Glanz, Rudolf: <u>The Jewish Woman in America: Two Female Immigrant Generations, 1820-1829</u>. Vol. 1: <u>The Eastern European Jewish Woman</u>. Vol. 2: <u>The German Jewish Woman</u>. Ktav Publishing House, 1976, 1977 respectively.

Goldberg, Steven: <u>The Inevitability of Patriarchy</u>. Morrow, 1973.

Goldman, Emma: <u>Living My Life</u>. 2 volumes. Dover, 1971, pap.

> Inspiring.

Goldstein, Alvin H.: <u>The Unquiet Death of Julius and Ethel Rosenberg</u>. Lawrence Hill, 1975.

Gordon, Barbara: *I'm Dancing as Fast as I Can.* Morrow, 1979.

Gornick, Vivian: *In Search of Ali Mahmoud.* Saturday Review Press/Dutton, 1973. Also pap.

> American Jewish liberal spends time talking to and romancing with Egyptian men but fails to go in search of Vivian Gornick, the Jew.

Greenberg, Dan: *How to Be a Jewish Mother.* Los Angeles: Price, Stern, Sloan, 1966.

> Good example of oppressive use of stereotype masquerading as humor. Know the enemy. Good for C.R.

Hasanovitz, Elizabeth: *One of Them.* Houghton-Mifflin, 1918.

> Autobiography of Russian immigrant who became a factory worker and, later, a union organizer; gives lengthy descriptions of sexual harassment.

Hilf, Mary Asia: *No Time for Tears.* Th. Yoseloff, 1964.

> Sometimes charming but often superficial and self-serving autobiography of Russian-born milliner who eventually established a model family and business in Wisconsin [S.W.].

Hellman, Lillian: *Pentimento: A Book of Portraits.* London: Quartet Books, 1976; also pap.

Hobhouse, Janet: *Everybody Who Was Anybody—A Biography of Gertrude Stein.* G.P. Putnam's Sons, 1975.

Hoffman, Michael J.: *Gertrude Stein.* London: G. Prior (World Authors Series), 1976.

Jacob, H.E.: *The World of Emma Lazarus.* Schocken, 1949.

Jastrow, Marie: *A Time to Remember: Growing Up in New York Before the Great War.* Norton, 1979.

Katz, Sanford N.: *Creativity in Social Work: Selected Writings of Lydia Rapoport.* Temple Univ. Press, 1975.

> A posthumous collection of 20 years of work in her profession.

Keats, John: *You Might as Well Live—The Life and Times of Dorothy Parker.* Simon & Schuster, 1970. Bantam, 1972, pap.

> "I was just a little Jewish girl, trying to be cute."

Kimball, Gussie: *Gitele.* Vantage, 1960.

> Woman supports her family by running a liquor store in the Fillmore district of San Francisco.

Kohut, Rebecca: *My Portion*. Albert & Charles Boni, 1927.

———————: *More Yesterdays*. Bloch, 1950.

Kramer, Sydelle and Masor, Jenny: *Jewish Grandmothers*. Boston: Beacon Press, 1976.

    Oral histories of ten Jewish women.

Lang, Lucy Robins: *Tomorrow Is Beautiful*. Macmillan, 1948.

    Russian immigrant's involvement with American radical movement, feminists and labor leaders.

Lebeson, Anita: *Recall to Life: The Jewish Woman in America*, T. Yoseloff, 1970.

    Excellently researched accounts of Jewish women from 1600s.

Levy, Harriet Lane: *920 O'Farrell Street*. Doubleday, 1947; Arno reprint, 1975.

    Memoirs by child of middle-class German Jewish immigrants who settled in San Francisco.

Mazow, Julia Wolf: *The Woman Who Lost Her Names*. Harper & Row, 1980.

    An anthology of writing—fiction and autobiography—by American Jewish women about their lives.

Maynard, Fredelle Bruser: *Raisins and Almonds*. Doubleday, 1972, pap.

    Recollections of childhood in Saskatchewan; strange assimilationist ending.

McCarthy, Mary: *Memories of a Catholic Childhood*. Harcourt, Brace, 1957.

    Episodes in her early life; final chapter on her Jewish grandmother.

Merriam, Eve: *Emma Lazarus—Woman with a Torch*. Citadel, 1956.

———————: *The Voice of Liberty*. Farrar, Straus and JPS, 1959.

    Biography of Emma Lazarus.

Meyer, Annie Nathan: *It's Been Fun*. Henry Shuman, NY 1954.

    Autobiography by the daughter of a distinguished Sephardic family who devoted herself to cause of education for women and who became one of the founders of Barnard College.

Meyerhoff, Barbara: *Number Our Days*. Dutton, 1978.

    Anthropological study of old poor Jews' community in Venice, Ca. Fascinating material on old Jewish women—their history, values, coping, sources of strength.

Morton, Leah [pseud.: Elizabeth Stern]: *I Am a Woman and a Jew*. Arno reprint, 1969.

Autobiography of Jewish feminist of the 1930's. See below, "Stern."

Nathan, Maud: *Once Upon a Time and To-Day*. Putnam's Sons, 1933. Arno Press reprint, 1974.

Neidle, Cecyle S.: *America's Immigrant Women*. Hippocrene Books, 1976, pap.

From 1609. Explores women's political, social, economic contributions, with some material on Jewish women.

Peck, Arlene G.: "The Southern Jewish American Princess in the Fabulous Fifties." In *The Ethnic American Woman—Problems, Protests, Lifestyles: An Anthology*. Blicksilver, Edith, ed. Dubuque, IA: Kendall Hunt, 1978.

Pesotta, Rose: *Bread Upon the Waters*. Dodd, Mead & Co., 1944.

Organizer (later vice-president) for the ILGWU describes her work throughout the U.S., Puerto Rico and Canada during the 1930's. A must for students of labor history [S.W.].

Philipson, Rabbi David, ed.: *Letters of Rebecca Gratz*. Phila.: JPS, 1929.

Picon, Molly: *Molly! An Autobiography*. Simon & Schuster, 1980.

Rosen, Ruth and Davidson, Sue, eds.: *The Maimie Papers*. Old Westbury, NY: The Feminist Press, 1977.

Correspondence between Maimie Pinzer, a Jewish prostitute in Philadelphia, and Fanny Quincy Howe, a prominent Bostonian. Maimie suffered morphine addiction, jails, hospitals and reformatories until she was able to support herself and help other women.

Sampter, Jessie E.: *A Guide to Zionism*. Folcroft, 1920. Reprint.

Author was a popular poet and essayist of the period 1920-1940.

Sandberg, Sara: *My Sister Goldie*. Doubleday, 1968.

——————: *Mama Made Minks*. Doubleday, 1964; Avon, 1966, pap.

Biography.

Schappes, Morris U., ed.: *Letters of Emma Lazarus*, 1868-1885. New York Public Library, 1949.

Schneiderman, Rose: "The Childhood of an Immigrant Working Girl," Blicksilver anthology, op cit.

Schwartz, G. and Wyden, B.: The Jewish Wife. Paperback Library, 1970.

>   Pop. sociology based on in-depth interviews. Good sources despite authors' value judgments.

Sheklow, Edna: So Talently My Children. Cleveland: World, 1966.

>   Portrays the skills and sacrifices of her immigrant mother.

Shulman, Alix: To the Barricades: The Anarchist Life of Emma Goldman. Crowell, 1971.

Solomon, Hannah G.: Fabric of My Life: Autobiography of a Social Pioneer. Bloch, 1946.

>   Autobiography of co-founder of National Council of Jewish Women.

Stein, Leon: The Triangle Fire. Lippincott, 1962.

Stern, Elizabeth G. (Levin): My Mother and I. Macmillan, 1922.

Suhl, Yuri: Ernestine Rose and the Battle for Human Rights. Reynal & Hitchcock, 1959.

>   This is the only biography of the famous Jewish suffragist, but currently out of print.

Syrkin, Marie: The State of the Jews. Washington: New Republic Books, 1980.

Tonner, Leslie: Nothing But the Best: The Luck of the Jewish Princess. Coward, McCann and Geoghegan, 1975.

>   Classist, superficial, reinforces oppressive stereotypes; know the enemy.

Tornabene, Lyn: What's a Jewish Girl. Simon & Schuster, 1966.

>   Oppressive companion volume to Greenberg and Tonner books.

Torres, Tereska: The Converts. Knopf, 1970.

>   Autobiography of this author of popular fiction, wife of Meyer Levin. An account of how it felt to be raised as a Catholic in a Jewish family converted to Catholicism. A sensitive record of a girl's childhood and growth within a dual identity.

Wald, Lillian: The House on Henry Street. Henry Holt & Co., 1915.

Wigoder, Deborah: Hope Is My House. Englewood Cliffs, NJ: Prentice-Hall, 1966.

>   Autobiography of an American convert to Judaism now living in Israel with her family.

Yezierska, Anzia: <u>Hungry Hearts</u>. Arno Press, 1979.
    Reprint of famous novel of immigrant woman of the Lower East Side.

Zohar, Danah: <u>Up My Mother's Flagpole</u>. Stein & Day, 1974.
    Wildly funny autobiography of convert.

B. <u>Periodicals and Book Chapters</u>

"Abraham" and "Sarah": "Two Perspectives on Being Gay," <u>Jewish Currents</u>, January, 1976.
    "Sarah" discusses her position as a lesbian and Jewish professional working with children, citing the hostile attitude of the Jewish community towards homosexuality.

Abzug, Bella: "Bella on Bella," <u>Moment</u>, February 1976.
    Bella talks of her life—her Jewish feelings; feminism and a variety of factors which shaped her political consciousness.

_____: "The Jewish Woman in Politics," Address to the First Jewish Women's Conference, JSPS, February 1978.

Ain, Stewart: "Esther Jungreis and Hineni," <u>Women's American Ort Reporter</u>, March/April, 1977.

Alpert, Rebecca Trachtenberg: "Survival Imperatives after the Holocaust," <u>Reconstructionist</u>, April 1977.
    Addresses the zero population growth problem from a feminist perspective.

Avery, Evelyn: "Role of Jewish Women in Literature." In <u>Rebels and Victims: The Fiction of Richard Wright and Bernard Malamud</u>. Kennikat Press, 1979.

Balser, Ruth: "Liberation of a Jewish Radical," <u>Chutzpah</u>,* Summer 1973.

Baron, Sheryl: "National Liberation and the Jewish Woman." In <u>Jewish Radicalism: A Selected Anthology</u>. Grove Press, 1973, also pap.

Barag, Gerda G.: "The Mother in the Religious Concepts of Judaism." In <u>The Psychodynamics of American Jewish Life: An Anthology</u>, Kiel, Norman, ed.: Twayne, 1967.

Bart, Pauline: "Portnoy's Mother's Complaint." Transaction Magazine, November/December, 1970. Also in Response* Anthology, op cit.

_____ : "Depression in Middle-Aged Women." In anthology Woman in Sexist Society, Gornick, V. and Moran, B., eds. Basic Books, 1971.

> Breakthrough research and analysis on fate awaiting traditional enabler. A must for CR.

Bauman, Batya: "On Coming Out Gay," Lilith, vol. I, no. 2.

> Moving, inspiring testimony.

Baumgold, Julie: "The Persistence of the Jewish American Princess," New York, March 22, 1971.

> Persistence of a stereotype, perpetuated by author as well. Know the enemy.

Beck, Evelyn Torton: "Isaac Bashevis Singer's Misogyny," Lilith, no. 6, 1979.

Bender, Esther: "Looking Back/Excerpts from a Life Story," National Jewish Monthly, November 1977.

> This is the "world of our mothers"—and an inspiration it is! Author is 74 years old and this is her first published work. [M.H.]

Berger, B.: "Observations: What Women Want," Commentary, March 1979.

Berman, Louis A.: "Sex Role Patterning in the Jewish Family," Chapter 8 in Jews and Intermarriage. Th. Yoseloff, 1968.

Berman, Susan: "Seven Grooms for Seven Sisters," New York, July 31, 1978.

> Cutesy pro-patriarchal feature on women rescued from Syrian ghetto to become brides for Brooklyn Jewish men.

Bissell, Sherry: "My Divorce and My Community," Sh'ma, April 1978.

Blau, Zena Smith: "In Defense of the Jewish Mother." In The Ghetto and Beyond. Rose, Peter I., ed. Random House, 1969, pp. 57-68.

Bluestone, Naomi: "Sunset, Sunset: The Life of Jewish Singles," Moment, September 1976.

Blumengarten, Louis H.: "I'm Ready But What Can I Do?" Sh'ma, January 1978.

> Another Jewish male moaning about how Jewish women don't appreciate him. [M.H.]

Boucher, Sandy: "Tillie Olsen: The Weight of Things Unsaid," Ms., September 1974.

Bronznick, Shifra: "Jewish Women's Liberation," Alliance,* April 1972.

Brooklyn Bridge Women's Group: "Jewish Women: Life Force of a Culture," Brooklyn Bridge, no. 1.

Brown, Laura: "Jewish Women—Mothers, Princesses, Sisters?" Hashofar,* October 1972.

Brown, Pryde: "Sexism in Textbooks and TV," Council Woman, Fall 1976.

> A group of New Jersey women form a corporation, "Women on Words and Images," to uncover sexism in elementary texts and TV.

Brozan, Nadine: "Jewish Women Discuss Impact of Feminism," The New York Times, November 21, 1979.

Cantor, Aviva: "The Sheltered Workshop," Lilith, no. 5, Spring 1979.

> Feminist critique of current volunteering behavior of Jewish organizational women.

_____: "Jewish Women and the Communal Agenda," Women's American ORT Reporter, January/February 1980.

Carson, Rubin: "Gentile vs. Jewish Marriage," Cosmopolitan, December 1972.

> Extremely insulting autobiographical account by Jewish male of his marriages, comparing what he refers to as Brand A (Jewish) and Brand B (non-Jewish) women. Sick and hateful. Know the enemy.

Charr, J.: "The Paschal Lamb: Women Offered for the Sacrifice," Reconstructionist, May 1979.

Chutzpah Anthology: "Dilemma of a Jewish Lesbian," San Francisco, New Glide Publications, 1977.

> Anonymous article.

Cohen, Steven Martin: "American Jewish Feminism—A Study in Conflicts and Compromises," American Behavioral Scientist, vol. 23, no. 4, April 1980.

Cohen, Steven Martin, Dessel, Susan C. and Pelavin, Michael A.: "Women's Power and Status in Jewish Communal Life: A Look at the UJA," Response,* Winter, 1975-76.

Cohn, Judy Birnbaum: "From USYer to Synagogue President," United Synagogue Review, Spring/Summer 1976.

Cook, Blanche Wiesen: "Female Support Networks and Political Activism: Lillian Wald, Crystal Eastman, Emma Goldman," Chrysalis, no. 3, 1977.

Datan, Nancy: "Coming of Age in Morgantown," Moment, January 1976.

Daum, Annette: "Women on the Move," Reform Judaism, October 1978.

Davis, Sarah: "Jews in Politics: Where Are the Women?" Council Woman, January 1976.

Denes, Magda: "Performing Abortions," Commentary, October 1976.

Dworkin, Susan: "A Song for Women," Moment, May/June 1975.

> Centers around five issues: equal access to God, equal opportunity for joy, equal treatment by history, equal access to power, and respect.

_____: "Henrietta Szold: Liberated Woman," Hadassah, February 1972.

> Interesting and sad. Do not be misled by title.

_____: "Women of Valor—New Voices, New Values, New Vitality," Hadassah, April 1973.

> Report on First Network National Jewish Women's Conference.

Edelhert, Martha: "Conversations and Reminiscences," Heresies, A Feminist Publication on Art and Politics, Winter 1978.

> Memories of Jewish grandmothers.

Epstein, Helen: "Are You Jewish? My Parents Are," Village Voice, February 24, 1972.

Evans, Jane: "Volunteerism: Are Women Pawns or Powers?" Pioneer Woman, September 1975.

> Pro-volunteerism.

Faust-Levy, Elie: "The Jewish Women's Movement," The American Zionist, June 1974.

Feinstein, Sara: "Opening Opportunities for Women in Jewish Communal Service," Journal of Jewish Communal Service, Winter 1975.

Feldstein, Donald and Bayer, Ellen R.: "Patriarchy—Is It Inevitable? Two Essays on The Inevitability of Patriarchy by Steven Goldberg," Journal of Jewish Communal Service, December 19, 1974, pp. 206-210.

Filsenburg, Rosa: "The Noah Syndrome," Davka,* Winter 1975.

    Single, divorced, separated and widowed women.

Fishman, Leora: "Jewish Women's Activities." In The Jewish Catalog, vol. I, Jewish Publication Society, 1973.

    Excellent.

Flexner, Eleanor: Century of Struggle. Atheneum, 1974.

    This excellent herstory includes information on Ernestine Rose, Rose Schneiderman, among others.

Forse, Chana: The "New Yeshivas," Women's American ORT Reporter, May/June 1979.

    About Bais Chana, a yeshivah for young women from Orthodox homes. Author of article spent two weeks at this Lubavitcher school in St. Paul, Minnesota.

Frank, Shirley: "The Population Panic," Lilith, vol. I, no. 4.

    Definitive feminist analysis of why Jewish leaders are pressuring women to have [more] children.

_____: "The Need for Jewish Day Care," Attah,* February 1973.

Garson, Sascha: "On Re-Becoming a Jew," Village Voice, November 25, 1971.

    Beautiful account of development of her Jewish consciousness.

Gertel, Elliot: "Passivity, Equality and the Jewish Woman," Congress Monthly, November 1976.

    Anti-feminist.

Gilson, Estelle: "Trude's a Holy Terror: Scholar, Critic, Rebel, Gadfly [A Profile of Trude-Weiss Rosmarin]", Present Tense, Winter 1978.

Gittleson, Natalie: "Anti-Semitism: It's Still Around," Harper's Bazaar, February 1972.

    She learned this great revelation through interviews with upper class assimilationist American Jewish women. Know the enemy.

Goodblatt, Robert: "Me, Myself and the Middle-Class Jew." In Voices from Women's Liberation, New American Library, 1971, pap.

    Makes good points about growing up as a Jewish female but marred by much misunderstanding of Judaism.

Gold, Doris B.: "Beyond the Valley of the Shmattes," Lilith, vol. I, no. 1.

    Incisive, thought-provoking look at Jewish women's organizations, raising serious questions about their real nature and purpose.

Gold, Doris B.: "Jewish Women's Groups: Separate—But Equal?" Congress Bi-Weekly, February 6, 1970.

Oppressive nature of sexist division of labor in Jewish community.

_____: "Women and Volunteering: New Thoughts on a Complex Issue," Women's American ORT Reporter, May/June 1977.

Book review of three works on subject.

_____: "Women and Voluntarism," In Woman in Sexist Society, Gornick, V. and Moran, B., eds. Basic Books, 1971. Also N.A.L., pap.

Germinal essay.

Goldberg, Doris: "One Family's Story," Moment, November 1977.

Family's experience with Tay-Sachs. Also rabbinic opinions concerning abortion and this disease.

Goldman, Rachel [Pseud.: Rosetta Reitz]: "The Liberation of the Yiddishe Mama," Village Voice, February 11, 1970.

Goldschneider, Calvin: "Socio-Economic Status and Jewish Fertility," Jewish Journal of Sociology, vol. VII, 1966, pp. 221-237.

Gordon, Maralee: "Feminist Frustration with the Forefathers." In Chutzpah: A Liberation Anthology, op cit.

_____: "Jewish Women—Up From Under," Chutzpah,* February/March, 1973.

_____: "Reports on the First Midwinter Jewish Women's Conference," Chutzpah,* Winter 1974.

Several pieces, including one on struggle with Chicago Federation.

Greenberg, Blu: "ZPG: Feminism and Jewish Survival," Hadassah, October 1978.

Tone is generally reformist—suggesting ways Jewish community can respond to feminist challenge and encourage more children, including the consideration of "planned single parenthood."

Greene, Diana: "What It's Like to Be a Jewish Girl," Cosmopolitan, November 1965.

Horrifying stereotyping. Borders on anti-Semitic. Know the enemy.

Greenspan, E.: "A Model Displaced Homemaker Program within a Jewish Vocational Service Agency," Journal of Jewish Communal Services, September 1979.

Grinstein, Alexander: "Profile of a 'Doll'—A Female Character Type." In *The Psychodynamics of American Jewish Life: An Anthology*, Kiel, Norman, ed. Twayne, 1967.

>Portrays what is called today a "JAP" without dealing with historical and sociological realities, i.e., sexism.

Grunfeld, Frederic V.: "Prophets Without Honor," *Present Tense*, September 1979. About Elsa Lasker-Schuler and other German-Jewish intellectuals.

Hapgood, Hutchins: "The Old and the New Woman," Chapter 3 of *The Spirit of the Ghetto*. Funk & Wagnalls, reissued 1965.

>Lower East Side Jewish women immigrants. Good source material on the "new Jewish woman," Circa 1900.

Harris, Marylou: "The Men Are Not Always Nice," *Present Tense*, Spring 1977.

>Statistics on singles and the Jewish community.

Hofstein, Saul: "Perspectives on the Jewish Single Parent Family," *Journal of Jewish Communal Service*, March 1978, pp. 229-240.

Hornik, Edith Lynn: "The Jewish Drinking Woman." In *The Drinking Woman*, Association Press, 1977, pp. 105-111.

"How to Get What We Want by the Year 2000," Lilith Forum, *Lilith*, no. 7, p. 18.

>Brief essays by eight Jewish women activists/academics on their expectations.

Hyman, Paula: "Is It Kosher to Be feminist?" *Ms.*, July 1974.

_____: "The Jewish Family: Looking for a Usable Past," *Congress Bi-Weekly*.

>Originally presented at a National Conference sponsored by the American Jewish Congress, Commission on Jewish Affairs.

_____: "The Volunteer Organizations: Vanguard or Rear Guard?" *Lilith*, no. 5, 1979.

>Evolution of national Jewish women's organizations from pro-feminist to lack of action on women's issues. Excellent.

Inwald, Doris: "Jewish Women at the National Women's Conference," *Congress Monthly*, December 1977.

Israel, Richard: "Letter to the Mother of a Lesbian Daughter," *Moment*, July-August, 1980.

Jacobs, Nancy L.: "The Changing Family: Its Implications for Early Childhood Centers," Journal of Jewish Communal Service, Fall 1977.

Jacoby, Susan: "World of Our Mothers: Immigrant Women, Immigrant Daughters," Present Tense, September 1979.

Jewish Heritage (Bnai Brith): "Special Jewish Family Issue," Summer 1972.

Jewish Week: "Judaism Called Immunization against Extremism of Lib," Speech by Elizabeth Douvan, October 25-31, 1973.

    Harbinger of campaign against Jewish feminism.

_____: "Women Once Denied Tenure for Fad to Head Jewish Studies Nationally," December 28, 1980, p. 1.

    Announcement of Dr. Jane Gerber's election to presidency and some background on Jewish studies field.

Jochnowitz, Carol: "The Award to Irene Paull—From Jewish Currents Dinner Honoring M.V. Schappes, May 15, 1977," Jewish Currents, June 1977.

    Speech and Paull's response combine to present a picture of courageous, sensitive, passionate writer and activist.

_____: "The Jewish Woman Today," Jewish Currents, March 1975.

Julianelli, Jane: "Bessie Hillman," Ms., May 1973.

    Biographical sketch of union organizer.

Kellen, Konrad: "Reflections on Rape," Midstream, February 1976.

    Blatantly misogynist attack on Brownmiller, dismissing and belittling violence against women. Dangerous: Know the enemy [M.H.].

Kessler-Harris, Alice: "Organizing the Unorganizable: Three Jewish Women and Their Union," Labor History, no. 17, Winter 1976.

Klemesrud, Judy: "Expecting Humor, Jews Get Feminism Lecture," The New York Times, August 7, 1975.

Krause, Corinne Azen: "Italian, Jewish and Slavic Grandmothers in Pittsburgh: Their Economic Roles," Frontiers: A Journal of Women Studies, Summer 1977.

    Brief account of economic role of Jewish women plus several oral herstories.

Kur, Carol: "Hadassah Way," Moment, March 1978.

Kushner, Rose: "Cancer Risks in Jewish Women," The National Jewish Monthly, December 1974.

Lamm, Bob: "Fear of Feminism," Lilith, vol. I, no. 1.

> What is it about Jewish women's liberation that Jewish men feel threatened by?

Lavender, Abraham D.: "Jewish College Women: Future Leaders of the Jewish Community?" The Journal of Ethnic Studies, Summer 1977.

_____: A Coat of Many Colors: Jewish Subcommunities in the US. Greenwood Press, 1978.

> Contains reprints of three articles on women and Judaism.

Lerner, Gerda: The Female Experience: An American Documentary. Indianapolis: Bobbs-Merrill Educational Publishing, 1977.

> Includes contributions by many Jewish women: Emma Goldman, Muriel Rukeyser and more.

Lester, Elenore: "The Riddle of Tillie Olsen," Midstream, January 1975.

> Discusses Olsen's works, pointing to her socialist vision, Jewish identity and concern for elderly women. Unfortunately, written with an anti-feminist bias. Beware. [M.H.]

Levine, Louis: "The Women's Garment Workers," Huebsch, 1924.

> References to Jewish women.

Lewis, Helen S.: "The Historic National Women's Conference in Houston," Jewish Frontier, March 6, 1978.

Lieberman, Betty: "Hadassah," Lilith, no. 5, Spring 1979.

> Insider's critique of the organization. (See also Hadassah's official response in Lilith, no. 6, 1979, Letters column.)

Lieberman, Sharon: "Circumcision Is No Insurance," Lilith, vol. I, no. 3.

> Explodes myths on cervical cancer.

Livingston, Nancy: "What Is a Pre-School Doing in a Jewish Community Center?" Journal of Jewish Communal Service, Fall 1977.

"Liza" and "Penny": "Anti-Semitism in the Lesbian Movement," Dyke, no. 5.

> Articles center on correspondence between Jewish and Protestant lesbians about anti-Semitism and racism.

Mailer, Norman: "The Jewish Princess," Atlantic Monthly, August 1973.

Makouska, Irina: "A Second Life," Council Woman, January 1976.

> Soviet Jewish woman in United States.

Malcolm, Sarah: "I Am a Second Generation Lesbian," Ms., October 1977.

Maller, Allen: "The Sexism of Intermarriage," Sh'ma, February 1976.

Maller, Allen: "Why Jewish Women Marry Gentile Men," <u>Women's American ORT Reporter</u>, March/April 1977.

> Both pieces stereotype Jewish women. [M.H.]

Margolis, Vera S.: "The Challenge of Change," <u>Journal of Jewish Communal Service</u>, Winter 1975.

Mason, Ruth: "Socialist Feminist Conference: A Jewish Woman's Caucus? What For?" <u>Jewish Radical</u>,* May 1975.

> An account of author's experience at a Socialist Feminist convention and the bond participants felt as leftists, women and Jews.

Mayer, Barbara: "Sex and the Jewish Girl," <u>Cosmopolitan</u>, December 1970.

> Interesting non-assimilationist testimony on the double standard.

Merriam, Eve: <u>Growing Up Female in America: Ten Lives</u>. Dell Pub. Co., 1971.

> Includes excerpts from <u>I Am a Woman—And a Jew</u>, the autobiography of Elizabeth Gertrude Stern (1890-1954).

Meyers, Janet: "Diaspora Takes a Queer Turn: A Jewish Lesbian Considers Her Past," <u>Dyke</u>, no. 5.

> Excellent piece, draws analogy between Jews in Christian world and lesbians in heterosexual world.

Michel, Sonya: "Grandmother's Legacy," <u>Jewish Currents</u>, March 1977.

> Review of <u>Jewish Grandmothers</u> (op cit.).

Miller, Alvin S.: "Sexism, Drop-outs and Jewish Federation," <u>Jewish Frontier</u>, September 1973, pp. 29-31.

Miller, Joyce D.: "Working Women: The Struggle for Equality," <u>Jewish Frontier</u>, November 1979, pp. 10-12.

——————: "Women from the Reagan Era," <u>Jewish Frontier</u>, June-July 1981.

Miller, Sally: "Theresa Malkiel," <u>American Jewish History</u>, December 1978.

> Life and work of labor leader and suffragist.

Mirsky, Norman: "Mixed Dating, Mixed Mating, Mixed Marriage," <u>Moment</u>, October 1980.

<u>Mizrachi Woman</u>, n.a.: "Do Jewish Women Need Liberation?" March 1973.

> Straightforward account of First National Jewish Women's Conference held February, 1973.

Monson, Rela Geffen: "The Case of the Reluctant Exogamists: Jewish Women and Intermarriage," Gratz College Annual of Jewish Studies, Phila., vol. 5, 1976.

    Factors determining Jewish women's intermarriage and those not marrying out.

_____: Review of Women in Judaism, a book by Leonard Swidler; The Reconstructionist, November 1976.

    This was a critical review.

Narell, Irena Penzik: "The Jewish Settlement of San Francisco," Hadassah, June 1975.

    Includes accounts of women pioneers.

Newman, Mordecai: "From 'Private Benjamin' to 'It's My Turn,'" Jewish Frontier, February 1981, pp. 24-25.

    Compares two recent films that portray Jewish female protagonists.

Newsweek: Ezrat Nashim: September 17, 1973. Also Jewish Feminism: May 31, 1976.

Nissinson, Marilyn: "Muma Leah," Present Tense, Summer 1976. Review of Jewish Grandmothers.

Novak, William: "Are Good Jewish Men a Vanishing Breed?" Moment, January-February, 1980.

    Novak puts his finger on the problem of the lack of suitable men for many Jewish women to marry. But he shies away from pinpointing the real problem—the men's sexism.

Oliver, Rose: "The Jewish Mother Myth," Congress Monthly, September 1977.

    Using scientific criteria, Oliver, a psychologist, examines the validity of the stereotype and explores its pathological effects on both mother and offspring. Excellent [M.H.].

Ozick, Cynthia: "The Jewish Half-Genius," The Jerusalem Post Magazine, July 7, 1978.

_____: "Notes Toward Finding the Right Question (A Vindication of the Rights of Jewish Women)," Lilith, no. 6, 1979.

    The definitive analysis of women in Judaism and future directions for the struggle.

Plaskow, Judith: "The Jewish Feminist: Conflict in Identities," Blicksilver anthology, op cit.

    Address to First National Jewish Women's Conference of April 1973 held in New York City.

Plaskow, Judith: "Christian Feminism and Anti-Judaism," Lilith, no. 7.

    Deals forthrightly with how many Christian feminists "project onto Judaism the failure of [Christianity] to renounce sexism; thereby avoid confronting the failures of [their] own tradition." A very important must-read.

Plaskow, Judith et al.: "Blaming Jews for Inventing Patriarchy," Lilith, no. 7, 1980, p. 11 ff.

    Forum entitled "Feminists and Faith" which includes article by Annette Daum, "Blaming Jews for the Death of the Goddess," and dialogue between the two on the subject.

Playboy: "Interview with Barbra Streisand," October 1977.

    Discusses growing up poor and Jewish in Williamsburg.

Pogrebin, Letty Cottin: "'Yentl': Better a Fool than a Woman," Ms., February 1976.

    Review of Leah Napolin's Broadway play.

Polner, Murray: Rabbi: The American Experience. Holt, Rinehart & Winston, 1977.

    Some material on women rabbis and rebbitzins.

Postal, Bernard: "In Early America Jewish Women Played Important Roles Too!" Pioneer Women, September 1975.

Pratt, Norma Fain: "The Jewish American Woman." In Women in American Religion, James, Janet W., ed. Phila.: Univ. of Pa. Press, 1980.

Preisand, Sally: "Not for Men Only," Council Woman, February 1974.

    Shows growing feminist consciousness of first American woman rabbi.

Raynes, Rose: "Jewish Currents Dinner, May 19, 1975," Jewish Currents, September 1975.

    Raynes' speech urging women to organize.

Reguer, Sara: "Life in America: The Jewish Mother and the 'Jewish American Princess': Fact or Fiction?" USA Today, September 1979.

Rockland, Mae Shafter, with Rockland, Michael Aaron: The Jewish Yellow Pages with More than 300 Illustrations: A Directory of Goods and Services. Schocken, 1976, pap.

    Lists many Jewish women craftspersons and artists.

Roiphe, Anne: "Christmas Comes to a Jewish Home," Moment, February 1979.

> This topic by the same author caused a furor in the New York Times when printed in the same year.

Rose, Ernestine L.: "Address on the Anniversary of West Indian Emancipation," Journal of Negro History, July 1949.

> Rose's address given in 1853, edited by Morris U. Schappes.

Rosen, Gladys: "Can the Women's Movement Save the Jewish Family?" Jewish Digest, July-August 1979.

_____: "The Impact of the Women's Movement on the Jewish Family," Judaism, September 1979.

Rosenberg, M.J.: "Rebecca Gratz," The National Jewish Monthly, July-August 1976.

Rosenbluth, Margie: "Growing Up Female, Jewish and Radical: The Jewish Heritage in Her Music," Jewish Currents, March 1978.

Rossman-Mallow, Adar: "The Jewish Sorority—Sisterhood Perverted," Chutzpah,* Winter 1974.

Rothchild, Janice: "The Rebbizinhood," Central Conference of American Rabbis' Journal, Winter 1973.

Schappes, Morris U.: "Some Jewish Foremothers of '76," Jewish Currents, March 1976.

> Sketches of Jewish women from American Revolutionary period.

_____: "Three Women," Jewish Currents, September 1975.
Rose, Lazarus and Lemlich (Shavelson).

_____: Critical Reviews of H.E. Jacobs' The World of Emma Lazarus in both Masses and Mainstream, July 1949, and in American Literature, January 1950.

Scheier, Paula: "Clara Lemlich Shavelson," Jewish Life (now called Jewish Currents), November 1954.

Schneider, Susan Weidman: "A Jewish Women's Community Behind Bars," Lilith, no. 5, Spring 1979.

> Jewish women in a New York State jail and their struggles. Based on visits and interviews.

_____: "In a Coma—I Thought She Was Jewish! Some Thoughts and Speculations about Jewish Women and Sex," Lilith, vol. I, no. 3.

> Historical-sociological-psychological analysis of sexist "jokes."

Schneider, Susan Weidman: "Jewish Feminism: At the Crossroads," Women's American ORT Reporter, May/June 1980, pp. 9-12.

    The editor of Lilith raises some questions about the Jewish women's movement and where it stands today.

_____: "Review of Response anthology," Women's American ORT Reporter, March-April 1974.

_____: "Report on Second Network Conference on Sex Roles in Jewish Life," ORT Reporter, May-June 1974.

_____: "Women and Jewish Education," Jewish Digest, December 1979.

    Reprint of essay which first appeared in Women's American ORT Reporter, May/June 1979.

Schoen, Elin: "Kiss, Kiss, Kvetch, Kvetch—The Jewish American Women Novelists (JAWN's)," New York, May 23, 1977.

    Nasty attack on recent fiction by women who are as marginally Jewish as their characters. Schoen nevertheless stresses Jewishness as key component. Unsympathetic to women's struggles. Know the enemy.

Schwartz, Mary Cahn: "The High Price of Failure," Lilith, vol. I, no. 1.

    How the success ethic forces lower middle class Jewish women to push their less successful husbands. Powerful. Should be read with Bart.

Segal, Sheila F.: "Feminists for Judaism," Midstream, August/September 1975.

    A good account of the changes being made.

Selavan, Ida Cohen: "Bobba Hannah, Midwife," American Journal of Nursing, April 1973.

    Beautifully researched and written piece on the woman who delivered most of Pittsburgh Jewish parent population. An example of the kind of research that should be done and soon.

Shapiro, Dee: "Grandma Sarah Bakes," Heresies, Winter 1978.

    Baking challah as woman's expression.

Shapiro, Manheim S.: "Changing Lifestyles, the Jewish Family and the Jewish Community," Congress Bi-Weekly, n.d.

    Originally presented at a national conference sponsored by the American Jewish Congress, Commission on Jewish Affairs.

Shapiro, Miriam: "The Women's Role: A Continuing Discussion," Conservative Judaism, Fall 1978.

Sh'ma: "Women as Federation Campaign Heads," February 1976.

    Experiential pieces by four women who headed fund-raising drives.

_____: "The Jewish Birthrate," Special issue, February 16, 1979.

_____: "What If There's No One Around?" January 1978.

    A Jewish male moans that there aren't any Jewish women around who are good enough for him [M.H.]. Unsigned article.

_____: "Living Through Divorce—A Search for Self," April 1976.

    Anonymous article.

Silver, Helen S.: "Liz Holtzman," Pioneer Woman, December 1975.

Silver, George A.: "Love Is Not Enough: Hadassah and Israel's Medical Care Dilemma," Midstream, March 1978.

    Analysis of how volunteer organization built a medical complex and school in Israel to meet its needs—not the Israelis'. Should be read with Doris Gold's articles on voluntarism (op cit.).

Silver, Roslyn: "We Learn from the Young—A Mother's Viewpoint," JSPS, March 1973.

    Vivian's mother's impression of and feelings about First Jewish Women's Conference. Very moving.

Silver, Vivian: "On Being a Jewish Woman," JSPS, January 1973.

    Address to conference of World Union of Jewish Students, Antwerp, December 1972.

Singer, Betty: "An Unlikely Navy Officer?" The Jewish Veteran, September/October 1976.

    Jewish woman's experience in United States Navy.

Sklarew, Myra: "The Landscape of Dislocation: A Letter from the Suburbs," National Jewish Monthly, April 1977.

Small, Rona and Goldhammer, Paul: "The Professional Role within a Self-Help Model: A Widow-to-Widow Project," Journal of Jewish Communal Service, Winter 1979-80.

Smolar, Boris: "Between You and Me—Jewish Women," Jewish Telegraphic Agency, September 10, 1976.

Snitow, Virginia and Levine, Jacqueline: "Role of Jewish Women," Congress Bi-Weekly, June 18, 1971. Also see Levine piece in Response Anthology (op cit.).

Sochen, June: "Some Observations on the Role of American Jewish Women As Communal Volunteers," American Jewish History, American Jewish Historical Society, September 1980, pp. 23-33.

> A feminist historian performs a needed task from a scholarly stance about a neglected subject of Jewish women's lives.

Solender, Elsa: "Where Are the Women?" Moment, June 1973.

> Uncritical picture of women entering leadership positions in Jewish philanthropic organizations, cloned from male counterparts [M.H.].

Stiller, Nikki: "The Shiksa Question," Moment, July-August 1980.

Stokes, Rose Pastor: "Two Chapters from an Unpublished Autobiography," Jewish Currents, June 1958.

Stone, Amy: "J.F.O. at the McAlpin," Network,* May 1975.

> New York Jewish Feminist Organization all-day conference.

_____: "Jewish Women Searching for Options, History, Equality and a Sense of Self," Women's American ORT Reporter, November/December 1976.

> Book review of Baum/Hyman/Michel, Koltun, Pries et al.

_____: "The Jewish Establishment Is Not an Equal Opportunity Employer: Discrimination in Employment, Advancement and Pay in Jewish Social Service Organizations," Lilith, vol. I, no. 4.

_____: "The Locked Cabinet: How and Why Women Are Excluded from the UJA's Young Leadership Cabinet," Lilith, vol. I, no. 2.

Strassfeld, Sharon M.: "On Working for the Jewish Community," Sh'ma, vol. 11, no. 207, February 6, 1981.

> Personal essay about the author's negative experience for unnamed agency (probably J.W.B. Book Council) where she worked only a year.

Swerdlow, Tess: "The Emmas: Progressive Jewish Women," Jewish Currents, November 1975.

> The women and work of Emma Lazarus Federation of Jewish Women's Clubs.

Syrkin, Marie: "The Role of Zionism in the Life of Modern Woman," Pioneer Woman," March/April 1977.

> The role of Zionist and other volunteer organizations is to "help women transcend the self-indulgence of the private life...."

Temerlin, Maurice: "Lucy—Growing Up Human." In Science and Behavior, Bantam, 1977.

> A shrink raises a chimp as his "daughter." Fascinating theory on Jewish mother patterns, chapter 2.

Timberg, Judy: "Are Jewish Women Oppressed?" The Jewish Radical,* Spring 1971. Reprinted in Jewish Radicalism.

> Anthology (op cit.).

Tornabene, Lyn: "The Jewish Male: Prince or Portnoy?" Cosmopolitan, May 1970.

Turk, Deborah: "Why Orthodox Women Oppose the ERA," Women's American ORT Reporter, March-April 1979.

> The same tired argument. Know the enemy.

Van der Haag, Ernest: "Forbidden Fruit—Jewish Men and Non-Jewish Women," Cosmopolitan, April 1970.

Viorst, Judith: "The 16.5 Days of Christmas: Confessions of a Jewish Mother," Redbook, December 1970.

> Assimilationist rationalizations. Know the enemy.

WAO Reporter: "A Symposium: Volunteerism: A Valid Option for American Jewish Women," Women's American ORT Reporter, March/April 1975.

> Pro and con.

_____: "Debates on the more/fewer children question," September/October 1976 and January/February 1977.

> Mary Gendler vs. Rabbi William Berman.

Water, Pearl [pseud]: "National Council of Jewish Women," Lilith, no. 5, 1979.

> An insider's critique. (See also NCJW's official response in Lilith no. 6, Fall 1979, Letters column).

Waxman, Chaim: "The Impact of Feminism on American Jewish Communal Institutions," Journal of Jewish Communal Service, vol. LVII, no. 1, Fall 1980, pp. 73-79.

> This paper was presented at NIC Federation of Jewish Philanthropies' Women's Conf., October 29, 1979. Waxman advises women to play it cool, i.e. "feminine."

Weiss-Rosmarin, Trude: "Women in the Jewish Community," Jewish Spectator, February 1972.

_____: "Women Against Women," Editorial, Jewish Spectator, Winter 1979.

Whelton, Clark: "The Triangle Fire," Village Voice, March 25, 1971.

White, Barbara: "But Can She Chant?" Moment, September 1977.
    Author's experience as cantor.

Willis, Ellen: "Liberal Anti-Semitism," Village Voice, May 22, 1974.
    Testimony from radical woman on growing Jewish consciousness.

Wolfe, Ann G.: "No Room at the Top," Council Woman, January 1976.

_____: "What DO These Women Want?" News and Views, American Jewish Committee, March-April 1979.
    See also "Jewish Women and Community Roles," Face to Face, op cit. Raises some questions about Jewish responses to feminism.

_____: "The Jewish Woman." In Dialogue on Diversity. American Jewish Committee, 1976.
    Author has pioneered in struggle of Jewish women for equal opportunities.

Wolfenstein, Martha: "Two Types of Jewish Mothers." In Childhood in Contemporary Society, Wolfenstein, M. and Mead, Margaret, eds. Univ. of Chicago Press, 1955.

Wolk, Rochelle Saidel: "Prophecy or Paranoia?" Lilith, no. 7, 1980, pp. 8-10.
    Current anti-Semitism summary and the relationships to anti-feminism. Contains information on opposition to feminism by known anti-Semites.

Yezierska, Anzia: "1,000 Pages of Research," Commentary, July 1963.
    Writer of the period of great immigration tells of growing old in New York City.

C. Fiction

Adler, Marjorie Duhan: A Sign Upon My Hand. Doubleday, 1964.
    After assimilationist marriage falls apart, she returns to her heritage.

Asch, Sholem: The Mother. Liveright, 1930.
    Immigrant mother struggles with second-generation daughter.

Baum, Camille: A Member of the Tribe. Lyle Stuart, 1971.

Birstein, Ann: American Children. Doubleday, 1980.

Brenner, Marie: Tell Me Everything. Dutton, 1976.

Broner, E.M.: Her Mothers. Holt, Rinehart & Winston, 1975, also pap.
    Mother searches for her daughter and foremothers, incl. Biblical and Israeli models. Book for every mother and every daughter. (Also see interview with Broner in Lilith, vol. I, no. 4.)

Brown, Rosellen: Autobiography of My Mother. Doubleday, 1977.

Drexler, Rosalyn: I Am the Beautiful Stranger. Sphere Books, 1969.
    Fictional diary of young teenager growing up in poor non-religious family in the Bronx.

Epstein, Seymour: Leah. Little, Brown, 1964. Also pap.
    Sensitive portrait of single 37-year-old Jewish woman living in New York.

Freeman, Cynthia: Portraits. Bantam Books, 1980.
    A four-generation family saga of immigrants to the U.S. from Poland.

Friedman, Bruce Jay: A Mother's Kisses. Simon & Schuster, 1966.
    A "landmark" book of the stereotypical Jewish mother (and striving son).

Gidding, Joshua: Old Girl. Holt, Rinehart & Winston, 1980.
    Story of an 81-year-old Los Angeles Jewish grandmother in a second and third generation Jewish community; told sympathetically by her grandson, in the form of a novel.

Goldreich, Gloria: Four Days. Harcourt Brace Jovanovich, 1980.

Goldstein, Ruth Tessler: The Heart Is Half a Prophet. Macmillan, 1976; Bantam, 1977.
    A Chassidic family in Williamsburg during the Great Depression, seen through the eyes of a young girl.

Gould, Lois: Necessary Objects. Random House, 1972. Also pap.
    Upper-class women.

Gould, Mary Jane: Crossroads Marseilles, 1940. Doubleday, 1980.

Green, Hannah [pseud. of Joanna Greenberg]: <u>I Never Promised You a Rose Garden</u>. Holt, Rinehart & Winston, 1964. Also pap.

> Sixteen-year-old traumatized by anti-Semitic incidents as well as other problems in her childhood, retreats into fantasy life. Institutionalized by her parents, she is treated by a woman psychoanalyst refugee from Nazi Germany. (Also see review of movie by Rochelle Lefkowitz, <u>Lilith</u>, vol. I, no. 4.)

Greenberg, Joanna: <u>Summering</u>. Avon/Bard pap., 1974.

> Collection of short stories includes "How Beautiful with Feet" and "L'Olam and White Shell Woman."

_____: <u>A Season of Delight</u>, William Morrow, 1981.

> Novel of Jewish woman, her son and daughter all in conflict.

Harris, Alice Kessler: <u>The Open Cage: An Anzia Yezierska Collection</u>, Persea Books, 1980. Reprint.

Hobson, Laura Z.: <u>Over and Above</u>. Doubleday, 1979.

> Mother-daughter conflict over Jewish identification and commitment.

Horowitz, Eugene: <u>Home Is Where You Start From</u>. Norton, 1966; Pocket Books, 1967.

> Sensitive portrait of a woman stifled in marriage in New York City during the first half of this century.

Jong, Erica: <u>Fear of Flying</u>. Holt, Rinehart, 1974; also pap.

> Best chapter is about Germany.

_____: <u>How to Save Your Own Life</u>. Holt, Rinehart, 1977; also pap.

> "<u>Pareve</u>" sequel, despite sexy scenes. (See review by Sonya Michel, <u>Lilith</u>, vol. I, no. 3.)

Kalechofsky, Roberta: <u>Solomon's Wisdom</u>. Marblehead, MA: Micah Publications, 1979.

> Ten stories based on history and legendary material from the Bible and rabbinic literature which is transferred to modern times.

Kaplan, Johanna: <u>Other People's Lives</u>. Knopf, 1975.

> Short stories collection of note.

_____: <u>O My America</u>! Harper & Row, 1980.

> The life of an American rebel Jewish writer seen through the eyes of his daughter. (Received <u>Present Tense</u> and Jewish Book Council Awards for 1980.)

Karp, Lila: The Queen Is in the Garbage. Belmont, 1971.

    Flashbacks of a Jewish woman's life including a relationship with a rejecting mother and other brutal experiences.

Kaufelt, David A.: A Late Bloomer. Harcourt Brace Jovanovich, 1979.

Kelly, Myra: Little Aliens. Scribner's, 1910.

    Short stories about Jewish ghetto.

_____ : Little Citizens. McClure & Phillips, 1904. Also pap.

_____ : Wards of Liberty. McClure & Phillips, 1907.

Kohan, Rhea. Hand-Me-Downs. Random House, 1980.

    The story of "notorious" Malka who becomes a legend in her little Polish village because she refused to be like anyone else.

Kossover, Toni: The Diary of a Career Girl. Bantam pap., 1974.

    It's unclear whether this is fiction or autobiography or combination of both, but it's nauseatingly true-to-life, a day-by-day account of divorcee with children, working for WWD, no Jewish consciousness and lousy life.

Kurtz, Irma: The Grand Dragon. Dutton, 1979.

Leahy, Syrell Rogovin: A Book of Ruth. Simon & Schuster, 1974; also pap., 1976.

    Jewish teacher's affair with priest.

Lelchuk, Alan: Miriam at Thirty-Four. Farrar, Straus & Giroux, 1974.

    Unappetizing treatment of a Jewish heroine.

Levine, Faye: Solomon and Sheba. Richard Marek Publishers/Putnam's, 1980.

List, Shelley Steinman: Did You Love Daddy When I Was Born? Saturday Review Press, 1972. Also pap.

Lukas, Susan: Fat Emily. Stein & Day, 1974.

    Struggle of college woman growing up in assimilated Los Angeles family. Interesting but leaves too much undescribed.

Morgan, Carole: Heirlooms. Macmillan, 1980.

    Three generations of Jewish women.

Olsen, Tillie: *Tell Me a Riddle*. Dell pap. (Laurel ed.), 1976.

    Title story of book of short stories. Searing story of her life told by old Jewish woman.

Ozick, Cynthia: *Levitation: Five Fictions*. Knopf, 1981.

    Five "fictions" probing the unsettled—and unsettling—worlds that men and women create out of obsession, fantasy and delusion.

Paley, Grace: *The Little Disturbances of Man*. Bantam pap., 1969.

    Short stories, many about Jewish women in New York.

Parent, Gail: *David Meyer Is a Mother*. Harper & Row, 1975.

    MCP falls in love with writer masquerading as a masseuse. He "mothers" their child.

_____: *Sheila Levine Is Dead and Living in New York*, Putnam, 1972.

    Jewish girl who wants to get married and can't, attempts suicide. Very contrived and unfunny.

Petesch, Natalie L.M.: *The Odyssey of Katinou Kalokovich*. United Sisters, 1974.

Piercy, Marge: *Small Changes*. Doubleday, 1973.

    Blockbuster novel revolving around lives of two women, Beth and Miriam. Miriam is Jewish, middle-class, has a math career, but settles into an extremely oppressive marriage. Great for CR.

Rapoport, Nessa: *Preparing for Sabbath*. William Morrow, 1980.

Raskin, Barbara: *Loose Ends*. Bantam pap., 1973.

    Mother of four abandoned by husband, lover and shrink tries to cope. Ending too pat but rest is harrowing.

Rechtman, Janet: "Chanukah: Camp Hill, Alabama," Blicksilver anthology, op cit.

Richter, Ida: *Compassion*. Silver Springs, MD: Malcolm House, 1973, pap.

    Novel of the Depression by 78-year-old woman, edited by her granddaughter, Sally Banes, and published by her and her father.

Roiphe, Ann: <u>Long Division</u>. Simon & Schuster, 1972. Also pap.
> Woman takes journey to Mexico encountering her Jewishness on the way.

Rose, Louise Blecher: <u>The Launching of Barbara Fabrikant</u>. McKay, 1974.

Rosenbluth, Sally: <u>Feast of Ashes</u>. Atheneum, 1981.

Rossner, Judith: <u>To One Precipice</u>. Morrow, 1966. [Out of print.]
> A first novel about a Jewish woman born into poverty.

Roth, Philip: <u>Goodbye Columbus</u>. Bantam, 1959.
> First fictional appearance of Jewish princess stereotype.

_____: <u>Portnoy's Complaint</u>. Random House, 1967; also pap.
> To be read with Pauline Bart's work.

Rothchild, Sylvia: <u>Sunshine and Salt</u>. Simon & Schuster, 1964.
> Generational conflict in New England town.

Schaeffer, Susan Fromberg: <u>Falling</u>. Macmillan, 1973.
> Successful psychoanalysis of woman raised by oppressive East European family. Copout ending.

_____: <u>Love</u>. E.P. Dutton, 1981.

Sinclair, Jo: <u>Wasteland</u>. Harper, 1946. [Out of print.]
> Jewish man undergoes analysis and describes his siblings, including his sisters—one married and unhappy; another a lesbian.

Slesinger, Tess: <u>The Unpossessed</u>. Simon & Schuster, 1934; Avon, 1966.
> Women stuck in traditional roles within male-dominated radical, political and intellectual circles.

Smith, Robert Kimmel: <u>Sadie Shapiro, Matchmaker</u>. Simon & Schuster, 1980.

Stillman, Roberta: <u>Blood Relations</u>. Boston: Little, Brown, 1977.
> Short stories about mothers, grandparents, children and isolated women and men.

Steel, Danielle: <u>The Ring</u>. Delacorte Press, 1980.
> A multi-generational romantic novel. The tragic story of Kassandra von Gotthard, a rich German woman and her love affair with a Jew, writer Dolff Stern.

Tagliacozzo, Rhoda: <u>Saving Graces</u>. St. Martin's Press, 1979.

> An Orthodox Jew and an Italian Catholic marry to escape from their respective backgrounds. But they discover they cannot reject their heritages without suffering. Their parents are unpleasant stereotypes.

Tenenbaum, Silvia: <u>Rachel, The Rabbi's Wife</u>. Morrow, 1977.

> Sex in suburbia. The book that had the Jewish Establishment incensed for its criticism of congregants and local leaders.

Weingarten, Violet: <u>A Woman of Feeling</u>. Knopf, 1972.

_____: <u>Mrs. Beneker</u>. Simon & Schuster, 1967; Pocket Books, 1977.

> Sometimes humorous, sometimes painful account of day-to-day life of an assimilated middle-aged woman.

Weinzweig, Helen: <u>Basic Black with Pearls</u>. William Morrow, 1981.

Winslow, Thyra Samter: <u>Picture Frames</u>. Scholarly Reprints, 1971.

> Writer was well known in the 40's for short stories of urban middle-class Jews and their problems. Above original appeared in 1935.

Worthen, Helena Harlow: <u>Perimeters</u>. Harcourt Brace Jovanovich, 1980.

> A woman's search for a betrayed Jewish heritage.

Wouk, Herman: <u>Marjorie Morningstar</u>. Doubleday, 1955; also pap.

> Aspiring middle-class actress ends up in suburbia, just like her proto-hippie boyfriend predicted. Note how author extols virginity and other middle-class values as being intrinsically Jewish. The book that ruined so many women's minds; good for CR. (See critique by Elenore Lester in <u>Lilith</u>, vol. I, no. 1.)

Yezierska, Anzia: <u>Bread Givers</u>. Persea Books,* 1978.

> Reprint of 1925 edition. The story of Sara Smolinsky's struggle for freedom; a vivid picture of immigrant life on the lower East Side. This book lives. It is timeless—it is a friend. [M.H.]

Yglesias, Helen: <u>How She Died</u>. Houghton-Mifflin, 1972.

_____: <u>Family Feeling</u>. Ballantine, 1977.

---

*Yezierska's short stories and novels are being reprinted by this publisher. Her major works were: <u>All I Could Never Be</u> (1932), <u>The Arrogant Beggar</u> (1927), <u>Children of Loneliness</u> (1923), <u>Hungry Hearts</u> (1920) and <u>Salome of the Tenements</u> (1927). (The last is based on Rose Pastor Stokes, a radical Jew who married a rich Christian liberal.)

IV. WOMEN IN ISRAEL

A. Books: Non-Fiction

Bar-David, Molly Lyons: <u>My Promised Land</u>. Putnam's Sons, 1953.

Ben-Zvi, Rachel Yanait: <u>Coming Home</u>. Herzl Press, 1964.
   Autobiography of pioneer of Second Aliya period.

Cohen, Geula: <u>Woman of Violence</u>. Holt, Rinehart, 1966.
   Autobiography of right-wing M.K.'s 15 years in Stern Group (part of pre-state Underground). Note: Cohen is violently anti-feminist today.

Dash, Joan: Op cit.(see section III).

Datan, Nancy, Antonovsky, Aaron and Maoz, Benjamin: <u>A Time to Reap: The Middle Age of Women in Five Israeli Subcultures</u>. Baltimore: Johns Hopkins Univ. Press, 1981.
   Medical and psychological surveys on middle-aged Israeli women's reaction to menopause.

Davidson, Margaret: <u>The Golda Meir Story</u>. Charles Scribner's Sons, 1976.

Dayan, Ruth and Dudman, Helga: <u>And Perhaps...</u>. Harcourt 1973.
   Frank autobiography (see also Stone interview, reference IV.B).

Dayan, Yael: <u>Three Weeks in October</u>. Delacorte Press, 1979.
   Thoughts about (and by) a Jewish woman in the Israeli army.

Dobrin, Arnold: <u>A Life for Israel: The Story of Golda Meir</u>. Dial Press, 1974.

Eisen, Naava: <u>The Working Woman in Israel</u>. Tel Aviv: Histadrut, 1975. Pamphlet.
   Women's status in the labor market. Honest about inequities.

Ginor, Fanny: <u>Socio-Economic Disparities in Israel</u>. Tel Aviv: University Publishing Projects, 1979.

Goshen-Gottstein, Esther: <u>Marriage and First Pregnancy: Cultural Influences on Attitudes of Israeli Women</u>. Tavistock, 1966.

Gruber, Ruth: <u>Raquela: A Woman of Israel</u>. Coward, McCann and Geoghegan, 1978; also pap., New American Library.

Hazleton, Lesley: <u>Israeli Women: The Reality Behind the Myths</u>. Simon & Schuster, 1978.

> Deep, honest look at the condition of Israeli women. Excellent and revealing. Missing: information on work life.

Katzenelson-Rubashow (Shazar), Rachel: <u>The Plough Woman: Records of the Pioneer Women of Palestine</u>. Nicholas L. Brown, 1932; pap. reprint by Pioneer Women and Schocken, 1975.

> Important and moving. Beware: reprint is missing one entire section of original. Also Marie Syrkins' anti-feminist introduction in which she refers to "early feminist extravagances."

Lindheim, Irma L.: <u>Parallel Quest</u>. Th. Yoseloff, 1962.

> Autobiography of woman from assimilated German-Jewish family who becomes a Zionist and settles in a kibbutz. (The author died April 10, 1978.)

Lytle, Elizabeth Edith: <u>Women in Israel</u>. Vance Bibliographies, 1979.

Maimon, Ada: <u>Women Build a Land</u>. Herzl Press, 1962.

> Excellent and important herstory of Working Women's Movement in pre-State Israel from early 1900s: first feminist wave. Key resource. Author fought feminist battles until her death in 1973.

Mann, Peggy: <u>Golda—The Life of Israel's Prime Minister</u>. Coward McCann, 1972. Pocket Books, 1973.

Meir, Golda: <u>My Life</u>. Putnam, 1975.

> Conceals more than it reveals, more history than personal experience.

Pincus, Chasya: <u>Came from the Four Winds</u>. Herzl Press, 1971.

> Moving life stories of men and women—alumni of Youth Aliyah.

Rabikowitz, Dalia (sp. also Ravikovitch): <u>The New Israeli Writers</u>. Funk and Wagnalls, 1969.

> This translated collection (from Hebrew) contains a story by Ravikovitch, "Uri and Rachel."

Rein, Natalie: <u>Daughters of Rachel: Women in Israel</u>. Viking/Penguin, pap. 1980.

> Analysis of women in Israel as seen through the eyes of a British feminist.

Rennert, Maggie: *Shelanu—An Israel Journal*. Englewood Cliffs, NJ: Prentice-Hall, 1979.

Samuels, Gertrude: *The Secret of Gonen*. 1969, n.p.

> A documentary book by an American newspaperwoman and war correspondent who covered the Six Days War.

Slater, Robert: *Golda: The Uncrowned Queen of Israel*. Jonathan David Publishers, 1980.

> A candid portrait of former Israeli Prime Minister, Golda Meir, drawn from newly released documents from the Israel State Archives.

Spiro, Melford E.: *Kibbutz: Venture in Utopia*. Cambridge: Harvard Univ. Press, 1956.

> See esp. pp. 221-235. An important analysis of the new kibbutz society, with a postscript written in 1970.

_____: *Gender and Culture: Kibbutz Women Revisited*. Schocken, 1980.

> A look at social relations in the modern kibbutz; a study of "counter-revolution" in kibbutz conceptions regarding marriage, family, division of labor by sex, etc.

Stern, Geraldine: *Israeli Women Speak Out*. Lippincott, 1979.

> Essays by ten women.

Syrkin, Marie: *Golda Meir: Israel's Leader*. Putnam, 1970.

Talmon, Yonina: *Family and Community in the Kibbutz*. Boston: Harvard Univ. Press, 1972.

Tiger, Lionel and Shepher, Joseph: *Women in the Kibbutz*. Harcourt Brace Jovanovich, 1975.

> Sexist anti-historical study of how kibbutz women got back into the kitchen. Know the enemy.

B. *Periodicals and Book Chapters*

Aharoni, Andree Ada: "Letter to Kadreya from Haifa: To Cairo with Love," *Jewish Frontier*, May 1971, pp. 6-9.

> Autobiographical "letter," after 20 years of life in enemy countries.

Aloni, Shulamit: "Israel's Women Need Women's Lib," *Israel Magazine*, April 1971.

> Attorney emphasizes problems arising from Rabbinate's control.

Aloni, Shulamit: "The Status of Women in Israel," Judaism, vol. 22, no. 2, Spring 1973, pp. 248-256.

Averbuch, Gloria: "Her Own Story," Jewish Currents, May 1977.

    Inspiring account of Hanna Weiselberg, among first women settlers on Kibbutz Ha-Ogen.

Bar-Yosef, Rivka and Shelach, Ilana: "The Position of Women in Israel." In Integration and Development in Israel. Eisenstadt, S.N. et al., eds. Jerusalem: Israel University Press, 1970.

Ben-Yosef, Avraham C.: "The Woman on the Kibbutz," Israel Horizons, February 1957.

Bell, R.: "A Women's Center Grows in Haifa," Jewish Digest, December 1979.

    The growth of feminism in Israel.

Blumberg, R.L.: "From the Fields of Revolution to the Laundries of Dis-Content." In Women in the World: A Comparative Study. Iglitzin, L. and Ross, R., eds. Santa Barbara: Clio Press, 1976.

Blumenthal, A.H.: "Wanted: Equality for Jewish Women," Jewish Spectator, Summer 1979.

Bondy, Ruth: "Grand-daughter Wants Conservative Femininity," Hadassah, May 1972.

    Critical of work situation in Israel today but puts much blame on women for accepting old roles.

Breitberg, S.: "Women's Art in Israel," Ariel, November 1979.

Carr, Judy: "Be Proud, My Daughter," Pioneer Woman, April 1976.

Cass, Joan B.: "We Don't Need Women's Lib in Israel," JSPS, November 1972.

    Descriptive critique of many Israeli women's attitude at that time.

Chesler, Phyllis: Interview with, by Aviva Cantor. Lilith, vol. I, no. 2.

    Insightful analysis, mainly focusing on Israeli women and role of Israel.

Davis, Esther: "Is Israel a Matriarchal Society?" Mosaic, no. 28.

Dayan, Yael: "Israeli Women—More Feminine than Feminist," New York Times Sunday Magazine, February 13, 1977.

    Apologetics. Pontificates as to why Israeli women are not now and cannot be and should not become feminists. Good CR for those who still believe in the woman-on-a-tractor-with-a-gun myth.

de Beauvoir, Simone: "Israeli Women," New Outlook, May 1967.

Dulzin, Annette: "The Influence of Women in Israel," Forum (WZO Quarterly, Jerusalem), no. 34, Winter 1974.

> One wonders how the author could live in Israel and yet reach the conclusion that conditions are really good for women.

Elizur, Judith Neulander: "Women in Israel," Judaism, Spring 1973.

Elkin, Lillian: "Golda Meir Tells the Story of Her Life," Israel Horizons, April 1976.

> Review of autobiography.

Ephron, Nora: "Women in Israel: The Myth of Liberation," New York, November 19, 1973, pp. 63-66.

> While some points made are true, article's whole purpose seems a snide attack on Israel and lack of compassion for its women. No sisterhood.

Epstein, Perle: "Women in a War-Torn Society," Present Tense, Summer 1975.

Fallaci, Oriana: "Interview with Golda Meir," Ms., April 1973.

> Classic, fascinating.

Freedman, Marcia: "Feminist Publishing in Israel," Women's Studies Newsletter, vol. VIII, no. 1, Winter 1980.

——————: "What Is a Nice Jewish Feminist Doing Here?" Israel Horizons, vol. 25, no. 2, February 1977, pp. 16-22.

> Excellent, radical feminist analysis of Israeli society [M.H.].

Friends Talk: An Israeli feminist magazine. Kaufman, Tamar, ed. No. 1, Winter 1978/9, Kol Ishah, 95 Yefinuf Street, Haifa, Israel.

> Bilingual, Hebrew-English.

Friedlander, Dov: "Family Planning in Israel: Irrationality and Ignorance," Journal of Marriage and the Family, January 1973.

Friedman, David: "Moetzet Ha-Poalot," Israel, September 1972.

Frye, Thelma Ruby: "From Pretoria: Golda vs. Apartheid," Present Tense, Spring 1979.

Furstenberg, Rochelle: "Abortion in Israel: Pros and Cons," <u>Hadassah</u>, March 1976.

>The situation in 1976. Good piece in spite of omission of number of annual illegal abortions: over 60,000.

_____: "The Feminine Role," <u>Jerusalem Post International Edition</u>, November 7, 1978.

_____: "War Widows in Israel," <u>Women's American ORT Reporter</u>, March/April 1976.

Glazer, Myra (Schotz): "The Journal of Santa Caterina," <u>Chrysalis</u>, prob. 1979.

>Personal account of feelings and experiences on desert hike in Israel.

Habonim: <u>Kibbutz: A New Society</u>, Kibbutz Aliya Desk Pamphlet.

>Includes: Horowitz, Emil: "Women and Family in the Kibbutz"; Gerson, Menachem: "The Family in the Kibbutz"; Golan, Yona: "The Woman in the Kibbutz."

Hashomer Hatzair: "Women on Kibbutz," <u>Mishmar</u> (Tel Aviv), April 1967.

Hava: "Women on Watch," Reprinted by JSPS, February 1973 from <u>Palestine Review</u>, November 18, 1938.

Hazleton, Lesley: "Kibbutz Women," <u>The New York Times</u>, March 4, 1976, p. 26, Section L.

Kahanoff, Jacqueline: "Grandmother Was a Militant Feminist," <u>Hadassah</u>, May 1972.

>About pioneer women of Second Aliya period.

_____: "To Be or Not to Be...Independent," <u>Pioneer Woman</u>, September 1975.

Kaufman, A.: "Rabbanit Bracha Kapach; Personification of Tzedaka," <u>Israel Digest</u>, August 24, 1979.

Krausz, Judy: "Rivka Gruber: A Legend in Her Own Time," <u>Pioneer Woman</u>, September 1976.

_____: "Yes, There's a Women's Movement in Israel," <u>Council Woman</u>, October 1975.

>Views of eight Israeli women.

Lahav, Pnina: "Golda's Ambiguous Legacy," <u>Lilith</u>, no. 6, 1979.

>Why she fought feminism while striving in her own life for feminist goals.

Lahav, P.: "The Status of Women in Israel—Myths and Reality," The American Journal of Comparative Law, no. 24, 1974.

Leibler, D.: "During War of Independence: Women in the Underground," Israel Digest, August 24, 1979.

Lerner, Diana: "Women at the Helm," Pioneer Woman, June 1977.

> Short biographical sketches of seven leading Israeli business women.

Levenberg, S.: "Golda Meir's 'Secret Weapon' on her 80th Birthday," Jewish Frontier, May 1978.

Louvish, Misha: "Golda Takes Charge," Jewish Frontier, April 1969.

> Discusses Golda's assumption of power after sudden death of Prime Minister Levi Eshkol.

Nardi, Shulamit S.: "Twenty-Two Women Honored on Israel's Birthday," Hadassah, June-July 1979.

Nesvisky, Matthew: "Women's Liberation and the Kibbutz," Jewish Spectator, October 1973.

Oyserman, Erika: "Israeli Women in Yom Kippur War," ORT Reporter, Winter 1973/74.

_____: "The Girls of the Golan," Pioneer Woman, February 1976.

Padan-Eisenstark, Dorit: "Are Israeli Women Really Equal?" Journal of Marriage and the Family, 1973.

_____: "Image and Reality: Women's Status in Israel." In Cross-Cultural Perspectives in Women's Status. Leavitt, R., ed. Mouton 1974.

Pogrebin, Letty Cottin: "A Feminist Goes to Israel," Ms., October 1977.

> Chronicle of trip in December 1976 by author and other American feminists. General introductory overview of the scene.

Precker, Michael: "Draft Is a Fact of Israeli Women's Lives," Bergen: NJ: The Sunday Record, March 23, 1980, p. 24 ff.

Rabb, Christine: "Women of Israel," Boston Globe Magazine, April 6, 1980.

> Describes harassment of women observed during trip to Israel.

Ravikovitch, Dalia: "Thank God I'm a Woman," Israel, April 1971.

>Pathetic; feminine mystique transferred to Israel where middle-class women use it to justify life of idleness, privilege and pronatalism.

Reisman, D.: "Jerusalem's Machon Gold: Educating Modern Religious Women," Israel Digest, December 14, 1979.

Rosner, Menachem: "Women in the Kibbutz: Changing Status and Concepts," Asian and Africa Studies, no. 3, 1967.

_____: "Women in the Kibbutz," American Journal of Orthopsychiatry, no. 41, July 1971.

Rothbard, Dvorah: "Beba Idelson: A Tribute," Pioneer Woman, January 1976.

Russell, Diana E.H. and Van de Ven, Nicole: The Proceedings of the International Tribunal on Crimes Against Women. Millbrae, CA: Les Femmes, 1976, pap.

>Includes testimonies from Israeli women.

Scott, Beverly: "Women in the 1975 Knesset," Hadassah, January 1975, p. 14 ff.

>Contains photos and profiles of the women listed.

Sharon, L.: Jerusalem's Mysterious Daughters," Israel Digest, July 26, 1979.

Sharon, Lynn: "Tova Sanhedrai, Fighter for Women's Rights," JSPS, April, 1973.

>Orthodox former Knesset member.

Sigler, B.: "Women Instructors in Today's Israeli Army," Jewish Digest, April 1979.

Soferr, Barbara: "Make Me a Match," Present Tense, Winter 1976.

Sokoloff, J.A.: "Dahlia Raz—Commander of Chen," Pioneer Woman, October/November 1977.

>Commander-in-Chief of the Women's Army Corps in Israel.

Stern, Sol: "Marriage Israeli Style," JSPS, January 1973.

Stiller, Nikki: "Peace Without Honor—The Battle of the Sexes in Israel," Midstream, May 1976.

Stiller, Nikki: "Women of the Kibbutz," <u>Midstream</u>, February 1976.

    Review of <u>The Plough-Woman</u> and Tiger/Sepher book (op cit.).

Stone, Amy: "Ruth Dayan: Independence But Not Feminism," <u>JSPS</u>, November 1977.

    Chilling interview revealing that she has learned nothing from her own tragedy as a woman.

_____: "Women on the Kibbutz: Still Working in the Kitchens and the Laundries," <u>Women's American ORT Reporter</u>, September/October 1976.

    Review of Tiger.

Syrkin, Marie: "The Role of Zionism in the Life of Modern Women," <u>Pioneer Woman</u>, March/April 1977.

_____: "Remembering Golda," <u>Midstream</u>, February 1979.

Tzur, Jacob: "Golda Meir," <u>Jewish Frontier</u>, January 1975, pp. 19-26.

    Article by Ambassador Tsur which first appeared in <u>Maariv</u>.

Ullian, Florence: "What Won't Be Done by Women Won't Be Done!" <u>Pioneer Woman</u>, September/October 1978.

    Report on Commission on Status of Women in Israel. Calls for Pioneer women to press for women's equality.

Weissman, Debbie: "A Woman's Diary of the Yom Kippur War," <u>Response</u>,* February 1974.

    How an American Ezrat Nashim member felt during the 1973 War.

Yochelson, Mindy: "Sex and the Jewish Woman," <u>Canadian Jewish Digest</u>, vol. XVI, no. 4, 1976.

Yuval, Annabell: "The Israeli Woman," <u>Judaism</u>, Spring 1973.

    Statistics.

C. _Fiction_

Broner, E.M.: A Weave of Women. Holt, Rinehart, 1978.

Dayan, Yael: New Face in the Mirror. World, 1959; also pap.

Gruber, Ruth: Raquela, A Woman of Israel.

> A Sabra nurse in the Brish interment camps, around which is woven the story of Israel and the formation of the State.

Mitovsky, Dina: Jerusalem Rock. M. Evans, 1980.

> A romance between two musicians: an American Jew and a Sabra. The Six-Day War makes them weigh the relative values of art and career vs. familial fidelity and national loyalty.

Oz, Amos: My Michael. English translation. Knopf, 1972; also pap.

> Beautiful sensitive novel of crack-up of Jerusalem student/housewife/teacher, 1950's. Classical novel on depression.

Rogan, Barbara: Changing States. Doubleday, 1981.

> Novel about Israeli girl's conflict with Holocaust survivor parents who oppose her involvement with Arab lover.

Topol, Allan: A Woman of Valor. Morrow, 1980.

> An Egyptian Jew and her long-rooted family are forced to emigrate after the establishment of Israel. Later, she becomes a first-rate anti-terrorist agent in Israel's elite corps.

Viertel, Joseph: The Last Temptation. Simon & Schuster, 1951.

> Young woman, raised to be clinging and dependent, survives the Holocaust, is forced to conduct an independent struggle and then faces the choice of giving in to her upbringing or continuing an independent life.

V. JEWISH WOMEN IN OTHER COUNTRIES

A. Books: Non-Fiction

Charles, Gerda, ed.: Modern Jewish Stories. Prentice-Hall, 1963.

    British novelist and literary critic whose works are often of Jewish content.

Cowan, Evelyn: Portrait of Alice. Taplinger, 1979.

    Jewish housewife syndrome, Great Britain.

_____: Spring Remembered: A Scottish-Jewish Childhood. Taplinger, 1968.

Gordimer, Nadine: Burgher's Daughter. London: Cape, 1979.

    Autobiographical account of South African writer.

Grant, Myrna: The Journey: The Story of Rose Warmer: Courage, Faith, Drama. London: Hodder & Stoughton, 1979.

Michel, Jean: Dora. London: Weidenfeld & Nicolson, 1979.

Rosenfeld, Lulla: Bright Star of Exile. London: Barrie & Jenkins, 1979.

Rusinek, Alla: Like a Song, Like a Dream. Scribners, 1973.

    Soviet Jewish activists' struggle.

Ruskay, Sophie: Horsecars and Cobblestones. Beechhurst Press, 1948; A.S. Barnes reprint, 1973.

    Describes her childhood in Montreal.

Tindall, Gillian: Fly Away Home. Walker & Co., 1971.

    Woman living in London with her family reexamines her identity as a Jew and her ties to Israel during the Six-Day War.

B. Periodicals and Book Chapters

Ben, Yaakov I.: "Beate Klarsfeld: A German Woman of Valor," Woman's American ORT Reporter, September/October 1977.

    Christian woman who fights Nazism and anti-Semitism.

Bershadskaya, Liuba: "24 Years in the Life of...," The New York Times Sunday Magazine, March 14, 1971. Reprint available from Students Struggle for Soviet Jewry.

    Autobiographical account.

Cowen, Ida G.: "Bene Israel Marriage in Bombay," Jewish Frontier, November 1975, pp. 18-19.

Darel, Sylvia: A Sparrow in the Snow. Stein & Day, 1973.

Soviet Jewish woman's autobiography, little Jewish content.

Frankel, William: "Women Fight for Equality," Jewish Chronicle (London), Colour Magazine, September 22, 1978.

Glanville, Brian: A Second Home. London: Secker and Warburg, 1965.

Young actress' attempt to escape an unfortunate romance [fiction].

Gotein, S.D.: "A Mediterranean Society: The Jewish Communities of the Arab World as Portrayed in the Documents of the Cairo Geniza," vol. III. In The Family, Univ. of Calif., 1978, pp. 160-359.

Herman, Ilana: "More Fighting than Death: A Syrian Jew Tells Her Story," Hadassah, June 1975.

Woman who escaped the Damascus ghetto tells of the constant terror in which the Syrian Jewish community has lived since the Six-Day War.

Klarsfeld, Beate: "She Won't Let Germans Forget," Israel Horizons, December 1975.

Leven, Schneir: "Breast Feeding: Religious Influences," Journal of Psychology and Religion, Spring 1979.

Comparison of Orthodox and secular mothers in South Africa. Very superficial.

Rosten, Leo: "Proverbs and Jewish Women." In Treasury of Jewish Quotations, Bantam, 1977.

Introduction offensive, as are many quotes which reflect negative attitudes to women.

Schenker, Jonathan: "Beate Klarsfeld: One Woman's Campaign," Pioneer Woman, October/November 1975.

Servan-Schreiber, Claire: "Simone Veil: 20 Million Frenchwomen Won't Be Wrong," Ms., February 1976.

Health minister's fight for legal abortion in France. She's a Holocaust survivor.

Werner, Alfred: "The Genius of Anna Ticho," Pioneer Woman, February 1976.

Life and work of the Israeli woman artist, then not well known.

VI. IN THE HOLOCAUST AND RESISTANCE

A. Books: Non-Fiction

Berg, Mary: Warsaw Ghetto: A Diary. Fischer, 1945.

Bilik, Dorothy Seidman: Immigrant-Survivors: Post Holocaust Consciousness in Recent Jewish American Fiction. Middletown, CT: Wesleyan University Press, 1980.

Birenbaum, Halina: Hope Is the Last to Die. Twayne Publishers, 1971; also pap.

Testimony. Quintessential Jewish mother, and about sisterhood in ghettos and camps.

Brand, Sandra: I Dare to Live. Shengold, 1979.

Testimony of a survivor.

Dribben, Judith Strick: A Girl Called Judith Strick. Pyramid, pap. 1972. [And Some Shall Live title by Keter Books, Jerusalem, 1969.]

Autobiography of author who spied for WWII Polish partisans and survived.

Eliav, Arie L.: The Voyage of the Ulua. Sabra Books, 1969.

Ship of women refugees makes its way to Palestine through British blockade.

Epstein, Helen: Children of the Holocaust: Conversations with Sons and Daughters of Survivors. G.P. Putnam's Sons/Bantam, 1979; also Bantam pap., 1980.

Feld, Merilla: I Chose to Live. Manor Books, 1979.

Autobiographical account of Holocaust era.

Fenelon, Fania: Playing for Time. Atheneum, 1977.

A member of women's orchestra at Birkenau camp speaks with much love for her sisters and her music.

Guber, Rivka: Village of the Brothers: Memoirs of the Members of Kfar Ahim. Shengold Publishers, 1979.

Memoirs of survivors of the Holocaust.

Gurdus, Luba Krugman: The Death Train. Shocken, 1979.

> Testimony of a Maidanek camp survivor, illustrated with her drawings.

Hart, Kitty: I Am Alive. London: Abelard-Schuman, 1961; also Corgi, pap., 1962.

> Testimony of an Auschwitz survivor.

Heyman, Eva: The Diary of Eva Heyman. Jerusalem: Yad Vashem, 1974.

> A 13-year-old Hungarian Jewish girl during the Holocaust years.

Holder, Maryse: Give Sorrow Words: M. Holder's Letters from Mexico. Grove, 1979.

> Survivor testimony.

Kats, Elizabeth: Child of the Holocaust. London: Collins, 1979.

Kirk, Robert: Women in Hitler's Germany: The Limits of Misogyny. Academy Chi Ltd., 1979.

Koehn, Ilse: Mischling, Second Degree: My Childhood in Nazi Germany. Greenwillow/Morrow, 1978.

> Testimony of a woman who is part Jewish.

Kovaly, Heda and Kohak, Efrayim: The Victors and the Vanquished. Horizon Press, 1973.

> Autobiography of Czech woman who survived Auschwitz and Slansky trials period.

Kuchler-Silberman, Lena: My 100 Children. Doubleday, 1961 [Transl. from Hebrew].

> Autobiographical account of woman who survived Holocaust, searched for surviving children and brought them to London.

Klein, Gerda Weissman: All But My Life. Hill & Wang, 1957.

> Survivor testimony.

Kluger, Ruth and Mann, Peggy: The Last Escape: The Launching of the Largest Secret Rescue Movement of All Time. Doubleday, 1973.

> Peggy Mann interviewed Ruth Kluger (1914-1980) in over 1000 hours of tapes to describe the work of this one woman in a one-member team that rescued Jews during WW II.

Langfus, Anna: The Whole Land Brimstone. Pantheon Books, 1962.

> Fictionalized testimony. The author committed suicide.

Leitner, Isabella: *Fragments of Isabella: A Memoir of Auschwitz.* Crowell, 1978.

Masters, Anthony: *The Summer That Bled: The Biography of Hannah Senesh.* St. Martin's Press, 1972.

> Biography of Senesh in context of 1944 Hungarian situation, including the Kastner case.

Meed, Vladka: *On Both Sides of the Wall* [Transl. from Yiddish; also issued by Ghetto Fighters' House and HaKibbutz Hameyuchad, Israel) 1977. Distr. Jewish Labor Bund.

Novitch, Miriam: *Sobibor—Martyrdom and Revolt.* Holocaust Library/Schocken, 1980.

> Collection of documents and testimonies about this infamous death camp, eight by women. Important resource.

Rabinsky, Beatrice and Mann, Gertrude: *Journey of Conscience. Young People Respond to the Holocaust.* Cleveland: Collins, 1979.

Rose, Leesha: *The Tulips Are Red.* Cranbury, NJ: A.S. Barnes, 1978.

> About Rose's work in the Dutch Underground.

Rosen, Donia: *The Forest, My Friend.* World Federation of Bergen-Belsen Association, 1971.

> Testimony.

Rosenbaum, Irving J.: *The Holocaust and Halachah.* N.Y.: Ktav, 1976.

> Special Responsa explained, including abortion in the unusual circumstances of the Holocaust.

Rothchild, Sylvia, ed.: *Voices from the Holocaust.* New American Library, 1981.

> Taped stories of 38 men and women Holocaust victims.

Senesh, Hannah: *Letters, Diary, Poems.* Herzl Press, 1972.

Suhl, Yuri: *They Fought Back.* Crown, 1967; also pap.

> Biographical accounts include Zofia Yaika, Mala Zimetbaum, Rosa Robota, Niuta Teitelboim (Wanda). Invaluable.

Syrkin, Marie: *Blessed Is the Match.* Phila.: Jewish Publication Society, 1947; pap. rept. 1977.

> Accounts of the resistance: Hannah Senesh, Zivia Lubetkin and others.

Tillion, Germaine: <u>Ravensbruck</u>. Anchor/Doubleday, 1947; pap.

> Excellent scholarly report by a survivor of the women's concentration camp. Most significant: her description of how the women's support systems increased survival rates contrasted with that of the men.

Traub, Barbara Fishman: <u>The Matrushka Doll</u>. Richard Marek, 1979.

> Holocaust survivor testimony—but not clear if this is fictionalized or true account.

Zassenhaus, Hiltgunt: <u>Walls: Resisting the Third Reich—One Woman's Story</u>. Boston: Beacon Press, 1974.

B. <u>Periodicals and Book Chapters</u>

Alstat, Philip R.: "A Day or Forever—Ghetto Poetess," <u>Jewish Week</u>, May 10-16, 1973.

> Story of Henrike Lazowert who insisted on sharing mother's fate in death camp.

Bandler, Michael J.: "The Passion of Hannah Senesh," <u>Midstream</u>, January 1975.

> Review of Masters' book.

Benkler, Rafi: "Haviva Reik," <u>Israel Horizons</u>, April 1964.

> Remembrances of the other, forgotten woman parachutist, from Hashomer Hatzair.

Birman, Tzippora: "From the Bialystock Ghetto," <u>Jewish Spectator</u>, September 1971.

Cantor, Aviva: "TV's Holocaust: The Selling of Assimilation," <u>Lilith</u>, No. 5, 1979.

> Historical feminist/Zionist analysis of Jewish oppression and gender roles, and how the TV mini-series was rooted in conflicts arising out of them.

Davidson, Gusta ("Justina"): Diary of the Cracow resistance. In Nirenstein, Albert: <u>A Tower from the Enemy</u>. Orion Press, 1959.

Farstendiger-(Navon), Sylvia: "Hannah Senesh," <u>Jewish Liberation Journal</u>,* November 1970.

Field, Carole: "Hannah Senesh—Heroic Little Grey Mouse," <u>London Jewish Chronicle</u>, April 28, 1972.

Foldes, Susan B.: "The Wrought Iron Gate," Jewish Frontier, September 1969, pp. 29-31.

> The temple gate as last witness of her youth before the Holocaust.

Goldkorn, Dorka: "Memories of a Ghetto Fighter," Jewish Life (now called Jewish Currents), April 1950.

Gordon, Susan: "Women in the Resistance," Davka, November 17, 1976, pp. 53-57.

Grossman, Chaika: "Revolt in the Bialystok Ghetto." In Massacre of European Jewry, anthology by Hatzair, Hashomer. Tel Aviv, 1963; also in Barkai, Meyer: The Fighting Ghettos. Tower pap., 1972.

Klibanski, Bronya: "Bialystock Underground," Jewish Spectator, November 1969.

Koevary, Hannah and DeNola, David: "A Jewish Heroine: Interview with Ruth Kluger," JSPS, December 1973.

> Strong stuff, critical of Jewish Establishment.

Korczak, Ruzka: "A Shomer Pesach in the Ghetto." In Massacre anthology, op cit.

_____: "Flames Out of Ashes," Israel Horizons, April 1967.

> Vilna uprising.

Mann, Peggy: "Ruth Kluger: An Appreciation," Lilith, No. 7, 1980.

> Ruth Kluger (1914-1980) rescued Jews during the Holocaust.

Melamed, Aliza: "From the Diary of a Young Warsaw Ghetto Fighter," Israel Horizons, April 1967. Also in Massacre anthology, op cit.

Miedzyrzecka, Vlad Ka Peltel (Vlad Ka Meed): "Underground Activity on the Aryan Side of Warsaw," Yad Vashem Bulletin No. 22, Jerusalem.

Porter, Jack Nusan: "Jewish Women in the Resistance," Women's American ORT Reporter, Nov.-Dec., 1978.

Rozycka, Eugenia: "Looking Through My Window," Yad Vashem Bulletin No. 18, Jerusalem.

> Book review of testimony of Orthodox woman and her form of resistance.

Silver, Eve: "Listen to My Story," Blicksilver Anthology, op cit.

Syrkin, Marie: "Zivia Lubetkin," Midstream. October 1978.

Syrkin, Marie: "Miss Arendt Surveys the Holocaust," *Jewish Frontier*, May 1963, pp. 250-267.

Weinreich, Alisa: "Return to Austria," *Jewish Frontier*, November 1969.

> Thoughts of the Holocaust haunt this woman as she returns to the "scene of the crime."

Zdrojewicz, Malka: Excerpts from testimony given at Yad Vashem by the woman in the famous picture on the *Davka* (Summer 1971) cover and poster. *Yad Vashem Bulletin No. 22*.

C. *Fiction*

Berger, Dena: *Tell Her Another Morning*.

Carmel, Ilona: *An Estate of Memory*.

> Three women in concentration camp. Testimony.

Ettinger, Elzabieta: *Kindergarten*, priv. pub.

Field, Herman and Mierzenski, Stanislaw: *Angry Harvest*. Crowell, 1958; also pap.

> Searing story of young Jewish woman who escapes from ghetto and is sheltered by Polish peasant.

Grosman, Ladislav: *The Bride*. Doubleday, 1970.

> Czechoslovakia under the Nazis.

Karmel-Wolfe, Henia: *The Baders of Jacob Street*. J.B. Lippincott, 1970.

> Traces lives of three Jewish women in Cracow under the Nazis.

Lauterstein, Ingeborg: *The Water Castle*. Boston: Houghton-Mifflin, 1981.

> The narrator of this novel is Reyna von Meintert, a Viennese girl who grows from childhood into young womanhood as the Third Reich rises and falls.

Levin, Meyer: "Anne Frank" (drama).

> This privately published play emphasizes her Jewish consciousness, unlike the commercial Hackett version which was the "universalist" one shown on Broadway. Available in pamphlet from author (Kfar Shmaryahu, Israel).

_____: *Eva*. 1959, pap.

> Novel based on a survivor's true story; much revolves around women's friendships in the camps.

Levner, Lily Gluck with Stuart, Sandra Lee: The Silence. Secaucus, NJ: Lyle Stuart, 1980.

Lustig, Arnost: A Prayer for Katherine Horovitsova. Harper & Row, 1973; Avon pap., 1975.

Young woman defies Nazis.

Schaeffer, Susan Fromberg: Anya. Macmillan, 1974; also pap.

Fictionalized Holocaust testimony, based on interviews with survivor.

Varon, Miriam Laserson: "Unscheduled Stop," Hadassah, June 1973.

Short story about two women in Holocaust and how child of one is saved by the other.

VII. JEWISH WOMEN IN POETRY*

A. Anthologies

Bankier, Joanna, ed. et al.: The Other Voice: Twentieth Century Women's Poetry in Translation. Norton, 1976.

Betsky, Sarah Zweig: Onions and Cucumbers and Plums: 46 Yiddish Poems in English. Wayne State Univ. Press, 1977.

> Originally published in 1958.

Birman, Abraham: An Anthology of Modern Hebrew Poetry. Ram's Horn Books, 1968.

Carmi, T.: Penguin Book of Hebrew Verse. Viking/Penguin, 1981.

> New collection with Hebrew and English translations from Biblical times to today, and collected from many countries. Some poetry by women.

Cooperman, Jehiel and Sarah: America in Yiddish Poetry. Exposition Press, 1967.

Cosman, Carol; Keefe, Joan and Weaver, Kathleen, eds.: The Penguin Book of Women Poets. Viking/Penguin, 1978.

> Some poems included are of Jewish women; pre-modern and contemporary; transl. from Yiddish, Hebrew, German.

Glazer, Myra, ed.: Burning Air and a Clear Mind: Contemporary Israeli Women Poets. Ohio Univ. Press, 1981.

> Glazer and others are translators of first-time-in-English Israeli women poets, many unknown in US.

Gross, David: Love Poems from the Hebrew. Doubleday, 1976.

Howe, Florence and Bass, Ellen: No More Masks! An Anthology of Poems by Women. Doubleday, 1973.

> Howe is now the chief editor at Feminist Press. Collection contains some work of interest to Jewish women.

---

*This section prepared with the assistance of MARCIA COHN SPIEGEL, resource in Jewish women's poetry. Ms. Spiegel recommends, in addition to above anthologies and single author collections, the work of these poets for their occasional poems of Jewish content: Lyn Lifshin, Eve Merriam, Deena Metzger, Linda Pastan, Naomi Replansky, Muriel Rukeyser, Jean Starr Untermeyer and Jackie Lapidus.

Howe, Irving and Greenberg, Eliezer: *A Treasury of Yiddish Poetry.* Holt, Rinehart & Winston, 1972.

    Pap. ed., includes poems by Rashelle Veprinski, Anna Margolin, Celia Dropkin, Rajzel Zychlinska, Dvorah Fogel, Kadia Molodowsky, Rosa Gutman-Jasny, Rachel Korn and Rekudah Potash.

Joseloff, Samuel Hart: *A Time to Seek: An Anthology of Contemporary Jewish American Poets.* Union of American Hebrew Cong., 1975.

Larkin, Joan and Bulkin, Elly: *Amazon Poetry: An Anthology.* Brooklyn, NY: Out & Out Books, 1977.

    Collection contains some poems by women who have written on Jewish themes, i.e. Martha Shelley, others.

Leftwich, Joseph: *The Golden Peacock.* Thomas Yoseloff, 1961.

Mazey, Robert: *Poems from the Hebrew.* Thomas Y. Crowell, 1973.

Mintz, Ruth Finer, ed.: *Modern Hebrew Poetry: A Bilingual Anthology.* Univ. of Calif. Press, 1966.

Schappes, Morris U., ed.: *Jewish Currents Reader.* Jewish Currents, 1966.

Schwartz, Howard and Rudolf, Anthony: *Voices from the Ark: Modern Jewish Poets.* Yonkers: Pushcart Press; also Avon pap., 1980.

    Contains about 25 Jewish women poets in its 1,210 pages.

Spiegel, Marcia Cohn: *The Jewish Woman: A Portrait in Her Own Words.* National Federation of Temple Sisterhoods, 1979.

    A dramatic reading containing excerpts from the works of various Jewish women poets.

Zeldis, Chayim, ed.: *May My Words Feed Others: Reconstructionist Anthology.* A.S. Barnes, 1974.

B. *Jewish Women Poets*

Allen-Shore, Lena: *May the Flowers Grow.* Shengold Publishers, 1969.

Blank, Amy K.: *The Spoken Choice.* Cincinnati: Hebrew Union College Press, 1959.

Bloch, Chana: *Secrets of the Tribe.* Sheep Meadow Press (Persea), 1981.

    Poems; some transl. from Yiddish and Hebrew; one section on Old Testament themes, others on birth, death, dreams, men/women relationships, pregnancy, childbirth.

Borenstein, Emily: *Night of the Broken Glass*. Mason, TX: Timberline Press, 1981.

    Poems of the Holocaust and a return to Jerusalem.

Brin, Ruth F.: *A Time to Search*. Jonathan David Co., 1959.

_____: *A Rag of Love*. Minneapolis: Emmet Publishers, 1969.

Burch, Claire: *Notes of a Survivor*. Westbeth Poets Press, 1972.

Dame, Enid: *On the Road to Damascus, Maryland*. Downtown Poets, 1980.

    Poems on Jewish mythology with feminist slant; some "persona poems" of Lilith and Biblical figures.

_____: *Interesting Times*. Downtown Poets, 1978.

    Among other themes, contains *Vilda Chaya*, about coming to terms with the 70's as a Jewish woman.

_____: *Confessions*. Merrick, NY: Cross-Cultural Communications.

    Dramatic monologues of women, including that of Lot's daughter and Adah Isaacs Menken, 19th-century Jewish actress and poet.

Farber, Norma: *A Desperate Thing*. Boston: Plowshare Press, 1973.

Fell Yellin, Sarah: *Flower Children and Other Poems*. Los Angeles: Mendellin, 1969.

    Translated from Yiddish by Herman Eichenthal.

Fogel, Ruby: *Apes and Angels*. Denver: Allan Swallow, 1966.

Gershon, Karen: *Selected Poems*. Harcourt, Brace & World, 1966.

_____: *The Pulse in the Stone*. Harcourt, Brace & World, 1970.

    Latter book is translated by the author from Hebrew.

Gold, Doris B.: *Honey in the Lion: Collected Poems*. Print Center/Brooklyn and Biblio Press, Fresh Meadows, NY, 1979.

    Jewish Women's Resource Center called this work "...shot through with Yiddishkeit and women's sensitivities."

Goldberg, Leah: *Selected Poems*. San Francisco: Panjandrum Press, 1979.

    Transl. from Hebrew by Robert Friend. Well known Israeli poet who died in 1980.

Gotlieb, Phyllis: <u>Ordinary, Moving</u>. Toronto: Oxford Univ. Press, 1969.

    Contemporary poems, several on Jewish themes.

Hadas, Pamela White: <u>In the Light of Genesis</u>. Phila.: Jewish Publication Society, 1980.

    Jewish Book Council awardee; well reviewed and praised collection.

Hadas, Rachel: <u>Starting from Troy</u>. David Godine, 1975.

    Some Biblical and modern poems showing Judaic influences.

Henig, Suzanne: <u>The Age of the Assassin</u>. Aeolian Press, 1976.

Jong, Erica: <u>Loveroot</u>. Holt, Rinehart & Winston, 1975.

Kaufman, Shirley: <u>From One Life to Another</u>. Univ. of Pittsburgh Press, 1979.

_____: <u>The Floor Keeps Turning</u>. Univ. of Pittsburgh Press, 1970.

    Collection by popular American Jewish poet now living in Israel. Was winner of United States Award of International Poetry Forum for second work.

Klepfisz, Irene: <u>Periods of Stress</u>. Brooklyn: Out and Out Books, 1975.

    Poems about WW II, aloneness, relationships and the American dream.

Kolmar, Gertrud: <u>Dark Soliloquy, Selected Poems</u>. Seabury Press, 1975.

    Poet died in Auschwitz. Biographical intro. by Henry Smith. Book shows poems in German with English translations. Kolmar writes about women and their passions; nature and animal topics also.

Kruger, Fania: <u>The Tenth Jew</u>. Dallas: Kaleidograph Press, 1949.

Kruger, Mollee: <u>Unholy Writ</u>. Bethesda, MD: Maryben Books, 1970.

    Humorous verse on Jewish life with some on Jewish women by an author whose columns have appeared in <u>The Jewish Week</u> and other Anglo-Jewish weeklies over the years. <u>More Unholy Writ</u> was a second edition.

Lazarus, Emma: <u>Songs of a Semite: The Dance to Death and Other Poems</u>. Irvington Publishers, 1970.

    Rept. of the famous 1882 edition.

_____: <u>Selections from the Prose and Poetry of Emma Lazarus</u>, Schappes, Morris U., ed. NY: Emma Lazarus Federation of Jewish Women's Clubs, 1978.

    First edition appeared in 1944.

Levenberg, Diane: *Out of the Desert*. Doubleday, 1979.
> Contemporary confessional poems with Jewish sensibilities by the then poetry editor of *Lilith* magazine. Widely reviewed.

Levertov, Denise: *With Eyes at the Back of Our Heads*. New Directions, 1959.
> This well-known American poet (whose family were WW II refugees) often writes of Jewish themes of survival. She has written more than ten books of poetry.

Marx, Anne: *Hear O Israel and Other Poems*. Framestown, NH: Golden Quill Press, 1975.

Mintz, Ruth Finer: *Jerusalem Poems—Love Songs*. Jerusalem: Masada Press, 1976.

_____: *The Darkening Green*. Denver, CO: Big Mountain Press, 1965.

_____: *Traveler Through Time*. Jonathan David Publishers, 1970.

Moise, Penina: *Secular and Religious Work*. Charleston, SC: Nicholas Duffy, 1911.

Morgan, Robin: *Monster*. Random House, 1972.
> This well-known feminist and activist is well known for her essays and critiques on women.

Ravikovitch, Dalia: *A Dress of Fire*. San Francisco: Panjandrum Press, 1976 [and London: Menard Press].
> Translated from Hebrew by Chana Bloch.

Sachs, Nelly: *O the Chimneys*. Sunburst/Farrar, Straus & Giroux, 1967.
> Translated from German. Sachs shared the Nobel with Agnon for her searing, singing, stunning poems of the Holocaust.

_____: *The Seeker*. Farrar, Straus & Giroux, 1970.

Salaman, Nina: *Rahel Morpurgo and Contemporary Hebrew Poets in Italy*. London: Allen & Unwin Ltd., 1924.

Sampter, Jessie: *Brand Plucked from the Fire*. Phila.: JPS, 1937.
> A popular Jewish poet of the 30's and 40's.

Schuler, Else Lasker: *Hebrew Ballads and Other Poems*. Phila.: JPS, 1980.

Segal, Edith. *I Call to You Across the Continent*. People Artists Publication, 1953.

Sklarew, Myra: <u>From the Backyard of the Diaspora: Poems</u>. Washington, DC: Dryad Press, 1976.

Starkman, Elaine Marcus: <u>Coming Together</u>. Walnut Creek, CA: Sheer Press, 1977.

_____: <u>Love Scene</u>. Walnut Creek, CA: Sheer Press, 1979.

Syrkin, Marie: <u>Gleanings: A Diary in Verse</u>. Santa Barbara, CA: Rhythms Press, 1979.

Tannenbaum, Judith: <u>The World Saying Yes</u>. Anchor Bay, CA: Nehama Press, 1980.

> Collaborated with father photographer. Contains poems about concentration camps, Israel and Jewish identity.

Tussman, Malka Heifetz: <u>Am I Also You?</u> Berkeley, CA: Tree Books, 1977.

> Translated from Yiddish by Marcia Falk.

Wechter, Vivienne Thaul: <u>A View from the Ark</u>. Barlenmir House, 1974.

Whitman, Ruth: <u>The Marriage Wig</u>. Harcourt Brace & World, 1963.

Yelin, Shulamis: <u>Seeded in Sinai</u>. Waldon Press, 1975.

VIII. SPECIAL MAGAZINE ISSUES AND PAMPHLETS

American Jewish Committee, New York: <u>Mainstream: A Periodic Newsletter on Jewish Women's Concerns</u>. Schub, Susie, ed.

> Very informative; begun in 1980.

American Jewish Committee, New York: "Single Parent Families," <u>National Jewish Family Center Newsletter</u>, Jewish Communal Affairs Department.

American Jewish Historical Society, Waltham, Mass.: Special Issue on the History of Jewish Women, September 1980. Sochen, June, ed.

<u>Ezrat Nashim</u>: "Study Guide on the Jewish Woman," Jewish Women's Resource Center, New York.

> Under headings of Halacha, Life Cycle, Women in Jewish Literature, Women in Jewish History and Israel. Lists sources and thought-provoking questions for discussion.

<u>Genesis 2</u>, Boston, Mass.: "Jewish Women," Special issue March 1971

<u>Hadassah Jewish Education Guide</u>, New York: "Women in Judaism" Fall 1979 and Winter 1980.

> Rosalyn Bell is author of the two-part series used by Hadassah members.

<u>Israel Digest</u>: Special Issue on the Jewish Woman. August 24, 1979.

Israel Information Center, New York: <u>Women in Israel</u>, March 1975.

> Special edition in honor of International Women's Year. Includes law, history, culture, kibbutz, army and minorities.

Jewish Frontier: Special Issue, Golda Meir on Her 75th Birthday. March 1974.

Articles by Marie Syrkin, et al.

_____: Special Issue on the Life of Golda Meir, 1898-1978. January 1979.

Includes article by Jacob Katzman, "Golda and America," pp. 8-12.

*Lerner, Anne Lapidus: "Who Has Not Made Me a Man: The Movement for Equal Rights for Women in American Jewry." Pamphlet, AJC. Reprinted from 1977 American Jewish Year Book.

Jewish women's changing roles in religious and communal life. Good summary.

Lilith's Rib: Offset newsletter published occasionally by Chicago area Jewish feminists, 1973 and later available from Chutzpah, Chicago.

Lubert, Steven et al.: Chutzpah: American Jewish Liberation Anthology. San Francisco: NewGlide Publications.

Rapaport, Lynne: "The Liberated Kibbutz Woman," Special Issue of Ari, April 1974.

Part 3 of a study by the author who lived in Kibbutz Na'an.

Roumani, Eve: "The Status of Women in Israel Today," Kedma, Israel Journal of Development (S.I.D.). Jerusalem: IWY Special Issue, 1975, pp. 28-31.

Swirsky, Michael, ed.: "Filmography on the Jewish Woman," Jewish Media Service, no. 14, Winter 1977.

Union of American Hebrew Cong.: Jewish Options for the 80's—Synagogue Consciousness-Raising Programs for the Decade of Women. Daum/Wurzburg, 1980.

For leaders and facilitators in Reform synagogues. (The UAHC Commission on Social Action has issued other materials for women in Reform synagogues, relating to prayer terminology and liturgy adapted to equality, including a 1979 experimental Passover Haggadah.)

Women's Caucus Religious Studies Newsletter: Jewish Woman and Religion, Berkeley, CA, Summer 1974.

---

*Available from Biblio Press.

IX. UNPUBLISHED PAPERS AND RECENT JEWISH WOMEN'S CONFERENCES*

A. Unpublished Papers

Brandow, Selma Koss: "The Status of Women in Israel: An Exploratory Study of the Woman's Movement." Paper presented to Eastern Sociological Society, April 1976.

Brandstadter, Evan D.: "Emancipation of the American Jewess," Paper on file at YIVO on women's struggle in Reform Judaism movement to 1900.

Frank, Blanche Beverly: "The American Orthodox Jewish Housewife: Generational Study in Ethnic Survival," Dissertation Abstracts International, February 1976.

Frymer, Hanita Blumfield: "The Maintenance of Ethnic Identity Among Jewish Women in an Urban Setting," Dissertation Abstracts, February 14, 1978.

Handelman, Susan: "The Image of the Feminine in Chabad Chassidic Philosophy." (Available from the author at: Department of English, University of Maryland, College Park, MD 20742.)

Levine, Ruth: "Great Expectations," Private paper.

Describes menopausal reactions in kibbutz women. (Excellent companion paper to Pauline Bart's work in the USA.)

Meyerson, Robert: "Hannah Arendt and the Jewish Army," Private paper, 1980.

See Biblio Press for access.

Marsella, Joan F.: "Portraits from the Sunny Side: Scenes and Dreams of Senior Jewish Women Residents of South Florida Beach Hotels," n.d. Southfield, R.I.

Ms. cited in Meyerhoff, Barbara, Number Our Days, 1979.

Powers, James L.: "Two Jewish Women," Student paper, 1974, Univ. of Southern Calif., Los Angeles.

Cited in Myerhoff, Barbara, op cit.

---

*See Jewish Women's Resource Center

B. Recent Jewish Women's Conferences*

Melton Center for Jewish Studies, Ohio State Univ., Columbus, Ohio: "Women in Jewish Culture: Tradition and Transformation" Forthcoming: October 29/30, 1981.

Union of American Hebrew Cong. (Reform) Task Force on Equality of Women in Judaism, 1-day retreat, Village Temple, NYC, May 17, 1981: "In God's Image."

American Jewish Committee 75th annual meeting, Washington, D.C.: Panel discussion, May 16, 1981: "The Newest American Revolution: Impact of the Women's Movement on the Jewish Woman and the Jewish Community."

Stephen Wise Free Synagogue, New York, April 5, 1981: "Working Women: Their Changing Roles within the Jewish Community."

Address by Susan Weidman Schneider, editor of Lilith magazine.

Organizing Committee for a New Jewish Agenda, December 25, 1980, Washington, DC.

Report by Ellen Willis, "Radical Jews Caught in the Middle," Village Voice, vol. XXVI, no. 6, February 4-10, 1981. Includes comment on resolutions taken and attitudes to feminism in general and current views on Jewish men/women relationships seen at event.

Women's League for Conservative Judaism, Biennial Conference: "Therefore Choose Life," November 16-20, 1980, Concord Hotel, Kiamesha, NY.

American Jewish Committee, New York: "Women of Faith in the 80's," November 9-10, Stony Point, New York

100 key women leaders from major religious groups (Catholic, Muslim, Jewish, Protestant, Evangelical) met to plan joint social and political action.

American Jewish Commitee, Boston chapter: "The Jewish Woman Today: Her Changing Options," November 2, 1980 at Brandeis University, Waltham.

Conference included speakers Sonya Michel, Bernice Sandler, Sophie Freud Lowenstein et al.

Brooklyn College Hillel, April 11-13, 1980.

Resolutions taken at first national conference on women in Israel.

---

*Arranged by date. Most recent is first.

Federation of Jewish Philanthropies, Synagogue Relations Commission: "The Jewish Woman in a Changing Society." October 28-29, 1979.

> Conference on Feminism and Judaism. Speaker: Betty Friedan. New York City.

American Jewish Committee: "Consultation on the Response of Women's Organizations to the Changing Role of Women," May 30, 1979, New York City.

Women's League for Conservative Judaism. Biennial Convention Proceedings: "And Be Thou a Blessing," November 12-16, 1978, Concord Hotel, Kiamesha, NY.

> Included the presentation of a citation to the eminent scientist, Dr. Rosalyn Yalow.

Council of Jewish Federations, New York: "The Jewish Woman as Community Leader," November 8-12, 1978. San Francisco.

American Jewish Committee, New York: "Consultation on the Portrayal of Women and Girls in Texts and Curricula of Jewish Schools." February 12, 1978.

UN Decade for Women, Houston Conference: "Jewish Organizations Pledge Support." (See Jewish Frontier, January 1978, Report by Helen S. Lewis, pp. 13-18.)

Socialist-Feminist Conference, July 4, 1975. JSPS Report, September 1975 by Ruth Mason.

> Reports on 1500 women on the left who attended, among them many Jewish women.

Jewish Feminist Organization Conference, April 1975. New York City.

> Reported by Eleanor Blau in the New York Times April 21, 1975, p. 12, "Feminists Decry Role of Women in Jewish Life."

American Jewish Committee, New York: "The Jewish Family and Jewish Identity," April 23-24, 1974.

> Included papers by Rabbi Herman Pollack and Zena Smith Blau.

International Council of Jewish Women Conference. Jerusalem, 1974. "From the Point of View of the Woman and the Mother."

> Seminar on Jewish Identity in the Modern World.

X. STUDIES AND SURVEYS

American Jewish Committee, Philadelphia Chapter: Monson, Rela Geffen: "Bringing Women In—A Survey of the Evolving Role of Women in Jewish Organizational Life in Philadelphia," 1977.

Council of Jewish Federations and Welfare Funds, New York: "Where Women Are in Federation" (Final Report), 1975.

Engel, Sophie B. and Rogul, Jane: "Career Mobility: Perceptions and Observations (from a survey of Women in Jewish Communal Service). Journal of Jewish Communal Service, Fall 1979, pp. 101-102.

Krause, Corinne: "The Status of Women in Jewish Organizations of Greater Pittsburgh." April 1980, American Jewish Committee, Pittsburgh Chapter and National Council of Jewish Women, Pittsburgh.

National Jewish Community Relations Advisory Council, New York, January 18, 1979: "Survey of the Status of Women in Professional and Lay Leadership Positions in Jewish Community Relations Agencies."

National Jewish Welfare Board, Conference of Jewish Communal Service, New York, June 5, 1977: "The Status of Women in Jewish Communal Service."

Lilith, no. 4, Spring 1978: "The Jewish Establishment Is Not an Equal Opportunity Employer."

Concise summary of surveys by National Jewish Welfare Board.

Jewish Women's Resource Center, 92nd Street Y Library, NY. Newsletter, Summer 1979: "Call for Equal Opportunity."

Jewish Education, vol. 46, no. 3, n.d.: "Women in Jewish Schools," Lang, Gerhard, et al.

National Jewish Welfare Board, New York: "Special Salaries: Male-Female Comparison," 1979.

Siegel, Morris and Lazerwitz, Bernard: "Sex, Generation and Class as Structural Variables in a Large Jewish Community," Journal of Jewish Communal Service, September 1971, pp. 91-101.

Weiner, Toby and Engel, Sophie B.: "The Status of Women in Jewish Communal Service," Presented at 79th annual meeting of National Conference of Jewish Communal Service. Washington, DC: June 5, 1977.

Findings of a survey on opportunities for woman in Jewish communal organizations (devastating!).

XI. BIBLIOGRAPHIES*

Cantor, Aviva: <u>On the Jewish Woman, 1900-1978</u>. Bibliography, Fresh Meadows: Biblio Press, 1979.

    This is now out of print; available in many libraries, both college and Jewish.

Haber, Barbara: <u>Women in America: A Guide to Books, 1963-1975</u>. (Appendix of books, 1976-1979). Univ. of Illinois, 1981.

    Many books cited are of interest to Jewish women studies. Praised by <u>Library Journal</u>.

Horowitz, Sima: <u>Jewish Women in the Community, A Bibliography</u>. American Jewish Committee, N.Y., 1977.

Lubavitch Foundation of Great Britain: <u>A Woman of Valour</u>. Brooklyn, NY: Kehot Pub. Soc.

    Essays and articles for the Orthodox Jewish woman.

Mazur, C. and Pepper, S.: <u>Women in Canada, 1965-1975</u>. McMaster University Press, 1976.

    Not ethnically identified but a useful list.

Santera, Victor D.: "The Contemporary Jewish Family—A Review of the Social Science Literature," <u>Journal of Jewish Communal Service</u>, June 1974, pp. 297-312.

    Contains extensive bibliography and includes headings such as "Who dominates in the Jewish family."

Schlachter, Gail and Belli, Donna: <u>Minorities and Women: A Guide to Reference Literature in the Social Sciences</u>. California: Reference Service Press, 1979.

<u>Women and Literature: An Annotated Bibliography of Women Writers</u>. 3rd edition, 1976; pap. Livingston College, New Brunswick, NJ.

    Contains some listings of Jewish women writers.

---

    *Consult the useful bibliography which ends <u>The Jewish Woman in America</u> by Baum, Charlotte; Hyman, Paula and Michel, Sonya. New American Library; pap., 1977.

Corrections

CORRECTIONS TO PART I EDITION: 1900-1979

Because Supplements to the first edition contained citations for 1980, the following should be noted as corrections and changes in the pages which follow:

I.A.

Guggenheim, Peggy.
Klein, Carole.   Please move these citations to Part II edition, III.A.
Lowenthal, Marvin.
Scharansky, Avital, et al. Please move to V.A.
Yezierska, Anzia. Please move to III.A.
Zbrowski, Karl should be Zbrowski, Mark.

I.B.

Axelrod, Albert S. Should be Axelrad; also correct Purah to Puah.
Friedman, Mordecai A. Please move to Part I edition, II.B.
Hill, Melvyn A. Please move to III.A.
Polt, Harriet. Please move to III.B.
Porter, Jack Nusan. Please move to III.B.
Ribalow, Harold U. This citation is now in Part II edition, III.A.
Schneider, Nina. This citation is now in Part II edition, III.C.

II.B.

Umansky, Ellen. Please delete reference to omission of Regina Jonas.
Weiner, Greta. This citation is now in Part II edition, II.B.

III.A.

Beck, Evelyn Torton, ed. Delete this title. (It is now in Part II as
    Nice Jewish Girls anthology.)
Mazow, Julia Wolf. This citation is now in Part II edition, III.A.
Meyerhoff, Barbara. Should be spelled Myerhoff.
Stern, Elizabeth G. Please delete (Levin).
Yezierska, Anzia. Please move this citation to III.C.

III.B.

Bissell, Sherry. Please move this citation to II.B.
"How To Get What...etc." Please move this citation to Part II edition,
    III.B.
Monson, Rela Geffen. _____. Delete words "a book" and substitute
    "op. cit."
Ozick, Cynthia. Please move these citations to II.B.
Plaskow, Judith. Please move first citation to II.B.
Plaskow, Judith. Please move two citations to Part II edition, II.B.

Polner, Murray. Please move to II.A.
Priesand, Sally. Please move to II.B.
White, Barbara. Please move to II.B.

III.C.

Harris, Alice Kessler.
    Please add: Introduction by Harris is incisive and very useful for historical context.
    Please move to Part II edition, III.C.
Kohan, Rhea. Please move to Part II edition, I.C.
Levine, Faye. Please move to Part II edition, III.C.
Rapoport, Nessa. This citation moved to Part II edition, III.C.
Rosenbluth, Sally. This citation moved to Part II edition, III.C.
Smith, Robert Kimmel. This citation moved to Part II edition, III.C.
Steel, Danielle. This citation moved to Part II edition, I.C.
Weinzweig, Helen. This citation moved to Part II edition, III.C.
Worthen, Helena Harlow. This citation moved to Part II edition, III.C.

IV.A.

Datan, Nancy, et al. This citation moved to Part II edition, IV.A.
Maimon, Ada. This book is out of print and has not been reissued by the publisher.
Rabikowitz, Dalia. Please move this citation to IV.C.
Rein, Natalie. Please change date of publication to 1979.
Samuels, Gertrude. Correct Six Days War to "Six Day War." Correct "n.p." to "n.d." (no date).
Slater, Robert. This citation moved to Part II edition, IV.A.
Spiro, Melford E. _Gender and Culture_, etc. This citation moved to Part II edition, IV.A.

IV.B.

Aharoni, Andree Ada. This citation moved to Part II edition, V.B.
Freedman, Marcia. "Feminist Publishing," etc. This citation moved to Part II edition, IV.B.
Stiller, Nikki. In annotation, Tiger/Sepher should be Tiger/Shepher.

IV.C.

Please move these citations to Part II edition, IV.C.:
Mitovsky, Dina; Rogan, Barbara; Topol, Allan.

V.A.

Gordimer, Nadine. Annotation should read:
    "Protagonist leaves, then returns to South Africa to reaffirm commitment to struggle against apartheid."

Corrections

Rusinek, Alla. Annotation should read:
"Soviet Jewish activist's struggle."

V.B.

Glanville, Brian. This citation belongs with V.C. (Fiction of other countries)
Goitein, S.D. This citation should be in I.A.
Werner, Alfred. Please move this citation to IV.B.

VI.A.

Fenelon, Fania. Annotation should read:
"French Jew describes struggle to survive with other members of the Auschwitz orchestra."
Kluger, Ruth, etc. Annotation should read:
"Peggy Mann interviewed Ruth Kluger (1914-1980) in over 1000 hours of tapes to describe work of this one woman in a Mossad team that rescued Jews during WW 2. Exciting, inspiring, heart-breaking. Should be made into a film."
Traub, Barbara Fishman. Please move this citation to VI.C., and substitute this annotation:
"Survivor returns to Hungarian birthplace and falls in love with Soviet soldier."

VI.B.

Mann, Peggy. Please substitute this annotation:
See biography, The Last Escape, op. cit., Kluger, Ruth, etc. in this section.
Miedzyrzecka, etc. should be: Vladka Peltel (now Vladka Meed, op. cit.).

VI.C.

Carmel should be Karmel. (See 1986 selections in Part II Books)
Lauterstein, Ingeborg. Please move this citation to Part II edition, VI.C.
Levin, Meyer: Anne Frank (drama). Delete "available in pamphlet," etc.
Levin, Meyer. Eva. Add: New edition, NY: Behrman, 1979.

VII.A. and B.

These citations have been moved to Part II edition, VII.A. and B.:
Carmi, Schwartz, Bloch, Borenstein, Dame, Hadas, Schuler, Tannenbaum.

IX.A.

Meyerson, Robert. Please move this citation to Part II edition, VIII.

ADDITIONS TO FIRST EDITION: 1900-1979

Please add these citations, which were inadvertently omitted at the time of publication, to Part I, first edition.

I.A.

Badt-Strauss, Berthe: White Fire: The Life and Times of Jessie Sampter. (Rept.) Arno Press, 1977.

Gratz, Rebecca: Letters. Arno, 1975. (Rept.)

Kohut, Rebecca: My Portion. Arno, 1975. (Rept. of 1925 ed.)

Koltun, Elizabeth, ed.: The Jewish Woman: New Perspectives. NY: Schocken, 1976.

Levin, Alexandra Lee: The Szolds of Lombard Street. Phila.: Jewish Publication Society, 1960.

Levy, Harriet Lane: 920 O'Farrell Street. NY: Arno Press, 1975.

Reprint of 1937 and 1947 editions.

I.B.

Adler, Ruth: "Peretz' Empathetic Linkage to Woman," Annual of Conference in Modern Jewish Studies. NY: Queens College. Fall 1977/Winter 1978.

Avery, Evelyn: "Where Have All the Men Gone? Women in the Italian-American and Jewish-American Novel," The Interaction of Italians and Jews in America, ed., Scapaci, Jean. NY: American Historical Assn., 1975.

Kaplan, Marion A.: "German-Jewish Feminism in the Twentieth Century," Jewish Social Studies, Winter 1976.

Brief biography of Bertha Pappenheim, founder of the Movement, plus the organization's history.

Roskies, David G.: "Yiddish Popular Literature and the Female Reader," Journal of Popular Culture. 1977, No. 10.

Additions

Sartre, Jean-Paul: <u>Anti-Semite and Jew</u> (Tr. G.J. Becker) NY: Schocken, 1948. (Also Black Cat edition, 1962)

>Sartre gives interesting analysis of use of "beautiful Jewess" by writers as use as a hostile sexual symbol, p. 48-49.

II.A.

Neuda, Fanny: <u>Hours of Devotion. Prayers for Women</u>, tr. from German by M. Mayer. NY: L.H. Frank, 1978.

Trible, Phyllis: <u>God and the Rhetoric of Sexuality</u>. Phila.: Fortress, 1978.

>Professor of Hebrew language and literature at Newton Theological School discusses (inter alia) non-patriarchal conceptions of divinity in ancient Judaism.

II.B.

Kalechofsky, Roberta: "Bruriah," <u>Response</u>, Summer 1978, p. 65ff.

Meyers, Carol: "The Roots of Restriction--Women in Early Israel," <u>Biblical Archeologist</u> 41, Sept. 1978.

Neusner, Jacob: "From Scripture to Mishnah: The Origins of Mishnah's Division of Women," <u>Journal of Jewish Studies</u>, Autumn 1979.

Rapoport, Nessa: "A Defense of Passion," <u>Response</u>, #24, Winter 1974-1975, pp. 79-86.

>A meditation of what the love between a woman and a man can teach of God's love for us; a defense against reason of the sacred and the passionate in experience, as ways of understanding our love of God.

III.A.

Blicksilver, Edith, ed.: <u>The Ethnic American Woman</u>. Dubuque, IA: Kendall-Hunt Publishing Co., 1978.

Nachman, Elana: <u>Riverfinger Women</u>. Plainfield, VT: Daughters, 1974.

>Jewish lesbian accounts.

Nathan, Maud: <u>Once Upon a Time and Today</u>. NY: Arno Press, 1974.

III.B.

Bellman, Samuel Irving: "The Jewish Mother Syndrome," Congress Bi-Weekly, Dec. 27, 1965.

Cohen, Sarah Blacher: "Mary Antin's The Promised Land: A Breach of Promise." In Annual of Conference on Modern Jewish Studies, NY: Queens College Press, Fall 1977/Winter 1978.

Friedman, Melvin J.: "Jewish Mothers and Sons: The Expense of Chutzpah." In Malin, Irving: Contemporary American Jewish Literature, Bloomington, IN: Indiana Univ. Press, 1973, p. 156ff.

Discussion of Jewish mothers in fiction of Philip Roth, Henry Roth, Bruce Jay Friedman, Herbert Gold, Isaac Singer, Salinger, Romain Gary, Wallace Markfield.

Segal, J.B.: "The Jewish Attitude Towards Women," Journal of Jewish Studies, Autumn 1979.

III.C.

Paley, Grace: Enormous Changes at the Last Minute. NY: Farrar, Straus & Giroux, 1974.

Collection of short fiction.

Roiphe, Anne: Torch Song. NY: Farrar, Straus & Giroux, 1977; Signet pap., 1978.

A young Jewish woman falls in love with a sexual pervert and lets herself be drawn into degradation, for no apparent rhyme or reason. In addition to anti-feminist perspective, this novel is also boring.

Silman, Roberta: Boundaries. Boston: Little Brown, 1979.

A young assimilated Jewish woman with three children in suburbia tries to resolve a host of conflicts after her husband's death.

Sinclair, Jo (pseud. for Ruth Seid): The Changelings. NY: McGraw Hill, 1955. Reprinted by Feminist Press, 1983.

Jewish lesbian novel.

Tenenbaum, Sylvia: Please add to citation, "Marred by phony reconciliation at end."

IV.A.

Cohen, Geula: Woman of Violence. Add after "today" in annotation:

> "Still, she was one of the members of Knesset to speak out vociferously when the Israeli government did little officially to help Jewish desaparecidos in Argentina's reign of terror."

IV.B.

Freedman, Marcia, Interviewed by Rubin, Barbara: "On Women and War," Response, Winter 1976-77, p. 41.

Ingber, Judith Brin: "The Russian Ballerina and the Yemenites: On Rina Nikova in Israel," Israel Dance, 1975.

Ms. Magazine, "If It's Tuesday, It Must Be the Tel Aviv Women's Center." March 1979, pp. 13-14.

Shokeid, Moshe: "Social Networks and Innovations in the Division of Labor Between Men and Women in the Family and in the Community: A Study of Moroccan Immigrants in Israel," Canadian Review of Sociology and Anthropology, 1971.

Weissman, Debbie: "A Woman's Diary of the Yom Kippur War," Response, Winter 1973-74, p. 87.

IV.C.

Banks, Lynn Reid: Children at the Gate. NY: Simon & Schuster, 1968.

Novel about Gerda, a divorcee and two children who need shelter. Setting is Israel.

V.A.

The Working Mother: A Survey of Problems and Programs in Nine Countries, Ithaca, NY: ILR Press, Cornell Univ., 1978.

Israel is one of the countries reviewed with data presented.

V.B.

Whitman, Karen: "Our Sister Rosa Luxemburg," Women: A Journal of Liberation, Summer 1970.

VI.A.

Friedlander, Albert H.: "Nelly Sachs--Poet of the Holocaust," Jewish Quarterly 19, Winter 1966-67.

Gurdus, Luba Krugman: The Death Train, Poems of the Holocaust. NY: Schocken Books, 1979.

    Bilingual verse, Polish-English.

VII.A.

Schappes, Morris, ed.: Emma Lazarus: Selections from her Poetry and Prose. NY: Emma Lazarus Federation of Jewish Women's Clubs, 1944, Rev. 1967.

Voices Israel, an annual journal of poetry in English. Haifa, Israel: The Voices Group, c/o Reuben Rose, 38 Nehemia St., Neve Sha'anan, Israel, 1979.

VII.B.

Levertov, Denise: A Life in the Forest. NY: New Directions, 1978.
    _____: Freeing of the Dust. NY: New Directions, 1975.
    _____: Footprint Poems. NY: New Directions, 1972.

Lifshin, Lyn: Tangled Vines: A Collection of Mother and Daughter Poems. Boston: Beacon Press, 1978.

Shelley, Martha: Crossing the DMZ. Oakland, CA: Sefir Publications. (Or Women's Press Collective, 1974).

Untermeyer, Jean Starr. Job's Daughter. NY: Norton, 1967.

X.

Response, Summer 1973.

    Special issue devoted to women in Jewish history, law, community, texts, Israel and life-cycle events.

PART II

SECOND EDITION

THE JEWISH WOMAN: 1980 -- 1985

BIBLIOGRAPHY

and

1986 SUPPLEMENT:

BOOKS AND PERIODICAL ARTICLES

N O T E : Chapters in books, included with "Periodicals" in the First Edition, are now listed under "Books" in this Second Edition.

See "Note on Bibliographical Criteria and Selection" after Introduction.

I. JEWISH WOMEN IN HISTORY/HERSTORY

A. Non-Fiction Books (Chapters, and Biography/Autobiography)

Araten, Rachel Sarna: Michalina. Spring Valley, NY: Philip Feldheim, 1985.

> True story of Jewish girl abducted in 1899 in Poland, converted to Catholicism, who learns her history at age 74.

Bitton-Jackson, Livia: Madonna or Courtesan?: The Jewish Woman in Christian Literature. NY: Seabury, 1982.

> Work focuses on myths that have shaped attitudes toward women throughout the ages.

Bristow, Edward J.: Prostitution and Prejudice: The Jewish Fight Against White Slavery 1870-1939. NY: Schocken Books, 1983.

> Should be read with feminist critique by Marcia Cohn Spiegel in Judaica Book News, Fall 1984.

Brooten, Bernadette, J.: Women Leaders in the Ancient Synagogue: Inscriptional Evidence and Background Issue. Chico, CA: Scholars Press, 1982.

Carswell, John: The Exile. London: Faber & Faber, 1983.

> A biography of the English woman Ivy Litvinoff, wife of Maxim Litvinoff, the Soviet diplomat, and her years in USSR under Stalin and in the Russian Embassy in Washington, DC.

Chagall, Bella: First Encounter. NY: Schocken Books, 1983.

> Chagall's wife's memoir of her adolescence in Russia and her first encounter with artist Marc Chagall.

Ginzburg, Eugenia: Within the Whirlwind. Tr. from Russian by Ian Boland. NY: Harcourt Brace Jovanovich, 1981.

> Dr. Ginzburg's memoirs of prison life in the Gulag penal settlements from 1937-1953.

Goitein, S.D.: "The Family." In Mediterranean Society, Berkeley/LA: Univ. of Calif. Press, v. III, 1978.

> Interesting information about the medieval Jewish family in the Mediterranean basin and some material about the status of women.

Hanna, Evelyn: Woman Against the World. NY: Ballantine, 1983.

   The story of Therese Lachman in 19th century Europe.

Hansen, Lilian Leah: Rosa--A True Story. NY: Vantage Press, 1985.

   Author's mother's adolescence in Victorian and Edwardian London and post-World War I hardships.

Hellman, John: Simone Weil: An Introduction to Her Thought. Phila.: Fortress Press, 1984.

Kaminskaya, Dina: Final Judgment--My Life as a Soviet Defense Attorney. NY: Simon & Schuster, 1983.

Loewe, Louis, ed.: Diaries of Sir Moses and Lady Montefiore. Facsimile, 1890 edition. London: Jewish Historical Society of England and the Jewish Museum, 1983.

Luxemburg, Rosa: Comrade and Lover: Letters to Leo Jogiches. Boston: M.I.T. Press, 1981, pap.

   The letters span the years 1893-1914.

McFarland, Dorothy Tuck: Simone Weil. NY: Frederick, Ungar, 1983.

Moskowitz, Faye: A Leak in the Heart. David Godine, 1985.

   The lives of three generations of Jewish women.

Namztlas, Judith (pseud.): A Wanderer's Reflections. Bryn Mawr, PA: Dorrance & Co., 1982.

   Flight from post-World War I Russia to U.S.A.

Rohrlich, Ruby and Baruch, Elaine Hoffman: Women in Search of Utopia. NY: Schocken Books, 1984.

Selavan, Ida C.: "Women of Valor." In The Jewish Almanac, eds. R. Siegel and C. Rheins, NY: Bantam Books, 1980.

Siegel, Beatrice: Lillian Wald of Henry Street. NY: Macmillan, 1983.

   Biography of founder of famous settlement house, based in part on interviews.

Strassfeld, Michael and Siegel, Richard, with Sue Levi Elwell and T. Drorah Setel: The Jewish Calendar 6746/1985-1986. NY: Universe Books, 1985.

> Devoted to the Jewish woman, it contains poetry, quotations, photos & citations of Jewish women from Biblical to modern times.

Taitz, Emily & Henry, Sondra: Written Out of History: Our Jewish Foremothers. Fresh Mdws., NY: Biblio Press, 1983.

> Revised and reprinted edition of 1978 work, known as Written Out of History: A Hidden Legacy of Jewish Women Revealed Through Their Writings and Letters. (Bloch Publishing Co.)

B. Periodical Articles

Anon.: "Jewish Women in the Middle Ages," Jewish Digest, October 1983, pp. 63-64.

Ashkenasy, H.: "Lise Meitner: Nuclear Physicist," Reconstructionist, February 1982, pp. 24-27.

Bristow, Edward: "The German-Jewish Fight Against White Slavery." In Leo Baeck Institute Annual, 1983.

Dresner, Ruth R.: "The Work of Bertha Pappenheim," Judaism, Spring 1981.

Duckat, Walter: "Hannah of Ludomir," American Mizrachi Woman, January 1982.

Frankel, G.: "Notes on the Costume of the Jewish Woman in Eastern Europe," Journal of Jewish Art, #7, 1980, pp. 50-51.

Frenkel, N.: "Music--By and For a Jewish Woman," Jewish Observer, Summer 1984, pp. 27-30.

Friedland, Charlotte: "Two Women, Two Worlds," Jewish Woman's Outlook, Oct./Nov. 1985, pp. 22-29.

> On Gluckel of Hamelin's memoirs.

Gordis, Robert: "In Ancient Egypt, Jewish Women Had More Rights," The Jewish Week (NY), June 10, 1983, p. 29ff.

Grossman, Cissy: "Womanly Arts: A Study of Italian Torah Binders in the New York Jewish Museum Collection," Journal of Jewish Art, 1980.

This is a Master's Thesis in Art History, Hunter College, 1979.

Kaplan, Marion A.: "For Love or Money: Strategies of Jews in Imperial Germany." In Leo Baeck Institute Yearbook, #28, 1983.

Lester, Elenore: "Sephardic Traditions Subject of Conference," The Jewish Week (NY) Oct. 26, 1984, p. 38.

Egyptian writer Ada Sharoni discusses prominence of Egyptian Jewish women in culture.

Meyers, Carol: "A New Look at Women of Ancient Israel," Brookline, MA: Genesis 2, Nov. 1981.

_____: "Procreation, Production and Protection--Male-Female Balance in Early Israel," Journal of the Amer. Academy of Religion, #51, Dec. 1983.

_____: "The Status of Women in Early Israel," Jewish Digest, Jan. 1982, pp. 30-34.

Na'amat Women (formerly Pioneer Women): Oral Histories of Members, Nov./Dec. 1985 issue.

Nulman, Macy: "Jewish Women and Jewish Music," American Mizrachi Woman, Feb. 1982.

Olshaker, Ed.: "A Profile of Emma Goldman," National Jewish Monthly, May 1982.

Scherer, Rebecca: "The Maid of Ludomir," Jewish Digest, Nov. 1981, pp. 73-76.

Shapiro, C.: "Post Script: Birth of the Bobbe Ma'ase," Jewish Observer, April 1983, p. 34.

Taitz, Emily: "Forgotten Jewish Heroines, " Women's American ORT Reporter, Jan./Feb. 1981.

Shoub, Myra Nelson: "Jewish Women's History: Development of a Critical Methodology," Conservative Judaism, Jan. 1982, pp. 33-46.

Applies methodology of women's studies to the problems involved in studying Jewish women. Excellent guidelines.

Spiegel, Marcia Cohn: "Three Women Poets," Women's League Outlook, Spring 1984, p. 16.

>A look at the lives and poetry of three 16th century women, Sarah Coppia Sullam, Deborah Ascarelli and Rachel Fischel.

Wengerhoff, Pauline: "A Memoir: Yom Kippur in Lithuania" (Tr. German by Henny Wenkart), Memoirs of a Grandmother. In The Jewish Advocate, Sept. 16, 1980.

Wolff, Lieselotte: Review of Marion Kaplan's The Jewish Feminist Movement in Germany, Jewish Currents, May 1982.

>See Part I--First Edition for Kaplan work cited.

C. Fiction: Historical Novels

Aharoni, Ada: The Second Exodus. Bryn Mawr, PA: Dorrance & Co., 1983.

>Novel about young Jewish woman's search for identity in Cairo before and after 1948, ending with her aliyah to Israel.

Bergelson, David: When All Is Said and Done (Tr. Yiddish by Bernard Martin), Athens, OH: Ohio Univ. Press, 1977, pap. (Rept. 1913 ed.)

>Novel about the decaying Jewish bourgeoisie in pre-Revolutionary Russia, in the Lermontov-Goncharov tradition. Heroine Mirele Hurwitz finds no man can rescue her from stultifying shtetl and small city Jewish life, but neither can she rescue herself. Translation leaves much to be desired and often distracts from the narrative, but worthwhile reading.

Brand, Sandra: Between Two Worlds. NY: Shengold, 1982.

>On eve of World War II, woman from Orthodox family elopes with assimilated Jew.

Broder, Bill and Broder, Kurian: Remember This Time. NY: Newmarket Press, 1983.

>The saga of a Russian Jewish family before their immigration.

Ellis, Julie: East Wind. NY: Arbor House, 1983.

>Jews in Hong Kong.

Gross, Joel: <u>Lives of Rachel</u>. NY: New American Library, 1984.

>Romanticized stories about Jewish women of one family in different historical periods. (Straight fluff but good read; a nice Bat Mitzvah gift.)

Joseph, Joan: <u>In Joy and In Sorrow</u>. NY: Dell Books, 1982.

>The story of a Jewish family in Portugal during the Inquisition and the courageous woman who helped shape its destiny in the New World.

Levine, Faye: <u>Solomon and Sheba</u>, NY: Richard Marek, 1980.

Litwoman, Jane: "Ahat, Shtayim, Shalosh," -- 3 stories plus notes on Biblical-period women. In <u>Womanspirit</u>, Winter Solstice 1983.

Poverman, C.E.: <u>Solomon's Daughter</u>, NY: Viking, 1981.

Prose, Francine: <u>Hungry Hearts</u>. NY: Pantheon, 1983.

>Humorous novel of a dybbuk in a Yiddish Theatre troupe touring Argentina in the 1920's.

Rayner, Claire: <u>Enduring Years</u>. NY: Delacorte, 1982.

>The story of Hannah Lazar in East End London through two World Wars.

Reibel, Paula: <u>Morning Moon</u>. NY: Wm. Morrow, 1985.

Rosshandler, Felicia: <u>Passing Through Havana</u>. NY: St. Martin's Press, 1984.

>Novel about a young girl's growth into womanhood in Cuba, where her family escaped from the Holocaust, and her coming to terms with being a Jew.

Shapiro, Rhonda Rieser: <u>A Place of Light</u>, NY: Poseidon, 1983.

>The story of two Jewish women of different generations and their search for love and spiritual fulfillment.

Tennenbaum, Silvia: <u>Yesterday's Street</u>. NY: Random House, 1981.

>Historical novel about a wealthy assimilated German Jewish family, spanning the first half of the 20th century.

Webb, Liliane: *The Marranos*. NY: Pocket Books, pap., 1982.

Wolfenstein, Martha: "Chayah." In *The Other Woman*, Susan Koppelman, ed. NY: Feminist Press, 1984.

The story is a reprint of the 1905 work.

II. JEWISH WOMEN IN RELIGIOUS LIFE AND LAW*

A. Non-Fiction Books and Book Chapters

Banks, Lynne Reid: Sarah and After: Five Women Who Founded a Nation. Garden City, NY: Doubleday & Co., 1975.

> Based on Biblical stories, author recounts tales of Sarah, Hagar, Rebecca, Leah, Rachel and Dina from each woman's perspective.

Biale, Rachel: Women and Jewish Law. NY: Schocken, 1984.

> This comprehensive source book covers those areas the author considers central to women's lives—marriage, divorce, abortion, rape—in Jewish law. (See review in Lilith #14 by Beverly Gribetz.)

Broner, E.M.: "Honor and Ceremony in Women's Rituals." In The Politics of Women's Spirituality, Charlene Spretnak, ed., NY: Anchor Press, 1982, pp. 237-241.

Cantor, Aviva: Egalitarian Haggadah. In Lilith #9, 1982.

Carlisle, Thomas John: Eve and After: Old Testament Women in Portrait. Grand Rapids, MI: Erdmans Publishing Co., 1984.

Central Conference of American Rabbis: Passover Haggadah, Second Revised Edition, 1982, (Baskin illustrations), NY: Viking Penguin & CCAR.

> A non-sexist worded Reform Haggadah.

Craven, Toni: Artistry and Faith in the Book of Judith. Chico, CA: Scholars Press, 1983.

> A study of the Apocryphal books.

Davidovich, David: Jewish Marriage Contracts Through the Ages. NY: Adama Books, 1985.

Eider, Shimon D.: Halachos of Niddah. Lakewood, NJ: Halacha Publications, 1981.

> English text with extensive notes regarding sources, on menstrual/ritual purity laws—Orthodox bias.

Elwell, Sue Levi: "Women in Jewish Civilization." In Woman and Religion, ed., Annette Baxter, NY: Markus Wiener, 1985.

Feldbrand, S.: From Sarah to Sarah. Bklyn.: S. Feldbrand, 1981.

> The stories of 120 women who have played vital roles in preserving "Torah-true Judaism." (Some material is "borrowed" from Biblio Press books.)

Fine, Irene: Midlife and Its Rite of Passage Ceremony, with a Midlife Celebration by Bonnie Feinman. San Diego, CA: Women's Institute for Continuing Jewish Education, 1983.

> Exploration of women's midlife transition experiences and special ceremony to mark it.

Friedfertig, Raizel Schnall, and Schapiro, Freyda: The Modern Jewish Woman: A Unique Perspective. Bklyn.: Lubavitch Educational Foundation for Marriage Enrichment, 1981.

> Hassidic bias.

Fuchs, Esther: "Who Is Hiding the Truth? Deceptive Women and Biblical Androcentrism." In Feminist Perspectives on Biblical Scholarship, Adela Y. Collins, ed., Scholars Press & the Society of Biblical Literature, Missoula, MT, 1985, pp. 37-44.

Gittelsohn, Ronald B.: The Extra Dimension: A Jewish View of Marriage. NY: Union of American Hebrew Congregations, 1983.

> Revised edition of author's My Beloved Is Mine.

Gottlieb, Freema. "Three Mothers." In Judaism, no. 30, Spring 1981, pp. 194-203.

> About Deborah, the prophetess as "national judge"; also Yael and the mother of Sisera.

Greenberg, Blu: How to Run a Traditional Jewish Household. NY: Simon & Schuster, 1983.

> A comprehensive, personalized guide informed by author's love of the tradition.

_____: On Women and Judaism: A View From Tradition. Phila.: Jewish Publication Society, 1982.

> Orthodox feminist wrestles with the tradition and ways women can struggle within it for feminist goals. Reformist. Valuable for scholarship and recommendations.

Religious Life and Law

Haddad, Yvonne Yazbeck and Findly, Ellison Banks, eds.: <u>Women, Religion and Social Change</u>. Albany, NY: SUNY Press, 1985.

> Study papers for symposium on women in various religions held at Hartford Seminary in Connecticut, Oct. 21-22, 1983.

Harris, Kevin. <u>Sex, Ideology and Religion</u>. NJ: Barnes and Noble, 1984.

Harris, Lis: <u>Holy Days</u>. NY: Summit Books, 1985.

> A positive view of a Hasidic family and its religious life by a Jewish outsider.

Haut, Irwin H.: <u>Divorce in Jewish Law and Life</u>. Bklyn: Sepher-Hermon, 1983.

> Author explains the Jewish law of marriage and divorce and attempts to offer solutions to the problem of the "agunah" both in USA and Israel. (Contains some information on new NY State divorce laws impinging on Jewish divorce)

Heschel, Susannah, ed.: <u>On Being a Jewish Feminist: A Reader</u>. NY: Schocken Books, 1983.

> Important anthology of new writings on search for spirituality. A key source.

Jackson, Bernard S. and <u>Jewish Law Assn. Int'l. Congress Staff</u>. Decatur, GA: Scholars Press, 1985.

> Papers published previously in 1980, including scholarly articles on the wife's right to divorce.

Jungreis, Esther: <u>Jewish Soul on Fire</u>, NY: William Morrow, 1982.

> Tepid, uncritical, sophomoric drivel about the wonders of Jewish family life.

Kukoff, Lydia: <u>Choosing Judaism</u>. NY: Union of American Hebrew Congregations, 1981.

> A convert's testimony.

Lacks, Roslyn: Women and Judaism: Myth, History and Struggle. NY: Doubleday, 1980.

>An examination of historical, cultural and mythological sources about the Jewish woman, with personal experience. Good general review of Jewish women's situation.

Lamm, Maurice: Jewish Way in Love and Marriage. San Francisco: Harper & Row, 1980.

Liptzin, Sol: Biblical Themes in World Literature. Hoboken, NJ: Ktav Publishing House, 1985.

>Influence of Biblical characters, ideas and events on world writing throughout the ages. Includes discussion of Hagar, Rebecca, Ruth, Michal, Abigail, Abishag, Shulamith and an essay on "The Rehabilitation of Lilith."

Lubavitch Women's Organization: Aura, A Reader on Jewish Womanhood. Bklyn.: 1984.

>Hassidic bias.

Miller, Yisroel: In Search of Jewish Woman. NY: Philip Feldheim, 1984.

Morgan, Moshe: A Guide to the Law of Niddah. Bklyn: Author, 1983.

>Ritual purity, Orthodox bias.

Morton, Nelle: The Journey Is Home. Boston: Beacon Press, 1985.

>Ten essays written during 1970's charting changes in women and religion, and differences and similarities among Christian and Jewish feminists.

New York Federation of Reform Synagogues: Out of the House of Bondage, Task Force on Equality of Women in Judaism, 1984.

>Supplement to the New Union Haggadah, includes glossary of substitute non-sexist terminology.

Nunnally-Cox, Janice: Foremothers: Women of the Bible. NY: Seabury Press, 1981.

Obukhova, Lydia (Tr. Mirra Ginsburg): Daughter of Night: A Tale of Three Worlds. NY: Avon, 1982.

Russian science fiction about creation myth involving Lilith, Adam and Eve (Odam and Neva).

Ochs, Carol: Women and Spirituality. Totowa, NJ: Rowman & Allanheld, 1983.

Religious spirituality based on a woman-centered model.

Patz, Naomi and Perman, Jane: In the Beginning: The Jewish Baby Book. NY: United Federation of Temple Sisterhoods (UAHC), 1983.

Rituals for newborn boys and girls, and fill-in pages to record baby's early events.

Rabinowicz, Rachel et al., eds.: "Feast of Freedom" Haggadah. NY: Rabbinical Assembly, 1982.

Revision of 1974 Conservative Haggadah, claiming to eliminate sexist language and "stressing the role women have had in the Jewish struggle for freedom." Does not live up to these claims. Nice art.

Raphael, Marc Lee, ed.: Approaches to Modern Judaism. Chico, CA: Scholars Press, 1983.

Contains essays on love and marriage.

Ross, Bette M.: Song of Deborah. NY: Fleming H. Revell, 1981.

Ruether, Rosemary Radford: Womanguides: Readings Toward a Feminist Theology. Boston: Beacon Press, 1985.

Stories from various religions as sources of women's experience; includes feminist Midrash on Lilith and Eve.

Ruether, Rosemary Radford and Keller, Rosemary Skinner, eds.: Women and Religion in America: Vol. I--The Nineteenth Century. San Francisco: Harper & Row, 1981.

_____: Vol. II--The Colonial & Revolutionary Period. San Francisco: Harper & Row, 1983.

Russell, Letty M.: Feminist Interpretation of the Bible. Phila.: Westminster, 1985.

San Diego Women's Haggadah. Women's Institute for Continuing Jewish Education, 1980. (Second edition published 1986)

Setel, T. Drorah: "Feminist Insights and the Question of Method." In Feminist Perspectives on Biblical Scholarship, Adela Yarbro Collins, ed. Decatur, GA: Scholars Press (n.d.).

New interpretations of Biblical texts.

Spitzer, Julie R.: Spousal Abuse in Rabbinic and Contemporary Judaism. NY: National Federation of Temple Sisterhoods, 1985.

Rabbi Spitzer deals with spouse abuse in general, the response of Jewish legal texts throughout history, overview of contemporary response and program ideas, plus bibliography and resource appendices.

Steinsaltz, Adin: Biblical Images -- Men and Women of The Book. NY: Basic Books, 1984.

Includes Eve, Sarah, Rebecca, Rachel, Leah, Miriam, Esther, et al.

Strassfeld, Sharon and Green, Kathy: The Jewish Family Book. NY: Bantam Books, 1981, pap.

New Jewish family practices. Part Two, "Celebrating" contains suggestions for non-sexist rituals.

Teubal, Savina, J.: Sarah the Priestess, The First Matriarch of Genesis. Athens, OH: Swallow/Ohio Univ. Press, 1984.

_____: "Women, the Law and the Ancient Near East." In Fields of Offerings: Studies in Honor of Raphael Patai on the Occasion of His Seventieth Birthday, Fairleigh Dickinson Univ. Press, 1982.

Trenchard, Warren C.: Ben Sira's View of Women; A Literary Analysis. Chico, CA: Scholars Press, 1982.

Trible, Phyllis: Texts of Terror: Literary-Feminist Readings of Biblical Narratives. Phila.: Fortress, 1984.

A reinterpretation of the stories of Hagar, Tamar and Jephtah's daughter.

Tolley, Jacquelyn, ed.: On Our Spiritual Journey: A Creative Shabbat Service. San Diego, CA: Women's Inst. for Continuing Jewish Ed., 1984.

Umansky, Ellen: "Feminism and the Reevaluation of Women's Role Within American Jewish Life." In Women, Religion and Social Change, ed. Haddad, Yvonne Yazbeck and Findly, Ellison Bank, Albany: SUNY Press, 1985.

_____: Lily Montagu and the Advancement of Liberal Judaism: From Vision to Vocation. Lewiston, NY: Edwin Mellen Press, 1983.

Biography of Lily Montagu, founder of The Jewish Religious Union in England and key figure in the establishment of the World Union for Progressive Judaism.

Umansky, Ellen, ed.: Lily Montagu: Sermons, Addresses, Letters and Prayers. Lewiston, NY: Edwin Mellen Press, 1985.

Weissler, Chava: "Voices from the Heart: Women's Devotional Prayers." In The Jewish Almanac, eds., R. Siegel and C. Rheins, NY: Bantam, 1980, pp. 541-545.

Wilson James, Janet, ed.: Women in American Religion. Phila.: Univ. of Penn. Press, 1980.

Essays on religious feminism.

Women's League for Conservative Judaism: Shabbat Manual, (n.d.).

Describes in non-sexist terms, the basics of Shabbat in the home and synagogue. Stereotype gender roles have been omitted.

Zakon, Miriam Stark, Tr.: Tzenah Ur'enah. (3 vols., Genesis, Exodus, Leviticus). NY: Mesorah Publications, 1983-84.

"Tzenah Ur'enah" was the Yiddish translation of the Biblical portions with lore and legends. Key source.

Zones, Jane Sprague, et al.: Taking the Fruit: Modern Women's Tales of the Bible. San Diego: Woman's Institute for Continuing Jewish Education, 1981.

Collection of women's midrashim (stories with ethical points) drawing on Biblical themes, written by eight women students at the above Institute. Good example of new Jewish women's creativity, drawing on and transcending traditional sources.

B. Periodical Articles

Adelman, Penina V.: "Prayer to Rahmana, Mother of Wombs," Reconstructionist, June 1985, pp. 26-27.

> A prayer for fertility.

Adler, Rachel: "I've Had Nothing Yet So I Can't Take More," Moment, Sept. 1983, pp. 22-26.

> One of the most important Jewish feminist pieces, questioning whether women are part of the Covenant. Analyzes treatment of women in Halacha as viewed only in terms of their relationships with women.

_____: "Second Hymn to the Shechinah," Response, Fall/Winter 1982.

Alpert, Rebecca: "A Prayer on the Occasion of a Miscarriage or Abortion," Reconstructionist, Sept. 1985, p. 4.

_____: "Sisterhood is Ecumenical: Bridging the Gap Between Jewish and Christian Feminists," Response, Spring 1984, p. 3ff.

> Commonalities of Jewish and Christian feminists exploring new non-sexist liturgy, restructuring religious institutions and re-evaluating beliefs in light of women's concerns.

_____: "The Reconstructionist Approach to Prayer: Some Questions and Answers," Response, Fall/Winter 1982.

Anon.: "Amy Eilberg Will Be Conservative Judaism's First Woman Rabbi," People weekly, April 29, 1985, p. 50.

Anon: "5744: Five Women Rabbis--Conservative Equality," Jewish Monthly, Aug./Sept. 1984, pp. 16-18.

Aronson, Leonard J.: "Women in the Minyan and in the Rabbinate," Jewish Spectator, Winter 1984, p. 56ff.

> The author believes that "if Jewish women come into the Minyan and into the rabbinate, Jewish men will leave and go fishing." (See response by Dr. Bernard Mandelbaum in Summer 1985 issue.)

Aschkenasy, Nehama: "A Non-Sexist Reading of the Bible," Midstream, June/July 1980.

Auerbach, Marilyn Iris: "Single but Equal," _Jewish Woman's Outlook_, Spring 1985, p. 5,10.

> The writer addresses herself to the problems of the Jewish unwed career woman whose religious needs are still not being met.

Back, T.T. et al.: "Women's Place at Sukkot," _Hadassah Magazine_, Oct. 1982, pp. 12-13.

Bergman, Helene Audrey: "Women in the Minyan," _Jewish Spectator_, Summer 1985, pp. 29-31.

Berman, Saul (interviewed by Shulamith Magnus): "Orthodoxy Responds to Feminist Ferment," _Response_, Spring 1981, p. 5ff.

> Fascinating interview with sympathetic Orthodox rabbi, revealing changes that have occurred in three areas: spiritual expression, legal (divorce), disabilities and exclusion from all but a service role. Outlines future steps needed to progress in those areas. Berman tends to be overly-optimistic, however.

Bocage, Angela: "Rosh Chodesh, A Celebration of Women," _Leviathan_, Univ. of Calif. at Santa Cruz, Spring 1981.

Borts, B.: "Report on Women in the Rabbinate," _European Judaism_, Winter 1981, pp. 30-31.

Braude, Ann: "The Jewish Women's Encounter with American Culture," In _Women and Religion in America: The Nineteenth Century_. San Francisco: Harper & Row, 1981.

Breslauer, S.D.: "Women, Religious Rejuvenation and Judaism," _Judaism_, Fall 1983, pp. 466-475.

> See also letter by H.P. Cramer in Summer 1984 issue.

Cantor, Aviva: "Jewish Feminism: 'Coming of Age'," _Women's American ORT Reporter_, Winter 1984, pp. 3-4.

> Report on progress in Jewish feminism since 1971 founding of Ezrat Nashim--first feminist group in Jewish community.

_____: "Profile of Amy Eilberg, First Woman Ordained as Conservative Rabbi at Jewish Theological Seminiary," _Ms. Magazine_, Dec. 1985.

> (See also: interview with Eilberg in _Lilith_ #14.)

Cantor, D.: "Get Ready, Get Set...Wait," Moment, Oct. 1983, pp. 38-42.

    On women rabbis.

Chipman, Jonathan: "Sex and the Tradition: A Rejoinder," Response, Fall 1977, p. 103ff.

Cohen, Shaye, J.D.: "Women in the Synagogues of Antiquity," Conservative Judaism, Nov./Dec. 1980.

Cohn-Sherbok, L.: "Towards a Feminist Theology," Jewish Spectator. Summer 1982, pp. 53-55.

Davidman, Lynn: "Reaching Out on the Upper West Side: Women Ba'alot Teshuvah at Lincoln Square Synagogue," The Melton Journal, No. 19, Summer 1985.

Dick, Judah: "Is an Agreement to Deliver or Accept a Get in the Event of a Civil Divorce Halachically Feasible?" Tradition, Summer 1983, pp. 91-106.

Durka, G.: "The Religious Journey of Women: The Educational Task," Religious Education, March/April 1982, pp. 163-178.

Editorial: "Women at the Seminary," Reconstructionist, Dec. 1983/Jan. 1984, p. 5.

Eisenpreis, B.: "Majority Discrimination," European Judaism. Winter 1981, pp. 32-33.

Eisenstein, Ira: "Conservative Rabbis Meet," Reconstructionist, Sept. 1984, pp. 29-80.

Elazar, Daniel J. and Monson, Rela Geffen: "Women in the Synagogue Today," Midstream, April 1981.

England-Schaffer, Naomi Y.: Review essay on Blu Greenberg's On Women and Judaism, Tradition, Summer 1983, pp. 132-144.

    Orthodox critique.

Falk, Marcia: "What About God?" Moment, March 1985, pp. 32-36.

    Considerations in creating new liturgy, by a poet and teacher at the Univ. of Judaism in L.A.

Fox, Karen L.: "Whither Women Rabbis?" Religious Education, July/Aug. 1981, pp. 361-368.

Frank, Blanche: "The American Orthodox Jewish Housewife: A Generational Study in Ethnic Survival," Contemporary Jewry, v. 5, no. 2, 1981.

> Summary of research project listed under "unpublished papers" in First Edition.

Friedman, Reena Sigman: "Jewish Women: The Struggle for Liberation," Jewish Frontier, Aug./Sept. 1984, pp. 11-19.

> Comprehensive overview of efforts in the religious sphere.

_____: "Women in the Rabbinate: A Moment of Real Change?" Jewish Frontier, Jan. 1982.

> Update on the situation in all "denominations," including the struggle in the Conservative movement.

Fuchs, Esther: "Status and Role of Female Heroines in the Biblical Narrative," Mankind Quarterly 23/2, Winter 1982, pp. 149-160.

_____: "The Literary Presentation of Mothers and Sexual Politics in the Bible." In Feminist Perspectives on Biblical Scholarship, Adela Y. Collins, ed., Missoula, MT: Scholars Press & the Society of Biblical Literature, 1985, pp. 117-136.

Furstenberg, Rochelle: "The Modern Mikve," Hadassah Magazine, Feb. 1982.

Garb, March; Penzner, Barbara and Waskow, Arthur: "Renaming: An Experiment in Liturgy," Menorah, Jan./Feb. 1983.

Gendler, Everett: "Ten Feminine Archetypes in the Jewish Bible," Response, Summer 1980, p. 75ff.

Gendler, Mary: "Sarah's Seed--A New Ritual for Women," Response, Winter 1974-75, p. 65ff.

Genesis 2: "Two Views on a Feminist Look at Halacha," Forum Based on Women and Jewish Law by Rachel Biale (op. cit.) May/June 1985, pp. 15-16.

Goldman, Ari L.: "Conservative Assembly Votes to Admit Women as Rabbis," New York Times, Feb. 14, 1985, p. A1ff.

Gordis, Robert: "The Ordination of Women," Midstream, Aug./Sept. 1980.

> (See also letters responding to this article in the April 1981 issue.)

Gottlieb, Lynn: "Av," Menorah, July/Aug. 1981.

    New Jewish rituals.

_____: "Speaking into the Silence," Response, Fall/Winter 1981, pp. 19-31.

    Women and prayer.

Greenberg, Blu: "Marriage in the Jewish Tradition," Journal of Ecumenical Studies, Winter 1985, pp. 3-20.

Greenberg, Irving: "The Religious Argument over Feminism," Pioneer Women (now Na'amat Women), May/June 1985, pp. 8-9.

Greenspahn, F.E.: "A Typology of Biblical Women," Judaism, Winter 1983, pp. 43-50.

Gross, Rita, M.: "Steps Toward Feminine Imagery of Deity in Jewish Theology," Judaism, Spring 1981, pp. 183-193.

Grossman, Dvora: "Why Jewish Women Don't Need 'Equality'," Women's American ORT Reporter, Spring 1984, p. 9.

    Typical Orthodox apologetics.

Grossman, S.: "Women and Jewish Law," Jewish Spectator, Winter 1981, pp. 26-28.

Guttman, A.: "The Woman Rabbi: An Historical Perspective," Journal of Reform Judaism, Summer 1982, pp. 21-25.

Handleman, S.: "Stranger in a Strange Land; Plight of the Single Orthodox Woman," Jewish Observer, Oct. 1983, pp. 17-21.

Harvey, Warren Zev: "The Obligation of Talmud on Women According to Maimonides," Tradition, Summer 1981, p. 122ff.

Heschel, Susannah: "Women Before the Law," New Traditions Magazine, Spring 1984.

Husbands-Hankin, Shonna: "Eshet Chazon: Woman of Vision," Menorah, April/May 1983.

    New Jewish rituals.

Hyman, Paula, and Agus, Arlene: "After a Decade of Jewish Feminism the Jewry Is Still Out." Interviewed in Lilith, Fall/Winter 1983, pp. 20-24.

> An evaluation by two founders of Ezrat Nashim.

Jensen, Charyl: "First Woman Rabbi Ten Years Later," Ms. Magazine, Feb. 1982.

> Feature on Rabbi Sally Priesand, first ordained Reform woman rabbi.

Jochnowitz, G.: "...Who Made Me a Woman:" Commentary, April 1981, pp. 63-64.

> Morning blessings in historic vernacular prayer books.

Jolles, Andree: "Blu and Yitz Greenberg--A Portrait," Present Tense, Spring 1984, pp. 13-16.

Judaism Symposium: "Women as Rabbis," Judaism, Winter 1984.

> Entire issue is devoted to this topic. Viewpoints of Robert Gordis, David Feldman, Blu Greenberg, Emanuel Rackman and others.

Kaufman, D.R.: "Women Who Return to Orthodox Judaism: A Feminist Analysis," Journal of Marriage and the Family, Aug. 1985, pp. 543-551.

Keeping Posted, "Divorce, Special Issue," NY: Union of American Hebrew Congregations, Oct. 1981.

Koltuv, Barbara Black: "Lilith," Quadrant, (Journal of the C.G. Jung Foundation for Analytical Psychology), Spring 1983, pp. 63-87.

> Author explores mythology of Lilith in ancient texts to shed light on her significance.

Klagsbrun, Francine: "At Last, A Conservative Woman Rabbi," Congress Monthly, May/June 1985, pp. 10-12.

Konheim, J.: "The Shammes Is a 'She'," Conservative Judaism, Fall 1982, pp. 81-83.

Lerman, Pamela Faith, and Waskow, Arthur: "Beyond the Shabbos Bride," Menorah, Jan./Feb. 1984.

    New Jewish rituals.

Levenberg, Diane: "A New Service for Havdalah," Reconstructionist, Dec. 1985.

_____: "The Motherhood of God: A Jewish Feminist Search," National Jewish Monthly, Feb. 1981.

Levett, Jay: "Women Rabbis: A Pyrrhic Victory?" Reconstructionist, Jan./Feb. 1985.

Litman, Jane (AKA Litwoman): "Is Judaism a Matriarchal Religion?" Lilith #10, Winter 1983, p. 32.

Lubavitcher Rebbe (Schneerson): "On Equal Rights," Wellsprings, Bklyn.: Lubavitch Youth Organization, Aug./Oct. 1985, pp. 8-9.

Mehren, E.: "A Two-Rabbi Marriage: A Unique Congregation," Ms. Magazine, Jan. 1984.

Mendels, Pamela: "Ms. Rabbi: Life Inside the Conservative Movement's First Co-ed Rabbinical Class," Jewish United Fund News (Jewish Federation of Chicago), April 1985, pp. 12-14.

Menorah Magazine: "The Covenant of Washing," April/May 1983.

    New Jewish rituals.

Moment Symposium: "What Kind of Job Is That for a Nice Jewish Person?" Moment, July/Aug. 1985, p. 30ff.

    Six recently-ordained rabbis, four men and two women, discuss their concept of the rabbinate and their commitment to a viable American Jewish community. Includes graduates of Reform, Conservative and Reconstructionist seminaries.

Morrell, Samuel: "An Equal or a Ward: How Independent Is a Married Woman According to Rabbinic Law?" Jewish Social Studies, Summer/Fall 1982, pp. 189-210.

Nave-Levinson, P.: "Women and Judaism," European Judaism, Winter 1981, pp. 25-28.

Neuberger, J.: "Women and Judaism," European Judaism, Winter 1981, p.29.

Neumark, Yosef: "Feminism vs. Judaism," Jewish Woman's Outlook, April/May 1984, pp. 13-17.

>The author, an Orthodox rabbi, believes that feminism is a scourge that has no place in Judaism. (Know the enemy.)

Peli, Pinchas H.: "Long Before Women's Lib," Jerusalem Post International Edition, July 20, 1985, p. 13.

>Claims the daughters of Zelophedad were the first women in Jewish tradition to struggle for "women's rights" more than 3,000 years ago.

Plaskow, Judith: "Christian Feminism and Anti-Judaism," Lilith, #7, 1980, pp. 11-12.

>Deals forthrightly with those Christian feminists who "project onto Judaism the failure of (Christianity) to renounce sexism, thereby avoiding confrontation with the failures of (their) own tradition." A very important must-read.

_____: "Language, God, and Liturgy: A Feminist Perspective," Response, Spring 1983, p. 31.

Plaskow, Judith, et al.: "Blaming Jews for Inventing Patriarchy," Lilith #7, 1980, p. 11ff.

>Forum on "Feminists and Faith" includes article by Annette Daum, "Blaming Jews for the Death of the Goddess," and dialogue between the two on the topic.

Read, Constance: "A Convert's Story," National Jewish Monthly, Feb. 1981.

Reisman, Y.: "Chinuch (Education): Whose Responsibility Is It?" Jewish Observer, Summer 1984, pp. 4-7.

>An Orthodox view.

Romain, S.S.: "Women Rabbis," European Judaism, Winter 1981, pp. 31-32.

Roundtable Discussion: "What Are the Sources of My Theology?" Journal of Feminist Studies in Religion, Spring 1985, pp. 119-131.

Rubin, Gary and Sheila: "Preserving Tradition by Expanding It: Creation of Our Simchat Bat," Response, Fall/Winter 1982, p. 61.

Saidel, Rochelle (formerly Wolk): "Marcia's Minyan," Hadassah Magazine, June/July 1981.

> Women organize a women's minyan to enable a friend to say Kaddish for her sister.

Sandberg, Martin I.: "Tefillin for Women?" Jewish Woman's Outlook, Summer 1985, p. 11ff.

Schneider, Susan Weidman: "Feminism Is Good for Jews: An Introduction," Present Tense, Spring 1984, pp. 4-7.

Schnur, Susan: "Becoming a Rabbi: An Act of Love, and Maybe of Revenge," New York Times, July 18, 1985, Sec. C, p. 2.

Schulweis, H.M.: "Rabbi Wanted, No Women Need Apply," Reform Judaism, Fall 1983, pp. 10-11.

Schwartz, H.: "Reimagining the Bible," Response, Spring 1983, pp. 35-46.

Schwartz, M.: "The Invisible Women of Passover," Moment, March/April 1981, pp. 100-102.

Schwartz, S.H.: "Conservative Judaism and the Agunah," Conservative Judaism, Fall 1982, pp. 37-44.

Schwarzbaum, Lisa: "Returning to Religion, Ritual and God," Glamour Magazine, Dec. 1984, p. 194.

Setel, T. Drorah: "Prophets and Pornography: Female Sexual Imagery in Hosea." In Feminist Interpretation of the Bible, Letty Russell, ed., Phila.: Westminster Press, 1985.

SH'MA: Opinion pieces on women and Judaism (and religious Judaism) appear frequently in this publication and are too numerous to list individually.

Silk, Mark: "Is God a Feminist?" New York Times Book Review, April 11, 1982.

> Discussion of recent feminist books on the subject. Sees Jewish feminist views as somewhat less rebellious about patriarchal conceptions than those of other feminists. Very superficial; oversimplifies.

Spiegel, Marcia Cohn: "Equal Justice Under Law: New Roles for the Jewish Woman," *Judaica Book News*, Fall 1984.

    Current books of interest to Jewish women relating to equal rights.

Spiegler, S.: "Adam's Rib: Feminists Rejoice," *Journal of Jewish Communal Service*. Fall 1983, p. 75.

Thistlethwaite, S.: "The Feminization of American Religious Education," *Religious Education*. July/Aug. 1981, pp. 391-400.

Umansky, Ellen: "Creating a Jewish Feminist Theology: Possibilities and Problems," *Anima*, Spring 1984, pp. 133-134.

_____: "(Re)Imaging the Divine," *Response*, Fall/Winter 1982, p. 110.

_____: "The Liberal Jew and Sex," *Response*, Winter 1976-77, p. 71.

_____: "Feminism and the Re-evaluation of Women's Roles Within American Jewish Life." In *Women, Religion and Social Change*. Haddad & Finley, NY: SUNY Press, 1985.

*Villenchik, (Williams) Penina: "Blessing for the Kindling of the Shabbat Lights," *Response*, Fall/Winter 1982.

    *Same as Adelman, Penina V. (1986 Supplement here)

Weiner, Greta: "The Morning Minyan," *Lilith* #7, 1980, pp. 27-28.

    Two sisters try to say Kaddish for their mother in traditional style. Essay on omission of women in mourning rituals is followed by one by Cohen, Sybil, with another view on kind of prayer to be used. (The prayer for women at funerals and how it denigrates them.)

Weiner, Nella Fermi: "Lilith: First Woman, First Feminist," *International Journal of Women's Studies*. Nov./Dec. 1979.

Weiss, A.: "Women and Sifrei Torah," *Tradition*, Summer 1982, pp. 106-118.

Weiss-Rosmarin, Trude: "Marriage Prisoners," *Jewish Spectator*, Winter 1984, pp. 5-8.

> The editor of the magazine offers an editorial.

_____: "Matrilny--A Survival of Polygyny," *Judaism*, Winter 1985, pp. 112-118.

_____: "Rabbis Without Power," *Reform Judaism*, Summer 1984, p. 11.

_____: "The Conservative Victory," *Jewish Spectator*, Spring 1981.

Wheeler, B.C.: "Accountability to Women in Theological Seminaries," *Religious Education*, July/Aug. 1981, pp. 382-390.

Wisse, R.: "Women as Conservative Rabbis?" *Commentary*, Oct. 1979 (discussion, Feb. 1980).

> Wisse is anti-feminist.

Wiest, S.: "Streisand and Women's Ordination," *Christianity Today*, Aug. 10, 1984, p. 68.

> An essay about *Yentl*, the motion picture starring Barbra Streisand, based on the Isaac B. Singer story.

Wolf, J.: "Baruch Ha'Shem, Not So Good: Some Concerns of Jewish Women," *Jewish Life*, Spring/Summer 1982, pp. 47-53.

Wolpin, N.: "The Further Reforming of Conservative Judaism," *Jewish Observer*, Nov. 1983, pp. 17-19.

Yates, G.G.: "Spirituality and the American Feminist Experience," *Signs* #9, Autumn 1983, pp. 59-72.

> A good general overview concerning women of all denominations.

Zola, G.P.: "J.T.S., H.U.C., and Women Rabbis," *Journal of Reform Judaism*, Fall 1984, pp. 39-45.

III. JEWISH WOMEN IN THE UNITED STATES AND CANADA

A. Non-Fiction Books and Chapters

Antin, Mary: The Promised Land--The Autobiography of a Russian Immigrant. (Rept.) Princeton Univ. Press, 1985.

Baetz, Ruth: Lesbian Crossroads: Personal Stories of Lesbian Struggles and Triumphs. NY: Wm. Morrow & Co., 1980.

See Jane Salter interview.

Bart, Pauline B. and O'Brien, Patricia H.: Stopping Rape: Successful Survival Strategies. Chicago, IL: Univ. of Illinois at Chicago, 1985.

Contains important chapter on "Ethnicity and Rape Avoidance: Blacks, White Catholics, and Jews." Also see interview with Bart in Lilith #15, in which she claims Jewish women are least likely of all ethnic/religious groups to successfully resist or escape rape.

Beck, Evelyn Torton: Nice Jewish Girls: A Lesbian Anthology. Trumansburg, NY: Crossing Press, 1982. (Orig. Persephone Press)

Excellent collection of writings by Jewish lesbians including Martha Shelley, Pauline Bart and Adrienne Rich. Heavily focused on anti-Semitism; deals forthrightly with it in the lesbian/feminist movement. See interview about book in Lilith #10.

Becker, Robin: Backtalk. Cambridge, MA: Alicejames Books, 1982.

Jewish lesbian views.

Bloch, Alice: Lifetime Guarantee: A Journey Through Loss and Survival. Watertown, MA: Persephone Press, 1981.

Coming to terms with the death of her sister, Barbara, of leukemia, at age 20. Also see interview with Bloch by Susanne J. Sturgis in Off Our Backs, Dec. 1981.

Bloom, Claire: Limelight and After: The Education of an Actress. NY: Penguin Books, 1983.

Bulkin, Elly; Bruce Pratt, Minnie and Smith, Barbara: Yours in Struggle: Three Feminist Perspectives on Anti-Semitism and Racism. Ithaca, NY: Firebrand Books, 1984 (previously published by Long Haul Press).

> Discussions by a white Christian Southerner, an Afro-American and an Ashkenazi Jew.

Bytensky, Bella: From Russia with Luggage. Thornhill, Ont.: Annick Press, 1981, pap.

> The story of a highly educated widowed working grandmother, who emigrated to Canada with her family in 1976.

Chernin, Kim: In My Mother's House: A Daughter's Story, NY: Harper & Row, 1983.

> Moving biographical/autobiographical portraits of women in Chernin's family. See also review by Julia Wolf Mazow, Lilith #13.

Chiswick, Barry R.: "The Labor Market Status of American Jews: Patterns and Determinants." In Van Horne, Winston A., ed., Ethnicity and the Work Force, Univ. of Wisc. (American Ethnic Studies) Milwaukee, WI, 1985, pp. 96-123.

> Includes data on Jewish women.

Cohen, Sarah Blacher, ed.: From Hester Street to Hollywood: The Jewish-American Stage and Screen. Bloomington, IN: Indiana Univ. Press, 1983.

> Includes essays on Fanny Brice, Sophie Tucker and Lillian Hellman.

DelFatlore, Joan: "Women as Scholars in Chaim Potok's Novels." In Studies in American Jewish Literature. Albany, NY: SUNY, 1985.

Dryfoos, Susan W.: Iphigene: Memoirs of Iphigene Ochs Sulzberger of The New York Times Family. NY: Dodd, Mead & Co., 1981.

Dye, Nancy Schram: As Equals and As Sisters: Feminism, Unionism and the Women's Trade Union League of NY. Columbia, MO: Univ. of Missouri Press, 1980.

> Efforts to organize immigrant garment workers. (Reviewed by I. Yellowitz in American Jewish History, Dec. 1981.)

Dykewomon, Elana: *They Will Know Me By My Teeth*. Northampton, MA: Megaera Press, 1976.

Views of a Jewish lesbian.

Edelman, Gary Edward: *Solidarity Forever: Rose Schneiderman and the Women's Trade Union League*. Arno Press, 1982.

Erens, Patricia: *Jews in American Cinema*. Bloomington, IN: Indiana Univ. Press, 1984.

Includes description of Jewish women characters in film.

Ettinger, Elzbieta: *Rosa Luxemburg: A Life*. Boston: Beacon Press, 1986.

Biography of German-Jewish social revolutionary, assassinated by Germans in 1919.

Ewen, Elizabeth: *Immigrant Women in the Land of Dollars: Life and Culture on the Lower East Side, 1890-1925*. NY: Monthly Review Press, 1985.

Author focuses on women's role in social change in Jewish and Italian immigrant communities of the period.

Falk, Candace: *Love, Anarchy and Emma Goldman*. NY: H. Holt & Co., 1984.

Drawing heavily on her love letters to B. Reitman, Falk gives us Goldman as an intensely human woman, struggling with the meaning of "free love" in which she believes as an anarchist but is tormented by her lover's obsessive infidelity. A major flaw is Falk's psychoanalyzing of Goldman, theorizing her loveless childhood led Goldman to be pained by her lover's faithlessness-- an oppressive and ridiculous assessment.

Feldman, Marla J.: *From Tzedek to Tzedakah*. NY: Natl. Fed. of Temple Sisterhoods, 1985.

A work by a rabbi on "economic and social issues of concern for women and children."

Frankfort, Ellen: *Kathy Boudin and the Dance of Death*. NY: Stern and Day, 1983.

About the Weatherwoman, a '60's revolutionary.

Freespirit, Judy: Daddy's Girl: An Incest Survivor's Story. Langlois, OR: Diaspora Distr., 1982.

    Jewish lesbian's childhood trauma.

Girgus, Sam B.: "Blut-und-Eisen: Anzia Yezierska and the New Self-Made Woman." In The New Covenant, Jewish Writers and the American Idea, Chapel Hill, NC: Univ. of N.C. Press, 1984, pp. 108-117.

Glass, Sharon: "Birth in My Family." In Birth Stories: The Experience Remembered, ed., Janet Isaacs Ashford, Trumansburg, NY: Crossing Press, 1984.

    A memoir of birth experiences in a Jewish family in NY and Los Angeles, 1920-60.

Goldman, Emma: Living My Life: The Autobiography of Emma Goldman. Laxton, UT: Peregrine Smith Books, 1982.

    The famous anarchist's autobiography; the only one-volume unabridged edition in print.

Goldscheider, Calvin & Zuckerman, Alan S.: The Transformation of the Jews, Chicago: Univ. of Chicago Press, 1984.

    An important sociological overview with data on fertility and intermarriage in USA, pp. 176-181; Israel fertility and intermarriage, pp. 211-213 and pp. 236-237, marriage in European communities. (Referenced frequently in current writings)

Guggenheim, Peggy: Out of This Century: Confessions of an Art Addict. London: Andre Deutsch, 1980.

Hobson, Laura Z.: Laura Z., A Life. Vol. 1, NY: Arbor House, 1983.

    Autobiography of the author of the classic Gentleman's Agreement and other groundbreaking novels.

Hoffman, Roy: Almost Family. NY: Dial, 1983.

    The story of the relationship between a Southern Jewish housewife, her black housekeeper and their families, from 1946 to 1975.

Holtzman, Will: Judy Holiday: A Biography. NY: G.P. Putnam, 1982.

    The "dumb blonde" actress had a genius IQ of 172.

Howard, Margo: Eppie: The Story of Ann Landers. NY: G.P. Putnam, 1982.

Jensen, Joan M. & Davidson, Sue, eds.: A Needle, a Bobbin, a Strike: Women Needleworkers in America. Phila.: Temple Univ. Press, 1984.

Analyzes changes in worklife and adaptation to new technologies.

Kateb, George. Hannah Arendt: Politics, Conscience, Evil. Totowa, NJ: Rowman & Allanheld, 1983.

Kaye/Kantrowitz, Melanie: Seed of a Woman. Buffalo, NY: Imp Press, 1981.

Jewish lesbian views.

Kaye/Kantrowitz, Melanie, and Klepfisz, Irena: The Tribe of Dina: A Jewish Women's Anthology. (Special publication of Sinister Wisdom magazine), 1985.

Collection of fiction, essays, art, poetry, photographs, interviews, etc. on Jewish feminism, lesbianism, women's history, etc.

Klein, Carole: Aline. Warner, 1980.

Biographical account of Aline Bernstein, Jewish stage designer, who was the lover of Thomas Wolfe, American writer.

Klein, Gerda Weissman: A Passion for Sharing--The Life of Edith Rosenwald Stern. Chappaqua, NY: Rossell Books, 1984.

Biography of the philanthropist.

Libo, Kenneth and Howe, Irving: We Lived There Too 1630-1930. NY: St. Martin's/Marek, 1984.

Includes accounts of Jewish women pioneers of the West.

Lowenthal, Marvin: Henrietta Szold, Life and Letters. Westport, CT: Greenwood Press (Rept.), 1975.

Lowenstein, Andrea Freud: This Place. Somerville, MA: Summerhouse Press, 1982.

Jewish lesbian account.

Malina, Judith: The Diaries, 1947-1957. NY: Grove Press, 1984.

Marcus, Jacob Rader: The American Jewish Woman: 1654-1980, A Documentary History, 2 vols. Hoboken, NJ: Ktav Publishing, 1981.

Useful as a source, but "colored by perception of women as concerned only with a morally pure home life," according to Myra Shoub Nelson. Use with caution.

Mazow, Julia Wolf, ed.: The Woman Who Lost Her Names: Selected Writings by American Jewish Women. San Francisco: Harper & Row, 1980.

Pioneer anthology, includes short stories, autobiographical sketches and excerpts from longer works. (out of print 1986)

Ribalow, Harold U.: "Susan Fromberg Schaeffer." In The Tie That Binds: Conversations with Jewish Writers. NY: A.S. Barnes, 1980.

Roazan, Paul: Helene Deutsch: A Psychoanalyst's Life. NY: Simon & Schuster, 1984.

Biography of famous psychoanalyst who developed misogynist theory of "female masochism."

Rochlin, Harriet and Fred: Pioneer Jews: A New Life in the Far West. Boston: Houghton Mifflin, 1984.

Includes much material on Jewish women pioneers. Also see Rochlin essay in Lilith #14 and other in San Francisco Review of Books, May/June, 1985.

Roiphe, Anne: Generation Without Memory: A Jewish Journey in Christian America. NY: Simon & Schuster/Linden, 1981.

Unfocused and uneducated mishmash attempting to capitalize on "scandal" that broke out after author wrote about celebrating Xmas in The New York Times. Assimilation chic; rationalizes her ignorance and unwillingness to learn anything about Judaism. Good candidate for ethnotherapy. (Know the enemy)

Ritterband, Paul, ed.: Modern Jewish Fertility. Leiden/Brill, 1981.

Rosenberg, Leah: The Errand Runner: Reflections of a Rabbi's Daughter. NY: John Wiley & Sons, 1981.

A young Jewish woman immigrant who attempts to integrate her Chassidic heritage with her Canadian environment.

Schneider, Susan Weidman: *Jewish and Female--Choices and Changes in Our Lives Today*. NY: Simon & Schuster, 1984 (pap. 1985).

The definitive, comprehensive work on the changes in Jewish women's lives today--issues, opinions and resources--in religious life, the family, the community. 640 pages includes a 125-page "Networking Directory."

Selavan, Ida Cohen, ed.: *My Voice Was Heard*. Hoboken, NJ: Ktav, 1981.

Second oral history project of the Pittsburgh section of the National Council of Jewish Women.

Shalom, Sabine: *A Marriage Sabbatical*. NY: Dodd, Mead, 1984.

A Florida housewife travels off the beaten track for six months, finds herself resourceful and courageous, but these discoveries do not affect her marriage to Sephardic husband upon her return.

Shulman, Alix Kates: *Red Emma Speaks: An Emma Goldman Reader*. NY: Schocken Books, 1983.

Collection of her speeches.

Silberman, Charles: *A Certain People*. NY: Summit, 1985. (pap. 1986)

On page 262, Silberman writes: "...The energy being released by the Jewish women's movement is likely to provide the most important source of Jewish renewal." Silberman devotes only 5 1/2 pages (of 366 pages of text) to this "most important" phenomenon. The data in these pages are as superficial and anecdotal as the rest of the book.

Simon, Kate: *Bronx Primitive*. NY: Viking, 1982. (Excerpt appeared in *Moment* magazine, April 1982)

Sochen, June: *Consecrate Every Day: The Public Lives of American Jewish Women, 1880-1890*. Albany: SUNY Press, 1981.

Non-analytical and historically fuzzy work on Jewish women in voluntary organizations. Tries unsuccessfully to fit all Jewish women who played any kind of public role into one Procrustean thesis that Judaism influenced them. Thesis unproved by author.

Solomon, Flora and Litvinoff, Barnet: <u>A Woman's Way</u>. NY: Simon & Schuster, 1985.

> The autobiography of Solomon.

Stein, Leon: <u>Triangle Fire</u>. NY: Carrol & Graf/Quicksilver, 1985.

> Originally published in 1962, the account of the tragic sweatshop fire at the turn of the century.

Stone, Sylvia: "Lifelong Volunteer in San Francisco." (Oral History) Berkeley: Univ. of California, Bancroft Library, Regional Oral History Office, 1983.

Straus, Dorothea: <u>Under the Canopy</u>. NY: George Braziller, 1982.

> The story of the author's twenty-year friendship with Isaac Bashevis Singer and her rediscovery of her Jewish heritage.

Syrkin, Marie: <u>The State of the Jews</u>. Wash.: New Republic Books, 1980.

Talbot, Toby: <u>A Book About My Mother</u>. NY: Farrar, Straus & Giroux, 1980.

> Account of a woman facing her mother's death.

Toder, Nancy: <u>Choices</u>. Watertown, MA: Persephone Press, 1980.

> Jewish lesbian views.

Wagenknecht, Edward: <u>Daughters of the Covenant: Portraits of Six Jewish Women</u>. Amherst, MA: Univ. of Mass. Press, 1983.

Walden, Daniel, ed.: <u>Studies in American Jewish Literature: Jewish Women Writers & Women in Jewish Literature</u>. Albany, NY: SUNY Press, 1983.

> Contains essays on Anna Margolin, Anzia Yezierska, Grace Paley, Cynthia Ozick and Norma Rosen.

Welch, Susan and Ullrich, Fred. <u>The Political Life of American Jewish Women</u>. Fresh Mdws., NY: Biblio Press, 1984.

> This first study examines the way Jewish women participate in politics and their beliefs about important political issues.

Wexler, Alice: <u>Emma Goldman--An Intimate Life</u>. NY: Pantheon Books, 1984.

Willis, Ellen: *Beginning to See the Light: Pieces of a Decade*. NY: Knopf, 1981.

A selection of articles, including some about her Jewish experiences in the 70's. Best essay is about her effort to accept Orthodoxy in Israel.

Young-Bruehl, Elisabeth: *Hannah Arendt: For Love of the World*. New Haven: Yale Univ. Press, 1983.

B. Periodical Articles

Abrams, Jeanne: "Unsere Leit (Our People): Anna Hillkowitz and the Development of the East European Jewish Woman Professional in America," *American Jewish Archives*, Cincinnati, OH: Nov. 1985, pp. 275-289.

A history of Anna Hillkowitz's work for the Jewish Consumptives Relief Society between 1905 and 1924.

Adler, Celia: "Celia Adler Recalls," (Yiddish) *Amer. Assn. of Professors of Yiddish*, v. 5, No. 2-3, 1983.

Recollections of great actress of American Yiddish Theatre.

Arich, Aliza and Hannah: "A Feeling of Family: Boston Gay and Lesbian Jews Attend World Conference," *Gay Community News*, Aug. 29, 1981.

Baer, M.F.: "A First Step Toward Women as Members," *Jewish Monthly*, Nov. 1984, pp. 14-15.

How to deal with women members in an "integrated" organization.

Beck, Evelyn Torton: "Interview with Faye Moskowitz," *Belles Lettres, A Review of Books by Women*, v. 1, #2, 1985, pp. 7-8.

Moskowitz is the author of autobiographical stories, *A Leak in the Heart*, published the same year. (op. cit.)

_____: "Daughters and Mothers: An Autobiographical Sketch," *Sinister Wisdom 14*, 1980.

_____: "Teaching About Jewish Lesbians in Literature: From 'Zeitel and Rickl' to 'The Tree of Begats'." In *Lesbian Studies*, ed., Margaret Cruikshank. Old Westbury, NY: The Feminist Press, 1982.

Becker, Robin: "Scenes from the Life of a Jewish Lesbian," Dyke.* A Quarterly, #5.

*This journal is now defunct.

Black, J.: "When Your Daughter Enlists," Reform Judaism, Summer 1984, pp. 10-11.

Bletter, Diane Katcher: "Front Page: Keeping Score," Present Tense, Summer 1983, pp. 7-8.

On stereotypes of the Jewish woman in popular entertainment.

Bogarin, Jonathan: "Grandma's Struggles, Our Strength." Jewish Currents, March 1980.

Braginsky, Judy: "She Sees Jewish Women in New Light," Life of Niles Township (Illinois, weekly), Jan. 21, 1982.

Report of course offering in Skokie, Illinois by a social worker, Shirley Gould, on "The Emerging Jewish Woman."

Bubis, Gerald B.: "Women in Leadership," Journal of Jewish Communal Service, Spring 1983, pp. 237-240.

Cantor, Aviva: "Feminism and Jewish Self-Determination," Israel Horizons, March 1981.

Speech to Agenda conference giving feminist analysis of lack of democracy in the Jewish community.

_____: "The Missing Ingredients--Power and Influence in the Jewish Community," Present Tense, Spring 1984, pp. 8-12.

Analysis of the role of Jewish women and their groups within the Jewish establishment, showing that substantive change is impossible as long as lack of democracy exists.

Cardin, Nina: "Review of Baum/Hyman/Michel, The Jewish Woman in America," Leviathan, Univ. of Calif. at Santa Cruz, Spring 1981.

Clar, R.: "First Jewish (Woman) Physician of Los Angeles," Western States Jewish Historical Quarterly, Oct. 1981, pp. 66-75.

"Chronicle," *Jewish Journal of Sociology*, v. 23, Dec. 1981, pp. 159-162.

> Editorial comment on seeming improvement in the number of women employed in two top executive categories.

Clayton, John: "Grace Paley and Tillie Olsen: Radical Jewish Humanists," *Response*, Spring 1984, p. 37ff.

Cohen, Esther: "Jewish Women Writers," *Women's American ORT Reporter*, Fall 1981.

> Review of seven books by Jewish women authors.

Cohen, Steven Martin: "American Jewish Feminism: A Study in Conflicts and Compromises," *American Behavioral Scientist*, April 1980.

> Based on interviews with ten Jewish feminist activists, author discovers interesting commonalities but tends to over-generalize from this narrow base.

Cohn-Sherbok, D.: "Women and 'Intellect'," *Jewish Spectator*, Fall 1983, pp. 24-25.

_____: "Defaming Jewish Women," *Jewish Spectator*, Summer 1983, pp. 58-59.

Coombs, A.: "Barbra Streisand: A Star Is Reborn," *Ladies Home Journal* #98, March 1981, p. 20.

> An article on Streisand's Jewish identity and her new Jewish commitment.

Danab, Mint: Review of *Nice Jewish Girls* (op. cit.) In *Womanspirit*, Winter Solstice 1983.

Daum, Annette: "Antisemitism in the Women's Movement," *Pioneer Women* (now *Na'amat Women*), Sept./Oct. 1983.

_____: "The Jewish Stake in Abortion Rights," *Lilith* #8, 1981.

> The definitive work on how Judaism's views of abortion conflict with the anti-choice organizations' and legislators' and what the Jewish community is doing and not doing to make this known. Excellent source for pro-choice activists.

Davis, Hanna B.: "Towards a New Understanding of Jewish Men," *Genesis 2*, March 1982.

Davis, Barbara Hillyer: "N.W.S.A. Diversity: Comments and Complaints from the Conferences," National Women's Studies Association Newsletter, Lawrence, KS: Univ. of Kansas, Winter 1983, pp. 8-11.

Includes paragraph on Jewish issues at N.W.S.A. Conferences.

Dresner, Ruth Rapp: "The Work of Bertha Pappenheim," Judaism, Spring 1981, pp. 204-211.

Essay on the founder of the Judischer Frauenbund of Germany.

Drew, Jill: "To Go to Berbir--A Journey to War," Sinister Wisdom #26, 1982.

Protest against Israeli invasion of Lebanon, this special issue evoked wide criticism and debate.

Dubrovsky, Gertrude: "Growing Up in Farmingdale," American Jewish History, Dec. 1981.

Jewish farmer's memoir.

Eisenpreis, B.: "Sisterhood at Seventy," Reform Judaism, Spring/Summer 1983, pp. 20-21.

Fein, H.: "Abused Women of Valor," Midstream, Nov. 1983, pp. 19-21.

Feinstein, Sarah: "It Had to Do With Apples," Lesbian Insider/Insighter/Inciter, July 1981.

Feron, James: "A Spirited Israeli-American Dialogue on Women's Issues Opens in Jerusalem," New York Times, Aug. 1, 1984.

Report on Israeli-American dialogue on status of Jewish women, attended by Betty Friedan and other American feminists.

Frank, S.S.: "Time for Personal Growth," Jewish Observer, Summer 1984, p. 3.

Fridkis, Ari Lloyd: "Desertion in the American Jewish Immigrant Family: The Work of the National Desertion Bureau in Cooperation with the Industrial Removal Office," American Jewish History, Dec. 1981.

"The problem of conflict between husband and wife was a major one for the American Jewish immigrant family."

Friedman, Nathalie: "The Changing Needs, Interests and Motivations of the Jewish Woman," American Mizrachi Woman, Jan. 1982.

Furstenberg, Rochelle: "A Unique Feminism," Midstream, Oct. 1982, pp. 35-39.

Gantz, Paula: "Our Golden Years," Lilith #10, 1983, pp. 6-9.

> What it means to be elderly and female in the Jewish community today.

Gold, Doris B.: "Women's History Day in Albany, NY," Jewish Currents, June 1985, pp. 12-14.

> Report on Women's History week conference, "Women Right History: Feminist Issues in HIstorical Perspective" and dialogue there between Betty Powell and Elly Bulkin, entitled "Black Feminist/Jewish Feminist."

Goldman, Aviva Dayan: "American Feminism, An Alien Philosophy," Response, Fall 1977, p. 106ff.

Goldsmith, E.: "Violence in the Jewish Family," Reform Judaism, Winter 1983-84, p. 20.

> Deals with wife-battering by Jewish husbands.

Golomb, Deborah G.: "The 1983 Congress of Jewish Women: Evolution or Revolution in American Jewish Women's History," American Jewish History, Sept. 1980.

Green, Tova: "Rediscovering My Jewishness," A Working Conference on Women and Racism: Newsletter of the New England Women's Studies Assn., March 4, 1981.

Hadassah Magazine editorial: "Reagan and Women's Rights: Can the President Be Moved?" May 1981, pp. 8-9.

Harrison, J.H.: "The Ubiquitous Jewish Mother," Jewish Digest, Dec. 1982, pp. 18-21.

Hirschhorn, Barbara: "Jewish Schools Are Changing," Present Tense, Spring 1984, pp. 19-24.

> The feminist revolution is bringing about change in Jewish education today. (Also see her article in Baltimore Jewish Times, Sept. 18, 1981)

Humphries, Ami: "Judaism's First Lady," Jewish United Fund News, Chicago, IL, June 1985, p. 7.

> Story of Shoshana Cardin, first woman president of Council of Jewish Federations.

Hyman, Paula: "Immigrant Women and Consumer Protest: The NYC Kosher Meat Boycott of 1902," American Jewish History, Sept. 1980.

Jochnowitz, Carol: "Jewish Women Now: The Invisible Bruise," Jewish Currents, May 1985, pp. 34-35.

> Jewish wife-beating.

Kanigel, R.: "Will Jewish Baby Boom Babies Ever Have Their Own?" Jewish Monthly, June/July 1983, pp. 9-12.

Katz, Judith: "Nadine Pagan's Last Letter Home," Sinister Wisdom #19, 1982.

> Jewish lesbian views.

Kaye, Melanie: "Fired or Not Rehired--Anti-Semitism, Homophobia and the Good White Knight," Off Our Backs, May 1982.

> Anti-semitism from white, black and Hispanic women at a Southwestern university.

Kessner, Carol: "Mordecai Kaplan on Women in Jewish Life," Reconstructionist, July/Aug. 1981, pp. 38-39.

> Views of movement's founder.

Klagsbrun, Francine: "Hooray for Jewish Mothers," Newsweek, "My Turn" column, March 28, 1983, p. 11.

Klein, Judith Weinstein: "Jewish Identity and Self-Esteem," NY: American Jewish Committee pamphlet, 1982.

> Groundbreaking work in ethnotherapy with crucial implications for Jewish women. See especially chapter, "Jewish Identity for Women."

Klepfisz, Irena: "Anti-Semitism in the Lesbian/Feminist Movement," Off Our Backs, April 1982.

Krausz, Judy: "First International Women Scholars Conference," Pioneer Women (now Na'amat Women), March/April 1982.

> Held in Israel, 12/28/81 to 1/8/82.

Kremer, G.H.: "Three Generations of Women Today," Jewish Digest, Oct. 1980.

Krummel, Regina P.: "A Secular Jewish Woman and Christianity," Jewish Currents, April 1984.

> Raises problem of educating a "secular Jewish" child.

Langer, M.E.: "Working Mothers," Journal of Jewish Communal Service, Winter 1982, pp. 176-182.

Lerner, Anne Lapidus: "The Making of a Person: The Vision of Two American Jewish Women Writers," Jewish Book Annual, JWB, 1981.

> Study of Anzia Yezierska and Esther M. Broner.

Lerner, Elinor: "Jewish Involvement in the New York City Woman Suffrage Movement," American Jewish History, June 1981.

Lester, Elenore: "Author Cynthia Ozick Advocates Jewish Ideas in Fiction," The Jewish Week (NY), April 8, 1983, p. 14ff.

> Author Ozick's Jewish roots and her views on writing, Jewish identity, motherhood and feminism.

Lev, Yehuda: "A Backward Glance: Remembering Our Parents Across the Long Long Years," Direction, April 1982.

> Memoir of his late mother, a lawyer.

Levenberg, Diane: "All She Could Never Be: Anzia Yezierska," Midstream, Nov. 1981.

Levin, M.: "The Feminist Mystique," Commentary, Dec. 1980.

> Ignorant, uninformed, but still dangerous example of the backlash against feminism. It's pathetic that a once-intellectual Jewish magazine has stooped to print this pathetic garbage. (Know the enemy.) See also "Feminism and Thought Control" (June 1982) and "Comparable Worth" (Sept. 1984).

Lilith Forum: "How to Get What We Want by the Year 2000," #7, 1980, p. 18.

    Brief essays by eight Jewish women activists/academics on their expectations.

Lowenthal, Rita and Spiegel, Marcia Cohn: "Leaders Feel Powerless," Lilith #7, Dec. 1980, p. 41.

    Women in both volunteer and professional leadership positions in Los Angeles explore their feelings of powerlessness.

Mallon, J.V.: "Jewish American Princess: Archetype or Stereotype?" Jewish Digest, Sept. 1984, pp. 70-73.

Mandelkern, Nick: "The Story of Pioneer Women," Pioneer Women (now Na'amat Women), Feb. & March, 1981.

    Fascinating history of founding, growth and change in the organization as it adapted to the needs of American-born members. Key resource.

Miller, J.D.: "Women Face the Reagan Era," Jewish Frontier, Dec. 1981, pp. 10-13.

Miriam, Selma: "Anti-Semitism in the Lesbian Community: A Collage of Mostly Bad News by One Jewish Dyke," Sinister Wisdom, 19, 1982.

Moment: "Interview with Marie Syrkin and Trude Weiss-Rosmarin," Sept. 1983, pp. 37-44.

Moore, Abigail S.: "History and Herstory: What's New on Jewish Women," Jewish Frontier, Jan. 1982.

    Review of new books by Marcus, Sochen and this Bibliography. Too uncritical, especially of Sochen.

Moore, Deborah Dash: "Studying the Public and Private Selves of American Jewish Women," Lilith #10, Winter 1983, pp. 28-30.

Morales, Rosario: "Double Allegiance: Jewish Women and Women of Color," A Working Conference on Women and Racism: Newsletter of the New England Women's Studies Association, May 1981.

Morris, Benny: "Portrait of a Radical Lawyer [Leah Tsemel], Present Tense, Spring 1981.

Mort, Jo-Ann: "Jews and the Abortion Debate," Jewish Frontier, March 1982.

_____: "Muriel Rukeyser: An Appreciation," Response, v. XII, no. 1, Summer 1979, p. 85ff.

Moskowitz, Faye: "Hers," New York Times, Oct. 1981.

This forum for women's writing included various essays on Jewish topics in four consecutive columns.

Pogrebin, Letty Cottin: "Anti-Semitism in the Women's Movement," Ms. Magazine, June 1982.

Groundbreaking, courageous essay about the subject; widely read and commented upon.

_____: "Will Our Children Remain Jewish in America?" Congress Monthly, May 1981.

_____: "Can Judaism and Feminism Afford to Be in Conflict?" New York Times "Hers" column, Aug. 25, 1983, Sect. C, p. 2.

Anti-Semitism in the women's movement and sexism in Judaism.

_____: "Women as the Litmus Test," Present Tense (symposium), Winter 1985, pp. 46-47.

Polikoff, Nancy: "Jewish Women--Connected," Off Our Backs, April 1982.

Review of Mazow anthology and Baum/Hyman/Michel Jewish Women in America. Superficial; misses the point most of the time. Also self-hating. Refers to one story in anthology as "...seemed too Jewish." (Know the enemy.)

Pratt, Norma Fain: "Culture and Radical Politics: Yiddish Women Writers, 1890-1940," American Jewish History, Sept. 1980.

Pressma, D.C.: "The Changing Role of Jewish Women: Implications for Family, Social Work Agency and Social Work Practice," Journal of Jewish Communal Service, Fall 1981, pp. 7-75.

Jewish women, 1950-1980.

Raphael, Marc Lee: "Female Humanity--American Jewish Women Writers Speak Out," Judaism, Spring 1981, pp. 212-224.

Reguer, S.: "Jewish Mother and the Jewish American Princess; Fact or Fiction?" USA Today, Sept. 1979.

Reisman, R.F.: "The Road to Nairobi," Anti-Defamation League Bulletin, Nov. 1984, pp. 9-12.

_____: "Females and Feminists." In Grandma Never Lived in America, The New Journalism of Abraham Cahan, ed., Rischin, Moses, Bloomington: Indiana Univ. Press, 1985, pp. 390-402.

Rosen, Gladys: "Teaching About the Role of Women," Pedagogic Reporter, Fall 1980, pp. 27-30.

In view of renewed emphasis on Jewish education, author argues that aspirations and potential of Jewish women must be studied in the classroom.

Ruby, Walter: "An Interview with Alma Singer" (wife of I.B. Singer), National Jewish Monthly, April 1982.

_____: "Ozick: Writing on Jewish Themes Not Ethnic or Parochial," (Interview) The Long Island Jewish World, June 29, 1984, p. 14.

Ozick's Jewish identity.

Salkin, Jeffrey: "Shylock in Drag?" Moment, March 1983, pp. 37-38.

On JAP (Jewish American Princess) jokes and other modern vulgarities--how Jewish women are "blamed."

Schreiber, Regina (pseud.): "Sisterhood Is Powerful Unless You're Jewish," Lilith #8, 1981.

Testimony by participant at UN women's conference in Copenhagen, describing experience there. Section includes testimony by other women.

Shimoff, Melanie B.: "Battered Women: A Problem for the Jewish Community," Women's American ORT Reporter, March/April 1981.

(Reprint of article first appearing in the Jewish World).

Shoro, Rima: "Remembering Sophia Parnok," Conditions: Six, 1980.

Smith, Beverly, with Judith Stein and Priscilla Golding: "The Possibility of Life Between Us: A Dialogue Between Black and Jewish Women," Conditions: Seven, 1981.

Spiegel, Marcia Cohn: "Sexual Stereotyping Again," Judaica Book News, Spring 1984, p. 16.

Review of Prostitution and Prejudice by Edward Bristow.

Spiegler, S.: "Adam's Rib: Feminists Rejoice," Journal of Jewish Communal Service, Fall 1983, p. 75.

Jewish social worker comments on developments in Jewish life as seen by "feminists."

_____: "Wife-Beating, Jewish Style," Journal of Jewish Communal Service, Winter 1983, pp. 169-170.

_____: "Woman Astronaut First Jew in Space (Late Judith Resnik)," Journal of Jewish Communal Service, Fall 1983, p. 76.

Stokes, Rose Pastor: "Voice from the Sweatshop," Lilith #8, 1981.

Chapter from unpublished autobiography of the Jewish radical, fictionalized by Anzia Yezierska in her "Salome of the Tenements." Manuscript is at Yale University.

Stone, Ellen: "Reproductive Freedom: A Jewish Issue," Genesis 2, March 1982.

Syrkin, Marie: "Does Feminism Clash with the Jewish National Need?" Midstream, June/July 1985, pp. 8-12.

Tax, Meredith: "Ancient Laws, Modern Times," The Village Voice, Jan. 1, 1985, p. 37.

Excellent review of Jewish & Female (by Susan Weidman Schneider) and On Being a Jewish Feminist (by Susannah Heschel), by the author of novel Rivington Street.

Tilchen, Maida: "JEB Talks--Picturing Lesbians," Gay Community News, Aug. 8, 1981.

_____: "Speaking Out: Jewish Feminists Discuss Anti-Semitism," Gay Community News, March 14, 1981.

(Re: Letter on Anti-Semitism by Nine Jewish Lesbians in Plexus, Berkeley/San Francisco, Jan. 1981.)

Tishman, Peggy: "An End to Exploitation of Women in the Jewish Establishment," Lilith #8, 1981.

Toll, W.: "The Female Life Cycle and the Measure of Jewish Social Change, Portland, Ore., 1880-1930," American Jewish History, March 1983, pp. 309-332.

Turitz, Leo E.: "Amelia Greenwald: The Jewish Florence Nightingale," American Jewish Archives, Cincinnati, OH, Nov. 1985, pp. 291-292.

> A brief history of nurse who was directed by President Herbert Hoover after WWI to establish the first school of nursing at the Jewish Hospital in Poland.

Wachtel, Nili: "Our Grandmothers, Our Mothers, Ourselves," Midstream, March 1982.

Weinberg, Sydney Stahl: "Working Daughters," Lilith #8, 1981.

> Jobs conferred adulthood on immigrant women.

Weiss-Rosmarin, Trude: "Second Thoughts on ERA," Editorial, Jewish Spectator, Fall 1982, pp. 7-9.

Yanina: "Reflections: A Black Lesbian Relates With Her Jewish Grandmother-in-Law," A Working Conference on Women and Racism: Newsletter of the New England Women's Studies Association, May 1981.

Ziemer, Susan: "In Memoriam." In Womanspirit, Winter Solstice 1983.

> Tribute to her grandmother.

C. Fiction

Barringer, Felicity: Flight From Sorrow--The Life and Death of Tamara Wall. NY: Atheneum, 1984.

> Expanded from this reporter's series, account of life of survivor of Siberia who became Washington lawyer, survived battering and died of cancer.

Brodkey, Harold: Women and Angels. Phila.: Jewish Publication Society of America, 1985.

Broner, E.M.: Her Mothers. Bloomington, IN: Indiana Univ. Press, 1985. (Rept. of 1975 Holt, Rinehart & Winston edition.)

Bulkin, Elly: *Lesbian Fiction: An Anthology*. Watertown, MA: Persephone Press, 1981.

>See especially Irena Klepfisz, Francine Krasno and Lynn Michaels.

Burnstein, Patricia: *Family Holiday*. NY: Morrow, 1982.

Busch, Frederick: *Invisible Mending*. MA: David B. Godine, 1984.

>Novel of New York Jews includes major character Rhona Glinsky. (Jewish Book Council Award for Fiction, 1985)

Bush, Lawrence: *Bessie*. NY: Seaview/Putnam, 1983.

>Beautiful fictionalized biography of his Communist grandmother. Moving, inspiring. See review in *Lilith* #14 by Julia Wolf Mazow.

Cohen, Arthur A.: *An Admirable Woman*. MA: David R. Godine, 1983.

>Inspired by the life of Hannah Arendt, this novel presents the story of Erika Hertz, a German Jewish intellectual driven from Germany and destined to become a legend in America. (Winner of Jewish Book Council Award for Fiction, 1984)

Cohen, Esther: *No Charge for Looking*. NY: Schocken Books, 1984.

>Humorous story of confused American Jewish woman who gets involved in the life of Nazareth while trying to write about Israel's Arabs.

Courter, Gay: *The Midwife*. Boston: Houghton Mifflin, 1981.

>Historical novel beginning during Czarist Russian pogroms and continuing in turn-of-the-century New York. Good, though shallow read.

Davidson, Sara: *Friends of the Opposite Sex*. NY: Doubleday, 1984.

>The story of a young Jewish woman who seeks roots. On a trip to Jerusalem she becomes aware of the importance of a link to ideas and values larger than herself.

Ellis, Julie: *Maison Jennie*. NY: Arbor House, 1984.

Epstein, Leslie: *Regina*. NY: Coward McCann & Geoghegan, 1982.

>Regina quits her family and therapist in order to make a comeback in the theater.

Evanier, David: The One-Star Jew. San Francisco: North Point Press, 1983.

>Short stories about character of young writer. Page 208 has the following sentence: "The Jewish Feminists have set up a booth [in Times Square] on the Holocaust and held up signs to advertise a rally 'In Memory of the Three Million'." (Know the enemy.)

Faessler, Shirley: Everything in the Window. Boston: Atlantic, 1980.

>A young Toronto Jewish woman marries non-Jew.

Ford, Gertrude: Eighty-One Sheriff Street. NY: Frederick Fell, 1981.

Freeman, Cynthia: Catch the Gentle Dawn. NY: Arbor House, 1983.

Friedman, Rosemary: Rose of Jericho. London: Victor Gollancz, 1984.

Geller, Ruth: Pictures From the Past. Buffalo, NY: Imp Press, 1981.

——————: Triangles. Trumansburg, NY: The Crossing Press, 1984.

>Young woman deepens her Jewish identity; lesbian relationships.

Gladstone, Frances: Anne's Youth. NY: Schocken Books, 1984.

Goldreich, Gloria: Leah's Children. NY: MacMillan, 1985.

>A family saga of the Goldfeders, spanning US, Europe and Israel, 1956-1978.

Goldstein, Rebecca: Mind-Body Problem. NY: Random House, 1983.

>A young Jewish woman and the process of her break with tradition.

Gussow, Don: Chaia Sonia. NY: Bantam Books, 1981.

>A family odyssey from the pogroms of Lithuania to New York's lower East Side, through the eyes of a woman and her five children.

Hellman, Aviva: Somebody Please Love Me. Garden City, NY: Doubleday, 1984.

>The life of a young woman from an Orthodox Jewish family in Brooklyn and her rise to the top of the fashion industry.

Isaacs, Susan: Almost Paradise. NY: Harper & Row, 1984.

 The marriage between a poor Jewish woman of humble origins and an upperclass non-Jew.

Kahan, Rhea: Hand Me Downs. NY: Random House, 1980.

 Jewish women in L.A., with Polish village background earlier.

Kaufmann, Myron S.: The Love of Elspeth Baker. NY: Arbor House, 1982.

 The story of a young woman abandoned by the father of her unborn child.

Koppelman, Susan, ed.: Between Mothers and Daughters: Stories Across a Generation. NY: The Feminist Press, 1984.

 Four stories by Jewish women authors are included.

Krantz, Judith: Mistral's Daughter. NY: Crown, 1983 (pap. Bantam).

 Awakening of Jewish consciousness in third-generation daughter.

Kreitman, Esther Singer: Deborah. Tr. M. Carr (Yiddish). NY: St. Martin's Press, 1984.

 Reprint of 1936 novel by daughter of famous Singer family—speaking with passion for the millions of women oppressed by traditional Jewish culture.

Levin, Sheila: Simple Truths. NY: Crown, 1982.

 Susan, the daughter of Holocaust survivors, comes to terms with her Jewishness through her involvement with Soviet Jewry.

Levine, Faye: Solomon and Sheba. NY: Richard Marek/Putnam, 1980.

Levinson, Norma: Room Upstairs. NY: Simon & Schuster, 1984.

Markus, Julia: American Rose. Boston: Houghton-Mifflin, 1981.

Mosco, Maisie: Glittering Harvest. NY: Bantam Books, 1981.

 The third volume of a generational saga. Sarah keeps her family together during WWII, and sees her grandchildren fighting for Israel in the Six Day War.

Novick, Marian: <u>At Her Age</u>. NY: Scribner's, 1985.

>75-year old woman escapes from nursing home.

Ozick, Cynthia: <u>Cannibal Galaxy</u>. NY: Dutton/Obelisk, 1984.

Pesetsky, Bette: <u>Stories Up To a Point</u>. NY: Knopf, 1982.

Pilcer, Sonia: <u>Maiden Rites</u>. NY: Viking Press, 1982.

Plain, Belva: <u>Crescent City</u>. NY: Delacorte, 1984; Dell, 1985.

>The life of a young German-born Jewish woman in New Orleans before and during the Civil War.

Potok, Chaim: <u>Davita's Harp</u>. NY: Knopf, 1985.

>A young Jewish woman goes through adolescence in 1930's Brooklyn, while her mother gives up Communism and marries an Orthodox Jew.

Rapoport, Nessa: <u>Preparing for Sabbath</u>. NY: William Morrow, 1980; Bantam Books, pap., 1982. (out of print, 1986)

>Moving first novel about young woman from traditional Toronto family, her struggles with love and independence. Parts about friendship with women and their highs and lows are the most vivid and often depressing parts of the book.

Rochlin, Harriet: <u>So Far Away</u>. Jove, pap. 1981.

>Unique historical novel--not a family epic but adventures of a worldly, idealistic young Jewish woman in San Francisco of the 1870's who chooses a groom over her family's objections and goes with him to live in the Arizona territory.

Rosen, Norma: <u>At the Center</u>. Boston: Houghton Mifflin, 1982.

Rosenbluth, Sally: <u>Feast of Ashes</u>. NY: Atheneum, 1981.

>A novel about a love obsession; begins in Italy; setting is in Israel mostly; on the eve of the Six Day War.

Rossner, Judith: <u>August</u>. Boston: Houghton Mifflin, 1983.

>The story of a female Jewish analyst and her teenage patient. The analyst's difficult marriage and love affair are infinitely more interesting than her patient's tzores.

Schaeffer, Susan Fromberg: Love. NY: E.P. Dutton, 1981.

Schneider, Nina: The Woman Who Lived in a Prologue. Boston: Houghton Mifflin, 1980.

>A woman in her 70's describes her life, begun as an upper class immigrant early in the century. She regrets having been pushed into traditional female roles without knowing enough to object; now she is ready to live her life for herself.

Schulman, Sarah: The Sophie Horowitz Story. Tallahassee, FL: Naiad Press, 1984.

>Billed as a "Lesbian detective novel."

Smith, Robert Kimmel: Sadie Shapiro, Matchmaker. NY: Simon & Schuster, 1980.

Spiegel, Penina: Millie Myerson and the Prince of Wales. NY: St. Martin's Press, 1982.

Steel, Danielle: The Ring. Delacorte Press, 1980.

>A multi-generational romantic novel. The tragic story of Kassandra von Gotthard, a rich German woman and her love affair with a Jew, writer Dolff Stern.

Stein, Toby: Only the Best; A Love Story. NY: Arbor House, 1984.

Stember, Sol Judith: A Love Story of Newport. NY: New American Library, 1983.

>Setting is Colonial America.

Tax, Meredith: Rivington Street. NY: Morrow, 1982.

>Blockbuster novel about "the world of our mothers" on the lower East Side.

Tonner, Leslie: Female Complaints. NY: Seaview, 1982.

>Novel about a group of divorced, middle-aged women.

Waldman, Bess: The Book of Tziril. Marblehead, MA: Micah Publns., 1981.

>Family chronicle seen through the life stories of four women.

Weinzweig, Helen: Basic Black With Pearls. NY: Morrow, 1981.

Worthen, Helen-Harlow: Perimeters. Harcourt, Brace, 1980.

    A woman's search for a betrayed Jewish heritage.

Yezierska, Anzia: The Open Cage. NY: Persea Books, 1980.

    Reprint collection of short stories by the famous immigrant novelist, with incisive introduction by historian Alice Kessler Harris.

Zeitlin, Marianne L: Mira's Passage. NY: Dell, 1981, pap.

IV. JEWISH WOMEN IN ISRAEL

A. Non-Fiction Books and Book Chapters

Adelson, Dorothy: Operation Susannah. NY: Pemberly Press, 1982.

>The story of Felicity Robbins, a public relations officer working for the Jewish Agency for Palestine in the days before Israel became a state.

Aharoni, Ada and Wolf, Thea: Thea: To Alexandria, Jerusalem, and Freedom. Bryn Mawr, PA: Dorrance, 1984.

>How two women, one a poet, another a nurse, made aliyah.

Azaryahu, Sara: Selected History Versus Women's Movement in Israel, 1900-1947. (Tr. from Hebrew), Haifa: Women's Aid Fund, 1980.

Bar-Yosef, Rivka: "Women Workers in Israel." In Women Workers in Fifteen Countries: Essays in Honor of Alice Hanson Cook. Ithaca, NY: ILR Press, 1985.

Cowen, Ida and Gunther, Irene: A Spy for Freedom--The Story of Sarah Aaronsohn. NY: Lodestar Books (Dutton), 1984.

>(Reissue of 1970's young adult novel published by Lewin-Epstein, Israel.) Biography of young woman executed by Turks as a spy for the British during WWI in Palestine.

Datan, Nancy, Antonovsky, Aaron and Maoz, Benjamin: A Time to Reap--The Middle Age of Women in Five Israeli Subcultures. Baltimore: Johns Hopkins Univ., 1981.

>Medical and psychological surveys on middle-aged Israeli women's response to menopause.

Dayan, Yael: My Father, His Daughter. NY: Farrar, Straus & Giroux, 1985.

>Daughter of the famous general writes about her relationship with him, and also gives her view of his life.

Golan, Aviezer and Pibkas, Danny: Shula: Code Name The Pearl. NY: Delacorte, 1980.

>Life story of a young Israeli woman, master spy and leader in pre-state underground.

Hazleton, Lesley: Where Mountains Roar: A Personal Report from the Sinai and Negev Deserts. NY: Holt, Rinehart & Winston, 1980.

Jordan, Ruth: Daughters of the Waves: Memories of Growing Up in Pre-War Palestine. NY: Taplinger, 1983.

Memoir of a young woman growing up in Haifa between the late 1920's and the early 1940's.

Keller, Mollie: Golda Meir. NY: Franklin Watts, 1983.

Keren, Thea: Sophie Udin—Portrait of a Pioneer. Rehovot, 1984 (privately published).

Life of Pioneer Women (now Na'amat USA) founder in US and Israel.

Lieblich, Amia: Kibbutz Makom. NY: Pantheon Books, 1981.

Interviews and oral history with founders of a pseudonymous kibbutz.

Meir, Menahem: Remembering Mama: A Son's Evocation of Life with Golda Meir. NY: Arbor House, 1983.

Palgi, Michal et al., and Marilyn Safir, ed.: Sexual Equality: The Israel Kibbutz Tests the Theories. Derby, PA: Norwood Editions, 1983.

An important analytical work by women members of kibbutzim who are also academics.

Safir, Marilyn; Mednick, Martha, and Izraeli, Dafna, eds.: Women's Worlds: From the New Scholarship. NY: Praeger Publishing, 1985.

Includes article on "Israeli Women and Military Service: A Socialization Experience," by Ann Bloom and Rivka Bar-Yosef.

Slater, Robert: Golda: The Uncrowned Queen of Israel. Middle Village, NY: Jonathan David, 1981.

Portrait drawn from recently released documents in the state archives.

Spiro, Melford E.: Gender and Culture: Kibbutz Women Revisited. NY: Schocken, 1980.

Social relations in the modern kibbutz--a study of "counter-revolution in kibbutz conceptions regarding marriage, family, division of labor by gender."

Tshelebi, Evliya: Evliya Tshelebi's Travels in Palestine, 1648-1650. (Tr. from Turkish by S.H. Stephen.) Jerusalem: Ariel, 1980, pap.

B. Periodical Articles

Amir, Aliza: "We Must Create a Revolution," (Interview) Youth and Nation, Winter 1981.

Subject was women in the kibbutz. Amir is Secretary-General of Kibbutz Artzi Federation.

Balka, Christie: "Beyond 'Zionism Equals Racism' in Nairobi," Sojourner, Cambridge, MA: Oct. 1985.

Focus on dialogue between Israeli and Palestinian women, as well as Israeli feminist issues, at U.N. Decade for Women Conference in Nairobi. Same author wrote on this topic in Genesis 2, Feb./March 1986, pp. 19-22.

Barach, J.: "The Girls with Soul," Israel Scene, Sept. 1982, pp. 24-25.

Bat-Ada, Judith: "Porn in the Promised Land," Lilith #11, Fall/Winter 1983.

Growth of pornography in Israel and its impact on increasing violence against women.

Beizer-Bohrer, Ruth: "Images of Women in Israeli Literature--Myth and Reality," Judaism, Winter 1984, pp. 91-100.

The literature reveals the gap between the ideological declaration of equality and the real attitudes of male chauvinism and discrimination.

Bernstein, D.: "Economic Growth and Female Labor: The Case of Israel," Sociological Review #31, May 1983, pp. 263-292.

_____: "The Plough Woman Who Cried into the Pots: The Position of Women in Pre-State Israeli Society," Journal of Jewish Social Studies, Winter 1983, pp. 43-56.

Breslauer, I.H.: "Israeli Women Soldiers," Jewish Spectator, Winter 1982, pp. 47-49.

Ben-Shaul, D'vora: "Women and the Press,: Jerusalem Post International Edition, March 13-19, 1983, p. 11.

Israeli women working in media assess their role in the profession and portrayal of women in media.

Broner, E.M.: "The Nairobi Difference," Moment, Oct. 1985, p. 22ff.

_____: "The Road to Nairobi," Moment, Nov. 1984, pp. 35-39.

The most complete account of the conference, dealing in detail with Jewish and Israeli women's relationships with non-Jewish and Third World women.

Congress Monthly, American Jewish Congress: Feb./March 1985.

This issue contains addresses and discussion summaries by American and Israeli women leaders presented at sessions of 20th annual "America-Israel dialogue" on feminism held in Jerusalem, Summer 1984 (Betty Friedan, Elizabeth Holtzman, Blu Greenberg, Cynthia Fuchs Epstein, Shulamit Aloni, Tamar Eshel, Rivka Bar-Yosef, Penina Peli, D. Izraeli).

Davidman, Lynn: Review of Janet Aviad, "Return to Judaism: Religious Renewal in Israel," Journal of the American Academy of Religion, Univ. of Chicago Press: June 1984, pp. 401-402.

Fainaru, Edna: "Israel's Gift of Song: Chava Alberstein," Hadassah Magazine, April 1982, p. 191.

_____: "Nitza Shapiro-Libai: Israel and its People are Changing," Present Tense, Autumn 1982, pp. 33-35.

Feldman, Yael S.: "Inadvertent Feminism: The Image of Frontier Women in Contemporary Israeli Literature," Modern Hebrew Literature 10:3-4, Spring/Summer 1985, pp. 34-37.

An essay based on the novel, Gai Oni (Valley of Sorrow) by Shulamit Lapid.

Freedman, Marcia: "Feminist Publishing in Israel," National Women's Studies Newsletter, v. VIII, #1, Winter 1980.

Fuchs, Esther: "The Beast Within: Women in Amos Oz's Early Fiction," Modern Judaism, IV/3, 1984, pp. 311-321.

In Israel

_____: "Casualties of Patriarchal Double Standards: Old Women in Yehoshua's Fiction," South Central Bulletin of MLA, Winter 1983, pp. 107-109.

Careful analysis of A.B. Yehoshua, leading Israel author's conceptions of old women.

_____: "Women as Traitors in Israeli fiction: Steps Toward Defining the Problem," Shofar, Fall 1985, pp. 5-16.

Valuable essay on the negative image of women in the works of outstanding Israeli authors, in treatment of War of Independence.

_____: "We Are All Magnetic Fields," an interview with Amalia Kahana-Carmon," Modern Hebrew Literature, #3/4, 1985, pp. 80-84.

_____: "The Sleepy Wife: A Feminist Consideration of A.B. Yehoshua's Fiction," Hebrew Annual Review 8, 1984, pp. 71-81.

Gilad, Lisa: "Contrasting Notions of Proper Conduct: Yemeni Jewish Mothers and Daughters in an Israeli Town," Jewish Social Studies, Winter 1983, pp. 73-86.

Goodhill, R.M.: "Women of the Kibbutz," Jewish Spectator, Fall 1981, pp. 57-58.

Izraeli, Dafna N.: "Israeli Women in the Work Force," Jerusalem Quarterly, Spring 1983, pp. 59-80.

_____: "The Zionist Women's Movement in Palestine, 1911-1927: A Sociological Analysis," Signs, Autumn, 1981.

Joseph, Shirley: "Forward Looking Strategies--How It Happened," Moment, Oct. 1985, pp. 28-29.

Nairobi conference--final resolutions.

Krausz, Judy: "Women Members of Knesset--Defending Social Programs During Hard Times," Pioneer Women (now Na'amat Women), Jan./Feb. 1985, p. 3ff.

Kronenthal, Rena: "Three-Day Seminar on the Status of Women," Pioneer Women (now Na'amat Women), May/June 1983, pp. 11-13.

Report on conference of Na'amat Status of Women Division.

Levavi, Lea: "Be a Man, Lend a Hand!" *Pioneer Women* (now *Na'amat Women*), March/Apr. 1985, p. 13ff.

    On Na'amat's campaign to get men to do some housework.

Livneh, Neri: "Female and Single in Israel," *Jewish Spectator*, Spring 1985, pp. 29-34.

    Reprint--translated from Hebrew by Margaret Weinberger Rotman.

London, Lauri: "The Myth of the Israeli Woman," *Ha'Etgar*, (U.C. at Berkeley, Cal.) Winter 1981, p. 15.

    A thoughtful review of both *My Michael* and *Elsewhere Perhaps*, by Amos Oz.

Lubelsky, Masha: "Masha Lubelsky Speaks Out On: Women in the 'Skills Revolution'," (Tr. from *Maariv*) *Pioneer Women* (now *Na'amat Women*), Jan./Feb. 1984, p. 19.

    Secretary-general of Na'amat stresses importance of technological revolution for women.

Malus, Elinor: "Kibbutzim: Not So Non-Sexist," *Israel Scene*, Jerusalem, Oct. 1985, p. 20.

Moriel, Liona: "Backroom Soldiers," *The International Jerusalem Post*, May 1-7, 1983, p. 18.

    Report of efforts by Col. Amira Dotan (commander of Women's Corps) to expand women soldiers' somewhat limited role in technological tasks of Israeli Army. (Dotan has since become the first woman general in the Israeli army.)

Morris, Benny: "Between Feminism and Tradition," *Hadassah*, June/July 1981.

    Women in the Israeli Army.

Palgi, Michal: "The Rise of Familism," *Shdemot*, cultural forum of the kibbutz movement, No. 24, 1985, pp. 18-23.

    An Israeli sociologist summarizes changes in kibbutz life based on increased family emphasis. (This issue of *Shdemot* is devoted to women in the kibbutz.)

Parker, S. & Parker, H.: "Women and the Emerging Family on the Israeli Kibbutz," *American Ethnologist*, #8, Nov. 1981, pp. 58-73.

Pomerantz, Marsha: "Writing and Keeping Books," Jerusalem Post Magazine, July 5, 1985, p. 7.

> An interesting piece about women writers in Israel and some of their problems of publishing via an interview with Shulamit Lapid, novelist and chair of the Hebrew Writers Assn.

Raday, F.: "Equality of Women Under Israeli Law," Jerusalem Quarterly, Spring 1983, pp. 81-108.

Ratok, Lily (Tr. Dalya Bilu): "Amalia Kahana-Carmon," Modern Hebrew Literature, Fall/Winter 1984.

Reinharz, Shulamit: "Toward a Model of Female Political Action: The Case of Manya Shochat, Founder of the First Kibbutz," Women's Studies International Forum, v. 7, no. 4, 1984, pp. 275-287.

> Excellent study, offers new information on Shochat's contribution to the creation of kibbutzim. Example of kind of research that needs to be done.

Rosenak, Michael: "In (Not Such) Splendid Isolation," Forum, World Zionist Org. 51/52, Spring/Summer 1984.

> Jewish education and thought symposium; includes material relevant to Jewish women.

Rosen, Sherry: "Jewish Intermarriage in Israel," Midstream, March 1982.

Rubin, N.: "Women's Place," Israel Scene, July 1982, p. 20.

Schneider, Susan W.: "Women in the Israeli Army," Lilith #8, 1981.

> Review of "To Be a Woman Soldier," a remarkable film by Shulie Eshel.

Segal, Shulamit: "Fixed Sex Roles in Kibbutz Facing a Challenge," Youth and Nation, Dec. 1980.

Seligman, Ruth: "Aesop's Fable, Israeli Style," Hadassah, April 1981, pp. 31-32.

_____: "Israeli-American Dialogue on the Status of Women," Pioneer Women (now Na'amat Women), Sept./Oct. 1984, p. 14ff.

_____: "Israeli Women at Work," Jewish Digest, Sept. 1983, pp. 73-79.

_____: "Women on Kibbutz," Pioneer Women (now Na'amat Women), Nov./Dec. 1985.

Shader, R.: "Crafts:--Workshop in Jerusalem That Is Providing Companionship and Work for Young Religious Women," Israel Scene, May 1983, pp. 16-17.

Shifrin, T.: "The Arts: A Woman in Love," Israel Scene, Dec. 1983, pp. 33-34.

Silver, Vivian: "Women on Kibbutz: An Unfinished Revolution," Jewish Frontier, April 1982, pp. 6-9.

Based on her research on status of women on kibbutz.

Steinberg, Ruth: "Schwester Selma," Jewish Observer, Summer 1985, pp. 12-17.

Biography of Selma Mayer, German-born nurse, who came to Palestine in 1916 and became central to the Shaare Zedek Hospital in Jerusalem.

Spiegler, S.: "Israel's E.R.A.," Journal of Jewish Communal Service, Summer 1982, p. 359.

Symon, Pamela: "Ensuring Women's Legal Rights," Israel Scene, Nov. 1985, pp. 16-17.

Na'amat's Division for the Status of Women fights for women's legal rights in Israel.

_____: "The Women's Place; Women and Politics," Israel Scene, Oct. 1984, pp. 31-32.

Tabory, E.: "Rights and Rites: Women's Roles in Liberal Religious Movements in Israel," Sex Roles, no. 11, July 1984, pp. 155-166.

Ullian, Florence: "Israel's Working Women: Over-Protected and Under-Employed," Pioneer Women (now Na'amat Women), Jan./Feb. 1981.

Yuval-Davis, Nera: "The Sexual Division of Labor in the Israeli Army," Feminist Studies, Fall 1985.

Zwi, Aza: "Poetry of Zelda," (Zelda Schneurson Mishkovsky) Ariel #165, 1986, pp. 58-70.

Analysis of the work of the poet born in Russia in 1914 who died in Israel in 1984.

C. Fiction

Amichai, Yehuda: *The World Is a Room*. Phila.: Jewish Publication Society, 1984.

    A collection of short stories that includes "Nina of Ashkelon."

Blair, Leona: *A Woman's Place*. NY: Delacorte Press, 1981.

    A family epic moving from the Holocaust to the Six-Day War in Israel seen by three women.

Broner, Esther M.: *A Weave of Women*. Bloomington, IN: Indiana Univ. Press, 1985 (Rept. of Holt, Rinehart edition)

    See Part I, first edition of this bibliography.

Gross, Joel: *This Year in Jerusalem*. NY: Putnam, 1983.

    An American woman falls in love with a leader of the Jewish resistance in 1947 Jerusalem.

Kashner, Rita: *To the Tenth Generation*. NY: G.P. Putnam's Sons, 1984.

    Well written but vile. Author would have us believe a woman could be so pathologically narcissistic as to purposely condemn her son to the pariah status of "mamzer" (bastard).

Mitovsky, Dina: *Jerusalem Rock*. M. Evans, 1980.

    A romance between two musicians: an American Jew and a Sabra. The Six-Day War makes them weigh the relative values of art and career vs. familial fidelity and national loyalty.

Rogan, Barbara: *Changing States*. Garden City, NY: Doubleday, 1981.

    Novel about Israeli girl's conflict with Holocaust survivor parents who oppose her involvement with Arab lover.

Shamir, Ruth: *All Our Vows*. NY: Shengold Publishers, 1983.

    A novel about a middle-aged and middle class Israeli woman's search for meaning in her life following the Yom Kippur War of 1973.

Topol, Allan: *A Woman of Valor*. NY: Morrow, 1980.

>Egyptian Jew, forced to emigrate after establishment of Israel, becomes anti-terrorist agent.

Zeldis, Chayym: *Forbidden Love*. NY: Berkeley Books, 1983.

>The love story of an Arab girl and an Israeli boy.

V. JEWISH WOMEN IN THE HOLOCAUST AND RESISTANCE

A. Non-Fiction Books and Book Chapters

Atkinson, Linda: *In Kindling Flame--The Story of Hannah Senesh 1921-1944*. NY: Lathrop, Lee & Shepard, 1985.

> Account of the martyred poet (for teenagers).

Bauman, Janina: *Winter in the Morning--A Young Girl's Life in the Warsaw Ghetto and Beyond, 1939-1945*. NY: The Free Press, 1985.

> Testimony drawing on her diaries.

David, Janina: *A Square of Sky and a Touch of Earth*. NY: Viking/Penguin, 1981.

> Testimony on the Warsaw Ghetto.

Ferderber-Salz, Bertha: *And the Sun Kept Shining*. NY: Holocaust Library, 1980.

> Testimony of Cracow Jewish survivor.

Friedenson, Joseph & Kranzler, David: *Heroine of Rescue: The Incredible Story of Recha Sternbuch*. Mesorah Publications, 1984.

> Woman and her husband rescued thousands of Jews from the Holocaust, operating out of Switzerland.

Gabor, Georgia M.: *My Destiny: Survivor of the Holocaust*. Arcadia, CA: Amen Publishing, 1981.

> Autobiography.

Hart, Kitty: *Return to Auschwitz*. NY: Atheneum, 1981.

> Survivor brings her son back to the death camp to confront her memories and awaken his consciousness. (See also first edition in Part I.)

Herbstrith, Waltraud: *Edith Stern, A Biography--The Untold Story of the Philosopher and Mystic Who Lost Her Life in the Death Camps of Auschwitz*. San Francisco: Harper & Row, 1985.

> German-Jewish woman convert to Catholicism becomes a Carmelite nun--deported when she refused to deny her Jewish heritage.

Hersh, Gizelle and Mann, Peggy: Gizelle, Save the Children. NY: Everest House, 1980.

Herzberger, Magda: The Waltz of the Shadows. NY: Philosophical Library, 1983.

An autobiography in the form of poetry, this book relates the story of a young girl's life during the Holocaust. The author has also included original music for one of the poems.

Hillesum, Etty: An Interrupted Life: The Diaries of Etty Hillesum, 1941-1943. NY: Pantheon Books, 1984. (Tr. from Dutch)

Diary of young Jewish woman in Amsterdam before and at beginning of the deportations, her spiritual struggles. Though Hillesum had little Jewish consciousness and was deeply attracted to Christianity, she chose to be deported with other Jews and died in Auschwitz.

Jackson, Livia E. Bitton: Elli: Coming of Age in the Holocaust. NY: Times Books, 1980.

Testimony.

Jewish Women's History Group (London): You'd Prefer Me Not to Mention It--The Lives of Four Daughters of Refugees. London: privately published, 1982?.

Testimony by four feminist children of survivors.

Katz, Esther, and Ringelheim, Joan Miriam, eds.: Proceedings of the Conference on Women Surviving: The Holocaust. NY: The Institute for Research in History, 1983.

The first conference to investigate women's history and lives during the Holocaust--roles in family, as concentration camp inmates and partisans. See also Ringelheim's article "Women and the Holocaust: A Consideration of Research," in Signs #10, Summer 1985.

Kotlar, Helen: We Lived in a Grave. NY: Shengold, 1980.

Kaplan, Marion: "Sisterhood Under Siege--Feminism and Anti-Semitism in Germany, 1904-1938." In Bridenthal, Renate et al., When Biology Became Destiny--Women in Weimar and Nazi Germany. NY: Monthly Review Press, 1984.

Also see references in other essays in this important book.

Laska, Vera, ed.: *Women in the Resistance and the Holocaust: Voices of the Eyewitnesses*. Westport, CT: Greenwood Press, 1983.

>Accounts of individual women, some Jews. Pioneering work. (Author spoke at conference on Women in the Holocaust sponsored by Institute for Research in History, NYC.)

Leitner, Isabella: *Saving the Fragments*. NY: New American Library, 1985. (Rept.)

>Her escape from Nazis during forced march, travails and emigration to U.S. (See author's previous listing in first edition--reissued by Dell, 1983.)

Lengyel, Olga: *Five Chimneys*. NY: Howard Fertig, 1983. (Rept.)

>Day to day record of a woman's nightmare of imprisonment in Auschwitz and Birkenau (originally published in 1947).

Levy-Hass, Hanna: *Inside Belsen*. NY: Barnes & Noble Books, 1982.

>The author kept a diary in Bergen-Belsen which is the first part of the book. The second part consists of interviews from the late 1970's which describe the author's life more fully.

Lubetkin, Zivia: *In the Days of Destruction and Revolt*. (Tr. from Hebrew writings 1946-47). Tel Aviv: HaKibbutz HaMeuchad and Am Oved, 1981.

>Key source. Must be read carefully because these are three different accounts not amalgamated into one. Lubetkin was one of the leaders of the Warsaw Ghetto uprising.

Michelson, Frida: *I Survived Rumbuli*. NY: Schocken Books, 1981.

>Testimony.

Milton, Sybil: "Woman and the Holocaust--The Case of German and German-Jewish Women." In Bridenthal, Renate, et al. (See Kaplan, Marion here op. cit.)

Negh, Claudine: *I Didn't Say Goodbye--Interviews with Children of the Holocaust*. NY: E.P. Dutton, 1985.

>By a French psychiatrist who worked with surviving children.

Nomberg-Przytyk, Sara: Auschwitz--True Tales from a Grotesque Land. Chapel Hill, NC: Univ. of N.C. Press, 1985.

Survivor testimony of an attendant in Mengele's "hospital."

Oberski, Jane: Childhood. NY: Doubleday, 1983.

A young Dutch boy's experiences including Bergen-Belsen--and his mother's great strength.

Rabinowitz, Dorothy: New Lives. NY: Avon Books, 1977.

Sketches of Holocaust survivors in the USA and their children.

Rubenstein, Erna F.: The Survivor in Us All: A Memoir of the Holocaust. Hamden, CT: Archon Books/Shoe String Press, 1983.

Salomon, Charlotte: Charlotte. NY: Viking, 1981.

Autobiography of the artist who died in the Holocaust, illustrated in color with her paintings, depicts her struggle to find an identity and reason to live.

Siegal, Aranka: Grace in the Wilderness--After the Liberation 1945-1948. NY: Farrar, Straus & Giroux, 1985.

Liberated from Bergen-Belsen, Hungarian-born girl finds healing in Sweden.

Tec, Nechama: Dry Tears: Story of a Lost Childhood. NY: Everest House, 1982.

Jewish girl survives by being hidden with Polish peasants.

Whitman, Ruth: The Testing of Hanna Senesh. Detroit: Wayne State Univ. Press, 1986.

Poems and prose about Senesh's last year of life, with background essay.

Wolf, Jacqueline: Take Care of Josette: A Memoir in Defense of Occupied France. NY: Franklin Wetts, 1981.

The story of a fourteen year old Jewish girl in hiding during the Nazi regime.

Wolff, Charlotte: Hindsight--An Autobiography. London: Quartet Books, 1980.

    Danzig-born Jewish doctor in family planning clinic in Berlin arrested, flees to Paris.

B. Fiction

Appelfeld, Aharon: Tzili--The Story of a Life. NY: Dutton, 1983. (Tr. from Hebrew)

    How Tzili's "simplicity," the pre-war despair of her family, initially helps her in her life in the forest during the Holocaust.

Condon, Richard: Infinity of Mirrors. NY: Berkeley Books, 1982.

Demetz, Hana: The House on Prague Street. St. Martin's Press, 1980; Bantam, 1983.

    Adolescent daughter of German father and Jewish mother, comes of age during the Holocaust in Czechoslovakia.

Feinstein, Elaine: The Border. NY: St. Martin's Press, 1984.

    Set in 1930's Austria and France, love story of Jewish intellectual couple making their way through Europe.

Frank, Anne: Anne Frank's Tales From the Secret Annex. Tr. by Ralph Manheim and Michael Mok. NY: Doubleday, 1984.

    The author's short stories, essays and reminiscences.

High, Monique Raphael. Keeper of the Walls. NY: Delacorte, 1985.

    Based on her grandmother's diaries, this novel takes place in France during the German occupation.

Ka-Tzetnik 135633 (Pseud.): House of Dolls. Chicago: Academy Press, 1982. (Rept. Tr. from Hebrew)

    Fictionalized account of a young Polish-Jewish woman forced into prostitution in a Nazi concentration camp.

Kaufelt, David: A Silver Rose. NY: Delacorte, 1982.

>Rennie Jablonski returns to Berlin in the late 1930's to find her father. She falls in love with a Nazi general, marries him and resigns herself to Nazism until her Jewishness is exposed.

Lauterstein, Ingeborg: The Wath Castle. Boston: Houghton Mifflin, 1981.

>Viennese girl grows to womanhood during the war.

Leahy, Syrelle Rogovin: Circle of Love. NY: Putnam, 1980.

>Hidden as a child in France, young woman returns to Germany to seek parents and finds--and loses--love, later rekindled in America.

Lustig, Arnost: The Unloved--From the Diary of Perle S. NY: Arbor House, 1985.

>Czech novel of concentration camp prisoner forced into prostitution.

_____ : Prayer for Katerina Horovitzova. Woodstock, NY: Overlook Press, 1985.

Siegel, Aranka: Upon the Head of the Goat. NY: Farrar, Straus & Giroux, 1981.

>Young adult novel of the destruction of the Hungarian Jewish community.

Thomas, D.M.: The White Hotel. NY: Viking Press, 1981; Pocket Books, 1982.

>A half-Jewish woman's struggle with Eros and Thanatos in pre-war Vienna and during the war, utilizing poetry, fantasy, psychoanalysis and Holocaust testimony. Babi Yar chapter is bone-chilling.

Weil, Greta: My Sister, My Antigone. NY: Avon Books, 1984.

Weinstein, Frida Scheps: A Hidden Childhood--A Jewish Girl's Sanctuary in a French Convent, 1942-1945. NY: Hill & Wang, 1985.

Zar, Rose: In the Mouth of the Wolf. Phila.: Jewish Publication Society, 1983.

>Author survives by living in hiding in Poland, later smuggling Jewish orphans out of the country.

VI. JEWISH WOMEN IN OTHER COUNTRIES

A. Periodical Articles and Book Chapters

Aharoni, Andree Ada: "Letter to Kadreya from Haifa: To Cairo with Love," *Jewish Frontier*. May 1971, pp. 6-9.

Coughlin, M.B., Rosenberg, R.: "Health Education and Beyond: A Soviet Women's Group Experience," Address, *Journal of Jewish Communal Service*. Fall 1983, pp. 65-67.

Cowen, Ida G.: "Meshedi Marriage Traditions," *Pioneer Women* (now *Na'amat Women*), October 1981.

Neuberger, J.: "Women and Judaism," *European Judaism*, Winter 1981, p. 29.

Shiels, Barbara: *Winners--Women and the Nobel Prize*. Minneapolis: Dillon Press, 1985.

> Chapters on Nelly Sachs (Lit. 1966), Maria Geoppert Mayer (Physics, 1963), Rosalyn Yalow (Physiology-Medicine, 1977).

B. Fiction

Alexander, Lynn: *Safe Houses*. NY: Atheneum, 1985.

> A novel about Hungary and Raoul Wallenberg which blends fiction, fantasy and truth.

Bermant, Chaim: *The House of Women*. London: Weidenfeld & Nicolson, 1983; NY: St. Martin's Press, 1983.

> The story of four sisters.

Friedman, Rosemary: *Proofs of Affection*. NY: Wm. Morrow/Quill Publications, 1982.

> Novel about Judaism in a British family.

Levinson, Norma: *The Room Upstairs*. London: Century, 1984.

> Single Jewish woman in London.

VII. JEWISH WOMEN IN POETRY

A. Anthologies

Bulkin, Elly and Joan Larkin: Lesbian Poetry: An Anthology. Watertown, MA: Persephone Press, 1981.

Carlisle, Thomas John: Eve and After: Old Testament Women in Portrait. Grand Rapids: Erdmans, 1984.

Carmi, T.: Penguin Book of Hebrew Verse. Viking/Penguin, 1981.

> Some poetry by women in this bilingual collection from Biblical times to today.

Falk, Marcia, tr.: Love Lyrics from the Bible. Decatur, GA: Almond Press, 1982.

Mozeson, Isaac, ed.: Ten Jewish American Poets. NY: Downtown Poets, 1982.

> Contains work of three Jewish women: Enid Dame, Layle Silbert and Doris B. Gold.

Rabson, Diane, ed.: On Being Jewish. Boulder. CO: Quarternight Press, 1985.

> Includes poetry by Jewish women.

Schwartz, Howard and Rudolf, Anthony: Voices from the Ark: Modern Jewish Poets. Yonkers, NY: Pushcart Press. Also NY: Avon, 1980.

> Includes work by 25 women.

Shirim: A Jewish Poetry Journal, Spring 1984.

> Issue is devoted to Jewish women poets.

Slobin, Mark, ed.: Tenement Songs--The Popular Music of Jewish Immigrants. Univ. of Illinois Press (with music cassette) 1982.

> This collection of early 1900's Yiddish songs features a few with striking feminist verses.

B. Jewish Women Poets

Bloch, Chana: Secrets of the Tribe. NY: Sheep Meadow Press (Persea), 1981.

>Poems include some translated from Yiddish; some on Biblical themes, birth, death, dreams, men-women relationships, pregnancy, childbirth.

Borenstein, Emily: Night of the Broken Glass. Mason, TX: Timberline Press, 1981.

>Poems of the Holocaust and return to Jerusalem.

Dame, Enid: On the Road to Damascus. Maryland, NY: Downtown Poets, 1980.

>Poems on Jewish mythology with feminist slant; some of Lilith and Biblical figures.

Dykewomon, Elana: Fragments from Lesbos. Langlois, OR: Diaspora Distribution, 1981.

Falk, Marcia: This Year in Jerusalem. Brockport, NY: State Street Press, 1985.

Hadas, Pamela White: In the Light of Genesis. Phila.: Jewish Publication Society, 1980.

>Much praised collection; received Jewish Book Council Award.

Holender, Barbara D.: Shivah Poems. Hartford, CT: Andrew Mountain Press, 1985.

Kaye, Melanie: We Speak in Code: Poems and Other Writings. Pittsburgh: Motheroot Publications, 1980.

Klein, Elizabeth: Approaches. Urbana, IL: Red Herring Press, 1980.

>A chapbook that contains several poems on Jewish themes.

Klepfisz, Irena: Keeper of Accounts. Persephone Press, 1982 (1986: Distr. Sinister Wisdom, Montpelier, VT)

>See Tribe of Dina anthology, III.A. here for Klepfisz, Dame, and other Jewish women poets.

Korn, Rachel: <u>Generations: Selected Poems of Rachel Korn</u>. (Tr. Rivka Augenfeld, et al.), Seymour Mayne, ed. NY: Riverrun, 1982.

Poems translated from the Yiddish.

Kruger, Mollee: <u>Daughters of Chutzpah: Humorous Verse on the Jewish Woman</u>. Fresh Mdws., NY: Biblio Press, 1983.

A wide-ranging collection of rhymed verse by a popular Jewish newspaper columnist.

Levertov, Denise: <u>Wanderer's Daysong</u>. Port Townsend, WA: Copper Canyon, 1981.

_____: <u>Light Up the Cave</u>. NY: New Directions, 1981.

_____: <u>Candles in Babylon</u>. NY: New Directions, 1982.

Pastan, Linda: <u>New and Selected Poems</u>. NY: Norton, 1982.

Rich, Adrienne: <u>A Wild Patience Has Taken Me This Far</u>. NY: Norton, 1981.

This important poet is increasingly identifying herself in recent poetry as Jewish and lesbian.

Schuler, Else Lasker: <u>Hebrew Ballads and Other Poems</u>. Phila.: Jewish Publication Society, 1980. (Tr. from German)

Sklarew, Myra: <u>From the Backyard of the Diaspora; Poems</u>. Washington, D.C.: Dryad Press, 1981.

Starkman, Elaine Marcus: <u>Love Scene</u>. Walnut Creek, CA: Sheer Press, 1980.

Tannenbaum, Judith: <u>The World Saying Yes</u>. Anchor Bay, CA: Nehama Press, 1980.

Poems about concentration camps, Israel, Jewish identity. (Collaboration with photographer father)

Whitman, Ruth: <u>Permanent Address: New Poems</u>. Cambridge, MA: Alicejames Books, 1980.

Wilner, Eleanor: <u>Shekhinah</u>. Chicago: Univ. of Chicago Press, 1984.

Mythic history of women.

Young, Elise: <u>Medusa's Hair: Poetry of Lesbian Re-Envisioning</u>. Middlefield, MA: Mountainwind Prod., 1980.

VIII. DISSERTATIONS/UNPUBLISHED PAPERS*

Beck, Evelyn Torton: "Between Invisibility and Overvisibility: The Politics of Anti-Semitism in the Women's Movement and Beyond," Univ. of Wisc.-Madison, Women's Studies Research Center, Working Paper Series No. 11, 1983.

    Available for $2 from Univ. of Wisconsin, Women's Studies Research Center, 209 N. Brooks St., Madison, WE 53715.

Berger-Sofer, Rhoda: "Pious Women: A Study of the Women's Roles in a Hasidic and Pious Community (Meah Shearim)" Doctoral diss., Anthropology, Rutgers Univ., 1979.

Blicksilver, Edith: "The Bintl Brief Woman Writer: Torn Between European Traditions and the American Life Style," Annual Conference on Modern Jewish Studies, Queens College, Fall/77-Winter/78.

Brooten, Bernadette J.: "Could Women Initiate Divorce in Ancient Judaism?" Unpublished Ernest Cadman Colwell Lecture, School of Theology, Claremont College, CA, 1981.

Buchwald, Lynne S.: "From the Beginning to the Beginning: Eve and Evil in the Bible and the Jewish Tradition," Roots and Realities: Changing Images of Women in Family and Community, National Women's Studies Conference, Phila.: Univ. of Penn., 1980.

Davidman, Lynn: "Strength of Tradition in a Chaotic World: Women Turn to Orthodox Judaism." Brandeis Univ., 1986 (Doctoral diss., Sociology) Available from University Microfilms International, Ann Arbor, MI.

Elwell, Sue Levi (now Rabbi): The Founding and Early Programs of the National Council of Jewish Women: Study and Practice as Jewish Women's Religious Expression. IN: Indiana Univ., 1972 (Doctoral diss.)

Engel, Sophie B., et al.: "Follow-Up Study, Status of Women in Jewish Communal Service," Conference of Jewish Communal Service, New York, Aug. 1981. Findings summarized in Lilith, Kol Ishah section, #8, 1981.

Epstein, Raymond: "A Jewish Response to Women's Rights," Council of Jewish Federations, 50th General Assembly, St. Louis, Nov. 10-15, 1981.

---

*Some unpublished papers are on file at the NYC Jewish Women's Resource Center. See also Hebrew Union College libraries for recent dissertation topics, some on Jewish women.

Dissertations, Unpublished Ms.

Felix, Cathy: <u>Views of Women in the Schools of Rabbi Akiva and Rabbi Ishmael</u>. Cincinnati: Hebrew Union College-Jewish Institute of Religion, 1980. (Doctoral diss.)

Fine, Irene: "Developing a Jewish Studies Program for Women: A Springboard to History," 1981. (Doctoral diss.) Available from University Microfilms International, Ann Arbor, MI.

Finkel, Gilberta: "History of Women's Liberation Movement in Israel," The Sorbonne, Paris, June 1981, Master's thesis.

Fisch, Linda Yellin: "Patterns of Religious and Feminist Socialization Among Jewish College Women," NY: Columbia University Teacher's College, 1983. (thesis)

This thesis examines the above patterns among a group of American female Jewish undergraduates at Barnard College between 1977-1979.

Friedman, Joan S.: "Women and Positive Time-Bound Commandments: A Comparison of Alfasi, Maimonides and the Tosafists," Cincinnati: Hebrew Union College-Jewish Institute of Religion, 1981. (diss.)

Jayanti, Miriam: "Women in Meah She'arim: An Alternative Reality," Jerusalem: The Hebrew University, 1982. (M.A. thesis)

This study of women in Jerusalem's ultra-Orthodox quarter includes sexuality, women's attitudes toward sexuality, transmission of sexual information, matchmaking patterns and girls' attitudes in choice of spouse.

Levenson, Edward R.: "Ambivalence Toward Women in Historical Judaism," Roots and Realities: Changing Images of Women in Family and Community, National Women's Studies Conference, Phila.: Univ. of Penn., 1980.

Loeb, Garry Allan: "The Changing Religious Role of the Reform Jewish Woman," Cincinnati: Hebrew Union College-Jewish Institute of Religion, 1981. (diss.)

Mathews, Carole and Rubenstein, Sandra: "Lesbian Jews: Reconciling a Dual Identity," Los Angeles: Hebrew Union College & Univ. of So. Calif., 1980. (M.A. thesis)

Meyerson, Robert: "Hannah Arendt and Jewish Arms," academic paper, 1980 (Query Biblio Press for access.)

Dissertations, Unpublished Ms.

Monson, Rela Geffen: "Bringing Women In: An Update 1974-1984; a Survey of a Decade of the Evolving Role of Women in Jewish Organizational Life in Philadelphia." Study sponsored by the Women's Issues Committee of the Philadelphia Chapter, American Jewish Committee, Philadelphia, PA, Feb. 1986.

A follow-up to the author's study done in 1975 and published in 1977 by the Philadelphia Chapter, American Jewish Committee.

Rubin, Ruth: "Jewish Woman and her Yiddish Folksong," Union Graduate School, Humanities Dissertation, 1976.

Scarf, Mimi: "Battered Jewish Wives: A Descriptive Study." Los Angeles: Hebrew Union College-Jewish Institute of Religion, 1980. (M.A. thesis)

Shoub, Myra (aka Myra Shoub Nelson): "And the Eldest Sold Herself: A Study of the Economic and Social Conditions Leading to Prostitution Among Lower East Side Immigrant Women at the Turn of the Century," 1981.

Swerdlow, Paul: "The American Jewess in the Second Quarter of the Twentieth Century." Cincinnati: Hebrew Union College-Jewish Institute of Religion, 1964. (diss.)

Wolf, Laura B.: "The Relationship Between Feminism and Depression in Adult Jewish Women." Houston: Univ. of Houston, 1982. (M.A. thesis)

IX. BIBLIOGRAPHIES, RESOURCES AND GUIDES*

American Jewish Committee, NY: "Women in the Middle East." Kit of materials for UN Conference on women held in Copenhagen, July 14-30, 1980.

> Statistics, magazine article reprints, showing "composite picture of women in the Arab world and in Israel, in education, health and employment."

American Studies Information Guide Series, Vol. 8: "Jewish Writers of North America." Detroit: Gale Research Co., 1981.

> Includes Jewish women writers.

Bibliography of Modern Hebrew Literature in Translation: Goell, Yohai. Jerusalem: Israel Program for Scientific Translations.

> Supplements issued each year. Source for books in all categories originating in Hebrew published in other languages, including English.

Brewer, Joan Scherer: Sex and the Modern Jewish Woman: Annotated Bibliography.

> Overview by Lynn Davidman; also "Sex and the Jewish Woman in 20th Century Fiction," by Evelyn Avery. Fresh Mdws., NY: Biblio Press, 1986.

Cargas, Harry James: The Holocaust: An Annotated Bibliography, 2nd edition, Chicago, IL: American Library Assn., 1985.

Chametzky, J.: "Main Currents in American Jewish Literature from the 1880's to the 1950's," Ethnic Groups, v. 4, #12-2, 1982, pp. 85-101.

Conservative Judaism, Spring 1986, v. 38, no. 3.

> Seven articles on aspects of feminist Biblical interpretation, Jewish women in medieval Europe, etc. Two are by women: Esther Altshul Helfgott and Emily Taitz.

"Divorce and Jewish Law," American Jewish Committee, 165 E. 56 St., New York, NY 10022, 1986. (2-pg. leaflet)

---

*See also Jewish Women's Resource Center, NYC, for their publications on birth ceremonies, marriage contracts, etc.

Edelheit, Abraham J. and Hershel: Holocaust Literature: A Bibliography. Boulder, CO: Westwood Press, 1986.

Elwell, Ellen Sue Levi & Levenson, Edward R.: The Jewish Women's Studies Guide. Fresh Mdws., NY: Biblio Press, 1982.

> A first collection of Jewish women's studies syllabi used by teachers of religion, literature and other subject fields, for use in universities and Jewish adult education programs, with introductory essay and bibliographies for each. (Second edition of this work forthcoming 1987.)

Fine, Irene: Educating the New Jewish Woman: A Dynamic Approach. San Diego, CA: Women's Institute for Continuing Education, 1985.

> A practical manual to help feminist educators plan programs of adult education for women. Includes examples of creative programs.

Genesis II: March 1980 issue.

> Special issue on Jewish women.

Hamelsdorf, Ora and Adelsberg, Sandra: Jewish Women and Jewish Law. Fresh Mdws., NY: Biblio Press, 1980.

> Companion to this (Cantor) bibliography; emphasis on traditional women citations. (Supplement added in current edition as update.)

Insdorf, Annette: Indelible Shadows: Film and the Holocaust. NY: Vintage Books, 1983.

> Critical study of 75 fictional & documentary films about the Holocaust produced in U.S. and Europe, many of which focus on women.

"Jewish Women in the Eighties," A Symposium held March 25, 1985, at Central Synagogue, New York City.

> Summary available from: Jewish Student Press Service, 15 E. 26 St., New York, NY 10010.

Jewish Women historic postcards.

> 2 dozen photographic postcards of important Jewish women in several fields. Helaine Victoria Press, 411 E. 4 St., Bloomington, IN 47401.

Jewish Women's Resource Center Newsletter: List of Feminist Haggadot. Winter/Spring 1981.

Jewish Women's Resource Center Newsletter: List of unpublished mss. on file. Winter/Spring 1981.

Jewish Women's Resource Center: "1985 End of the UN Decade for Women Conference Symposium," held May 9, 1985. Summary available.

Journal of Feminist Studies in Religion, Decatur, GA: Scholars Press, Jan. 1986.

    A semi-annual journal, edited by Judith Plaskow & Elisabeth Schussler-Fiorenza.

Keeping Posted, leader's edition, "The New Jewish Woman," v. XXV, no. 5, n.d. Union of American Hebrew Congregations, 838 Fifth Ave., New York, NY 10021.

    A collection of viewpoints, including one from Lilith Magazine of 1983.

Kuzmack, Linda Gordon and Salomon, George: "Working and Mothering--A Study of 97 Jewish Career Women with Three or More Children." American Jewish Committee, NY, 1981.

    29 page summary includes comments on combining careers and parenting. Lists ways the Jewish community can help.

National Jewish Resource Center: "The Holocaust: An Annotated Bibliography and Resource Guide," Zachor, 421 Seventh Ave., New York, NY 10001.

*Nordquist, Joan: Audiovisuals for Women. Jefferson, NC: McFarland & Co., 1981.

    *For information on films and other visual materials on Jewish women, write to Media Dept., JWB, 15 E. 26 St., New York, NY 10017.

Potter, Clare, ed.: The Lesbian Periodicals Index. P.O. Box 10543, Tallahassee, FL 32302: Naiad Press, 1986.

Rice Sherri L., Posner, Marcia, and Gold, Doris: How to Start a Jewish Women's Book Collection. Fresh Mdws., NY: Biblio Press, 1985.

    To be included in JWB Jewish Book Council pamphlet of same name, Sept. 1987.

Rosenbach, A.S.W.: <u>American Jewish Bibliography</u>, Univ. Press of
    Virginia, 1981.

Schatz, Julius: <u>A Selected Bibliography of Audio-Visual Resources for
    International Women's Year, 1975</u>. NY: American Jewish Congress.

<u>Shdemot</u>, cultural forum of the kibbutz movement, no. 24, 1985.

> A special issue devoted to sexual equality in the kibbutz; has
> articles by V. Silver, M. Palgi, D. Dayan and others. Available
> from Kibbutz Aliya Desk, 27 W. 20 St., New York, NY 10011.

<u>Shmate Magazine</u>, Issue #2, June/July 1982, Focus on Women, Gay Men, and
    Lesbians.

<u>Sojourner</u>, July 1983, Special issue on Jewish women.

Union of American Hebrew Cong., NY: <u>Jewish Options for the 80's--
    Synagogue Consciousness-Raising Programs for the Decade of Women</u>.
    Daum/Wurzburg, 1980. (out of print 1986)

> For leaders and facilitators in Reform synagogues. (UAHC's
> Commission on Social Action issued other guides for women,
> relating to prayer terminology and liturgy, including an
> experimental Haggadah for Passover 1979.)

Women's League for Conservative Judaism: Women of the Bible: A Study
    Guide, Spring 1984 (by Marcia Cohn Spiegel).

> A discussion guide using literary analysis to examine lives of
> Biblical women, Eve, Sarah, Hagar, Rebecca, Rachel, Leah, Miriam,
> Ruth and Naomi. Uses JPS <u>New Translation of the Holy Scriptures</u>
> and Ginsberg's <u>Legends of the Bible</u>, and poetry by Jewish women.

Women's Tefillah Network Newsletter, P.O. Box 236, Brooklyn, NY 11230.

> Umbrella group of halachic women's prayer groups in USA and
> Canada.

X. SUPPLEMENT--SELECTIONS OF 1986 *

A. Books

Adelman, Penina: <u>Miriam's Well: Rituals for Jewish Women Around the Year</u>. Fresh Mdws., NY: Biblio Press, 1986.

A first collection of new Rosh Hodesh and holiday-oriented rituals for women.

Alkalay-Gut, Karen: <u>Mechitza</u>. Merrick, NY: Cross-Cultural Communications, 1986. (poetry chapbook)

Antin, Mary: <u>From Plotzk to Boston</u>. NY: Markus Wiener Publishers, Dist. Schocken Bks., 1986 (Rept. pap.)

Aschkenasy, Nehama: <u>Eve's Journey: Feminine Images in Hebrew Literary Tradition</u>, Phila.: Univ. of Penn. Press, 1986.

Traces female images from Bible to modern Hebrew literature.

Bargad, Warren F. & Chyet, Stanley, F., Tr.: <u>Israeli Poetry: A Contemporary Anthology</u>. Bloomington, IN: Indiana Univ. Press, 1986.

Brayer, Menachem: <u>The Jewish Woman in Rabbinic Literature: A PsychoHistorical Perspective</u>. Hoboken, NJ: Ktav, 1986.

_____: <u>The Jewish Woman in Rabbinic Literature: A Psycho-Social Perspective</u>. Hoboken, NJ: Ktav, 1986.

Bulka, Reuven: <u>Jewish Marriage: A Halachic Ethic</u>. Hoboken, NJ: Ktav, 1986.

An overview of the topic by the Orthodox editor of the journal, <u>Psychology and Judaism</u>.

Carson, Anne: <u>Feminist Spirituality and the Feminine Divine: An Annotated Bibliography</u>. Freedom, CA: Crossing Press, 1986.

A guide to article on goddess-think, witch lore and feminist spirituality; emphasis on 1970 to 1985. A few references to Jewish feminist religion.

D'Alpuget, Blanche: <u>Winter in Jerusalem</u>. NY: Simon & Schuster, 1986.

---

* See Jewish Book World, JWB Jewish Book Council, Winter 1986-87 number for additional listings.

1986 Supplement

Dame, Enid: Lilith and Her Demons. Merrick, NY: Cross-Cultural Communications, 1986.

   Poetry chapbook.

Ettinger, Elzbieta: Rosa Luxemburg: A Life. Boston: Beacon Press, 1986.

Freed, Lynn: HomeGround. NY: Summit Books, 1986.

   Fictionalized account of growing up in a theatrical family in South Africa.

Fuchs, Esther: Israeli Mythogynies: Women in Hebrew Fiction. NY: SUNY Press (forthcoming June 1987).

_____: Sexual Politics in the Biblical Narrative: Toward a Feminist Critical Hermeneutics of the Hebrew Bible. Bloomington: Indiana Univ. Press (forthcoming 1987).

Ghatan, Yedidah H.E.: The Invaluable Pearl: The Unique Status of Women in Judaism. NY: Bloch Publishing Co., 1986.

   Citing historical Jewish heroines and women's role in Jewish law, author argues that the Bible and rabbinic literature have always placed women at a higher spiritual plane than men. Usual apologetica.

Goldman, Alex J.: The Rabbi Is a Lady. NY: Hippocrene Books, 1986.

   Conservative synagogue has rabbi's widow officiate at High Holy Day services, with ensuing complications.

Grade, Chaim: My Mother's Sabbath Days: A Memoir. NY: Knopf, 1986. (Tr. from Yiddish)

   Memoirs of family struggles in pre-WWII Vilna, with widowed mother as central figure.

Hay, Peter: Ordinary Heroes: Chana Szenes and the Dream of Zion. NY: Putnam, 1986.

   Possibly the first account of Hanna Senesh's personal life as well as her Zionism, from her aliyah to her death. A minor criticism: editor should have insisted, however, that spellings of names be the same throughout.

Hazelton, Lesley: <u>Jerusalem, Jerusalem</u>. Atlantic Monthly Press, 1986.

>Deeply personal and poignant account of British-born Jew's struggle to come to terms with her love of Israel and her feeling both at-home and not-at-home there because of the changes in its society.

Howard, Doris, ed.: <u>Dynamics of Feminist Therapy: Treatment, Theory and Ethnic Issues</u>. NY: Haworth Press, 1986.

>Contains chapter on "Anti-Semitism and Sexism in Stereotypes of Jewish Woman" by Rachel Josefowitz Siegel.

Isaacman, Clara: <u>Clara's Story</u>. Phila., PA: Jewish Publication Society, 1987.

>Romanian Jews in hiding in Antwerp. (for young adults)

Karmel, Ilona: <u>An Estate of Memory</u>. NY: Feminist Press. (Rept.)

>First issued in 1969, this holocaust novel is a new edition with an afterword by Ruth K. Angress, professor of German at the Univ. of California at Irvine.

Kerdeman, Deborah & Kushner, Lawrence: <u>Invisible Chariot: An Introduction to Kabbalah and Jewish Spirituality</u>. Denver, CO: Alternatives in Religious Education, 1986.

>Adult text on kabbalah and the Jewish mystical tradition; included here because of a woman's participation in kabbalah instruction.

Koltuv, Barbara Black: <u>Book of Lilith</u>. NY: Nicolas-Hays, Inc. (Dist. S. Weiser, York Beach, ME), 1986.

>Anthology of ancient and modern sources and commentary on tales about Lilith.

Kovaly, Heda Margolius: <u>Under a Cruel Star--A Life in Prague 1941-1986</u>. Cambridge, MA: Plunkett Lake Press, 1986.

>Deeply moving testimony of woman who escapes to Prague from a concentration camp, marries a Communist later executed in Slansky trials. Her struggles to survive the collapse of the couple's hope for a humane society, to survive illness and despair with her orphaned child, are heartbreaking.

Levin, Bonnie, and Neu, Diann: A Seder of the Sister of Sarah: A Holy Thursday and Passover Feminist Liturgy. Silver Spring, MD: WATER (The Women's Alliance for Theology, Ethics and Ritual), 1986.

Combined liturgy booklet for Passover and Holy Thursday by Jewish and Christian feminists.

Merkin, Daphne: Enchantment. NY: Harcourt Brace Jovanovich, 1986.

Novel about mother-daughter struggle.

Morton, Leah (pseud. Stern, Elizabeth G.): I Am a Woman and a Jew. NY: Markus Wiener, dist. Schocken Books, 1986.

(Reprint of 1969 Arno Press facsimile edition) Biography of woman who overcame sex and class bias to fight her way as a Jew into the Gentile worlds of social work, journalism and management, between 1900 and 1927.

Newhouse, Nancy R., ed.: Hers--Through Women's Eyes: Essays from Hers Column of the NY Times. NY: Harper & Row, 1986.

Contains several essays by Jewish women writers and journalists on feminism and Jewish identity.

Newman, Leslea: Good Enough to Eat. Ithaca, NY: Firebrand Books, 1986.

Unhappy bulimic woman in her 20's.

Opfell, Olga: The Lady Laureates: Women Who Have Won the Nobel Prize, 2nd ed. Metuchen, NJ: Scarecrow Press, 1986.

Includes Jewish women Nelly Sachs and anti-feminist scientist Rosalyn Yalow.

Paley, Grace: Leaning Forward. Penobscot, ME: Granite Press, 1986.

Poems "inflected with the speech of Jewish-American New York" on men, women, parents, displaced people..."

Plain, Belva: The Golden Cup. NY: Delacorte Press, 1986.

Henrietta De Rivera, Sephardic Jewish suffragette, is attracted to a Jewish radical; their "tempestuous marriage."

Rich, Adrienne: Your Native Land, Your Life. NY: W.W. Norton, 1986.

Includes long poem "Sources," an exploration of Jewish identity.

San Diego Women's Haggadah, 2nd Edition. San Diego, CA: Women's
    Institute for Continuing Jewish Education, 1986.

    See 1987 editions of Judaica Book News for review by Lorna Green
    of this work and other women's haggadahs.

Scherer Brewer, Joan: Sex and the Modern Jewish Woman: An Annotated
    Bibliography. Fresh Mdws.: NY: Biblio Press, 1986.

    The first compilation of a dozen aspects of Jewish women's
    sexuality. Applicable to several fields.

Schulman, Sarah: Girls, Visions and Everything. Seattle: The Seal Press,
    1986.

Scliar, Moacyr: Embrace. Available Press/Ballantine, 1986.

    Daughter of Hungarian Jews educated in Catholic school by
    Brazilian nuns.

Sharger-Handelman: Israeli War Widows--Beyond the Glory of Heroism.
    South Hadley, MA: Bergin & Garvey Publishers, 1986.

Sharma, Arvind, ed.: Women in World Religions. Ithaca, NY: SUNY Press,
    1986.

    Eight religions presented, including essay on Judaism, by Denise
    Carmody.

Simon, Kate: A Wider World: Portraits in an Adolescence. NY: Harper &
    Row, 1986.

    Autobiographical story of Jewish adolescence in 1930's Bronx.

Simon, Rita J. and Brettel, Caroline B., eds.: International Migration:
    The Female Experience. Totowa, NJ: Rowman & Littlefield, 1986.

    Includes chapter on "The Social and Economic Adjustment of Soviet
    Jewish Women in the United States," by Simon, Louise Shelley, and
    Paul Schneiderman.

Singer, June Flaum: The Markoff Women. NY: M. Evans Co., 1986.

    A novel.

Tauber, Rhea: Rhea's World. NY: Philosophical Library, 1986.

    Growing up in immigrant Brooklyn home.

Trupin, Sophie: <u>Dakota Diaspora: Memories of a Jewish Homesteader</u>. Berkeley, CA: Alternative Press, 1986.

Weatherford, Doris: <u>Foreign and Female: Immigrant Women in America, 1840-1930</u>. NY: Schocken Books, 1986.

Experiences and contributions of immigrant women--including Jews--drawing on their diaries and letters.

B. <u>Periodical Articles</u>

Ackelsberg, Martha: "Spirituality, Community, and Politics: <u>B'not Esh</u> and the Feminist Reconstruction of Judaism," <u>Journal of Feminist Studies in Religion</u>, Spring 1986.

Addresses challenge of feminism to traditional Jewish religious life and communities.

Arzt, Aliza and Berkenfield, Janet: "The Soul of a New Siddur," <u>Genesis 2</u>, Feb./March 1986, pp. 16-18.

The authors, members of a Massachusetts havurah and Siddur project, describe their approach to revising liturgy, especially regarding gender problems in God-language.

Avery, Evelyn M.: "Sex and the Jewish Woman in 20th Century Fiction." In <u>Sex and the Modern Jewish Woman: An Annotated Bibliography</u>. Fresh Mdws., NY: Biblio Press, 1986, pp. 17-37.

A survey of 60 years of fiction portraying the Jewish women's sexuality by both male and female authors.

Brodbar-Nemzer, Jay Y.: "Sex Differences in Attitudes of American Jews Toward Israel." In <u>Contemporary Jewry</u>, v. 8, Arnold Dashefsky, ed., New Brunswick, NJ: Transaction Books, 1986.

Cantor, Aviva: "My Children Are Disappeared: An Argentine Mother's Story," <u>Lilith</u> #15, 1986.

Based on interviews with Renee Epelbaum, one of the madres of the Plaza de Mayo, and Jewish communal leaders in US and Canada, Cantor's report shows that Holocaust history repeated itself: The Jewish world knew of the bloodbath in Argentina, 1976-1983, the special torture of Jews arrested there, but kept silent--again. The report tells why.

Charme, Stuart: "Sartre's Jewish Daughter: An Interview with Arlette Elkaim-Sartre," Midstream, Oct. 1986, pp. 24-28.

   Nowhere does article mention that A.E. was Sartre's lover whom he wanted to marry but ended up adopting to salvage his long-time relationship with Simone de Beauvoir (whom he refused to marry on principle).

Charytan, Margaret: "Feminism and Jewish Day School Studies," The Jewish Week, (NY) May 30, 1986, p. 21.

   Efforts to develop day school curriculum which includes Jewish women role models in an effort to address Jewish girls and thus develop Jewish women scholars.

Geller, Laura, ed.: "Women's Spirituality and Our Tradition," Sh'ma, #17/325, Jan. 9, 1987.

   Report on a West Coast 1984 Women's Spirituality Conference and developments since that date.

Goldstein, Rabbi Elyse M.: "Take Back the Waters: A Feminist Re-Appropriation of Mikvah," Lilith #15, Summer 1986, pp. 15-16.

   A Reform rabbi describes her own mikvah experience and proposes the building of "alternative mikvaot" run by and for women to reclaim the ancient ritual immersion for non-Orthodox women.

Gordon, Eric: "Being Jewish and Gay: A Conference Report," Jewish Currents, June 1986, pp. 14-15.

   First New York community-wide conference on Lesbian and Gay Jews in the Jewish Community.

Green, Leona S.: "The Haggadah Revisited," Sh'ma, 16/314, May 16, 1986.

   A critique of alternative Haggadot published in recent years.

Grossman, Edward: "Trust the Teller: Interview with Cynthia Ozick," Jerusalem Post International Edition, Oct. 4, 1986, pp. 17-18.

   Writer Cynthia Ozick discusses her views on Judaism, Israel, writing.

Hazleton, Lesley: "A Citizen of the World and of No Particular Place," Hers, New York Times, May 29, 1986, p. C-2.

   Author ponders her role as Wandering Jew.

Hyman, Frieda Clark: "The Education of a Queen," Judaism, Winter 1986, pp. 78-85.

> An analysis of the scroll of Esther and the personality of Esther herself.

Jochnowitz, Carol: "How We See Each Other," Jewish Currents, July/Aug. 1986, pp. 32-33.

> Report on conference "Jewish Women and Jewish Men: Our Changing Relationships," sponsored by Jewish Women's Resource Center.

_____: "The Thirteenth Tribe," Jewish Currents, Sept. 1986, pp. 29-30.

> A critical review of The Tribe of Dina: A Jewish Women's Anthology.

Kessner, Carole S.: "From Parnassus to Mt. Zion: The Journey of Emma Lazarus," Jewish Book Annual #44, JWB 1986.

> Lazarus' discovery of Judaism.

Kirschenbaum, Carol: "A Late Believer," Savvy, Nov. 1986.

> An intermarried Jewish mother rediscovers her Judaism.

Kolt, Frances: "Women's Prayer Groups," The Forum, New York University Jewish Student Newspaper, Jan./Feb. 1986, p. 10.

> Orthodox women's prayer groups spur controversy among Orthodox community and its leaders.

Magida, Arthur J.: "How Are Women Changing the Rabbinate," Baltimore Jewish Times, Aug. 8, 1986, pp. 56-61.

Midstream Symposium: "Does Judaism Need Feminism?" April 1986.

> Participants include Lucy Dawidowicz, Daniel J. Elazar, Elyse M. Goldstein, Marie Syrkin and Emanuel Rackman.

Moriel, Liora: "The Fight for the Right to Serve," International Jerusalem Post, Oct. 11, 1986, p. 17.

> Report on Leah Shakdiel's fight with Israel's religious establishment to serve on her town's religious council.

New, Elisa: "Angry Harvest," Tikkun, v. 1, no. 2, Fall 1986.

>Overly complex film review of Annieszka Holland's magnificent film does not mention book of the same name. (See first edition here under "Holocaust.")

Ozick, Cynthia: "The Role an Author Plays in Jewish Communal Life," The Jewish Week (NY), July 18, 1986, p. 19.

>Ozick's views on the Jewish writer's communal role.

Plaskow, Judith: "Standing Again at Sinai, Jewish Memory from a Feminist Perspective," Tikkun, v. 1, no. 2, 1986, pp. 28-34.

>Important feminist theologian's essay--how we can deal as feminists with the traditional Jewish concept embodied in Exodus 19:15 that women are uncovenanted. (See also R. Adler's article in 1980.)

Rabin, Roni: "The Two Wives of Avraham Cohen," Inside (magazine of Phila. Jewish Exponent), Fall 1986.

>Bigamy in Israel; how 25 men got permission from religious authorities in 1984-1985 to marry a second wife.

Roiphe, Anne: "The Jewish Family: A Feminist Perspective," Tikkun, v. 1, no. 2, Fall 1986.

>Wrap-up of major issues, overly optimistic point of view, trying to show that it is so obvious that feminism is good for the Jews; why can't they see it?

"In Israel, a Confluence of State, Temple and Gender Issues," Interview with Leah Shakdiel, New York Times, Oct. 12, 1986, p. E-7.

>Shakdiel's fight to serve on religious council of Yeruham, her Negev development town.

Shafransky, Renee: "The Goy of Sex," The Village Voice, May 20, 1986, p. 31ff.

>Ambivalence and conflict over mixed mating by a Jewish girl living with a WASP.

Shapiro, Haim: "The Search for a Role," The International Jerusalem Post, Oct. 11, 1986, p. 16.

>Feminist Jewish theology--Report on Eveline Goodman-Tau, initiated group on "The Role of Women in Religion" for the International Council of Christians and Jews.

Spiegel, Marcia Cohn: "Jewish Women Speak to God," Reconstructionist, Winter 1986.

>A survey of the prayers of Jewish women through the ages. (Forthcoming book by the author and Deborah Lipton Kremsdorf, poems and prayers, from Jewish Women's Institute for Continuing Jewish Education, San Diego.)

_____: "Alcoholism: Jewish Women Confront a Growing Problem." In Addictions in the Jewish Community, Stephen Jay Levy and Sheila B. Blume, eds., NY: Federation of Jewish Philanthropies, 1986.

Taitz, Emily: "Kol Ishah--The Voice of Woman: Where Was It Heard in Medieval Europe?" Conservative Judaism, v. 38, no. 3, Spring 1986.

>A thorough, interesting overview of the laws and practices of women in medieval times concerning women's "voice" in the community and in the synagogue.

Tikkun Symposium: "What Kind of Tikkun (Repair)?" Tikkun Magazine, v. 1, no. 1, Summer 1986.

>Essayists include Rabbi Laura Geller and T. Drorah Setel.

Umansky, Ellen: "Paula Ackerman: Reform's Lost Woman Rabbi," Genesis 2, Cambridge, MA, June/July 1986, pp. 18-20.

>Twenty years before first Reform rabbi was officially ordained, Paula Ackerman became spiritual leader of a Mississippi Reform Congregation after her husband died.

Wilentz, Gay: "White Patron and Black Artist: The Correspondence of Fannie Hurst and Zora Neale Hurston," Library Chronicle of Univ. of Texas at Austin, no. 25, 1986, pp. 21-43.

>Among other biographical items, this essay deals with Fannie Hurst's ambivalent Jewishness.

Young, Leila Rosen: "Women in Synagogue Life: Models of Congregational Change," Conservative Judaism, Summer 1986, pp. 74-78.

Change in the Conservative movement combines a respect for halacha with a greater role of women's participation in synagogue life.

REFERENCE *

Periodicals and Organizations Cited

Agudath Israel of America, 5 Beekman St., New York, NY 10013.
American Academy of Jewish Research, Jewish Theological Seminary of America (see J)
American Assn. of Professors of Yiddish, 802 Kiely Hall, 530 Kissena Blvd., Queens College, Flushing, NY 11367.
American Ethnologist, 1703 New Hampshire Ave. NW, Washington, DC 20009.
American Jewish Archives, 3101 Clifton Ave., Cincinnati, OH 45220.
American Jewish Committee, 165 E. 56th St., New York, NY 10022.
American Jewish History, 2 Thornton Rd., Waltham, MA 02154.
American Mizrachi Woman (see Amit Women)
American Zionist, 4 E. 34th St., New York, NY 10016.
Amit Women, 817 Broadway, New York, NY 10003.
Anima, 1053 Wilson Ave., Chambersburg, PA 17201.
Ariel, Jerusalem Post Publications Ltd., POB 3349, Jerusalem 91002, Israel.
Assn. for Jewish Librarians, National Foundation for Jewish Culture, 122 E. 42nd St., New York, NY 10017.
Assn. for Jewish Studies, Harvard University, Widener Library, Cambridge, MA 02138.
Baltimore Jewish Times, 2104 Charles St., Baltimore, MD 21218.
Belles Lettres, POBox 987, Arlington, VA 22216.
Biblical Archaeologist, Box HM, Duke Sta., Durham, NC 27706.
Bloch Publishing Co., 37 West 26th St., New York, NY 10010.
Bnai Brith, 1640 Rhode Island Ave., NW, Washington, DC 20036.
Canadian Jewish News, 562 E. Eglinton Ave., #401, Toronto, ON M4P 1P1, Canada.
Canadian Review of Sociology & Anthropology, Concordia University, 1455 Bd. de Maisonneuve W., Montreal, Que. #3G 1M8, Canada.
Chutzpah, POB 60192, Chicago, IL 60660.
Commentary, 165 E. 56th St., New York, NY 10022.
Conditions, Box 56, Van Brunt Sta., Brooklyn, NY 11215.
Cong. Solel, 1301 Clayvey Rd., Highland Park, IL 60035.
Congress Monthly (formerly Cong. Bi-Weekly), 15 E. 84th St., New York, NY 10028.
Conservative Judaism, 3080 Broadway, New York, NY 10027.
Contemporary Jewry, Dept. of Sociology, University of Alabama, Birmingham, AL 35294.
Emma Lazarus Women's Federation, 150 Fifth Ave., New York, NY 10011.
Emunah Women of America, 370 Seventh Ave., New York, NY 10018.
Ethnic Groups (See Gordon & Breach Publications)
European Judaism, Kent House, Rutland Gardens, London SW 71, BX, U.K.
Feminist Studies, Women's Studies Programs, University of Maryland, College Park, MD 20742.
Forum (See World Zionist Organization)
Gay Community News, 167 Tremont St., Boston, MA 02111.
Genesis 2, 99 Bishop Allen Drive, Cambridge, MA 02139.
Gordon & Breach Scientific Publications, 42 William IV St., London, WC2, U.K.
Hadassah Magazine, 50 W. 58th St., New York, NY 10021.
Ha'Or, c/o Queens College, Jewish Studies Dept., Flushing, NY 11367.
Helaine Victoria Press, 411 E. 4th St., Bloomington, IN 47401.
Herzl Press, 515 Park Ave., New York, NY 10019.
Hora, Israel Folk Dance Inst., 515 Park Ave., New York, NY 10022.
Ichud Habonim, 575 Sixth Ave., New York, NY 10011.
Institute for Jewish Policy, Synagogue Council of America, 155 Fifth Ave., New York, NY 10010.
International Journal of Women's Studies, Eden Press, 4626 St. Catherine St. W., Montreal, P.Q. H3Z 1S3, Can.
Isha le Isha/Woman to Woman, Haifa Feminist Movement, 9A Leonardo da Vinci St., Haifa, Israel.
Israel Dance (See Hora)
Israel Digest, POB 92, Jerusalem, Israel.
Israel Horizons, 150 Fifth Ave., New York, NY 10011.
Israel Library Assn., Histadrut Bldg., 7067 Arlozoroff St., Jerusalem 26111, Israel.
Israel Today (Israel Scene), 6742 Van Nuys Blvd., Van Nuys, CA 91405.

---

* Please refer to Books in Print available in most libraries to locate book publishers.

* Certain publications cited in the First Edition may now be defunct if not listed here. Some may be available at the Jewish Student Press Service. (Address in directory above)

Please note Index to Jewish Periodicals, a yearly guide, is available at some Judaica library collections, to locate articles beyond date of this Bibliography.

A list of major Judaica library collections in the USA is available from the Association of Jewish Librarians, National Foundation for Jewish Culture, 122 E. 42nd St., New York, NY 10036.

Jerusalem Post International Edition, 120 E. 56th St., New York, NY 10022.
Jewish Advocate, 251 Causeway St., Boston, MA 02114.
Jewish Book Annual (See Jewish Book Council)
Jewish Book Council, JWB, 15 E. 26th St., New York, NY 10010.
Jewish Currents, 22 E. 17th St., New York, NY 10011.
Jewish Digest, 1363 Fairfield Ave., Bridgeport, CT 06605.
Jewish Exponent, 226 S. 16th St., Philadelphia, PA 19102.
Jewish Frontier, 15 E. 26th St., New York, NY 10010.
Jewish Heritage (See Bnai Brith)
Jewish Journal of Sociology, 187 Gloucester Pl., London NW1, 6BU, U.K.
Jewish Monthly, Bnai Brith, 1640 Rhode Island Ave., NW, Washington, DC 20036.
Jewish Observer, 5 Beekman St., New York, NY 10038.
Jewish Occupational Council, 114 Fifth Ave., New York, NY 10011.
Jewish Publication Society, 1930 Chestnut St., Philadelphia, PA 19103.
Jewish Quarterly Review, Broad & York Sts., Philadelphia, PA 19132.
Jewish Social Studies, 250 W. 57th St., New York, NY 10022.
Jewish Spectator, POB 2016, Santa Monica, CA 90406.
Jewish Student Press Service, 15 E. 26th St., New York, NY 10010.
Jewish Telegraphic Agency, 156 E. 46th St., New York, NY 10036.
Jewish Theological Seminary of America, 3080 Broadway, New York, NY 10027.
Jewish Veteran, 1712 New Hampshire Ave., NW, Washington, DC 20009.
Jewish Week/American Examiner, 774 Nat'l Press Bldg., Washington, DC 20004.
Jewish Week, 1 Park Ave., New York, NY 10016.
Jewish Women's Outlook (See Women's League for Conservative Judaism)
Jewish Women's Resource Center (NCJW) 9 E. 69th St., New York, NY 10022.
Jewish World, 115 Middle Neck Rd., Great Neck, NY 11021.
Jonathan David Publishers, 68-22 Eliot Ave., Middle Village, NY 11379.
Jonathan Publications, 660 Prospect Ave., Hartford, CT 06105.
Journal of the American Academy of Religion, Univ. of Chicago Press, 5801 Ellis Ave., Chicago, IL 60637.
Journal of Ecumenical Studies, Temple University, (022-38) Philadelphia, PA 19122.
Journal of Feminist Studies in Religion, Scholars Press, Decatur, GA 30031.
Journal of Jewish Art, Center for Jewish Art, Hebrew University, Jerusalem, Israel.
Journal of Jewish Communal Service, 111 Prospect St., East Orange, NJ 07017.
Journal of Marriage and the Family, 1219 University Ave., SE, Minneapolis, MN 55414.
Journal of Popular Culture, Bowling Green State Univ., Bowling Green, OH 43403.
Journal of Reform Judaism (Same as Reform Judaism)
Judaica Book News, 303 W. 10th St., New York, NY 10014.
Judaism Magazine, 15 E. 84th St., New York, NY 10028.
Keeping Posted, Union of American Hebrew Cong., 838 Fifth Ave., New York, NY 10036.
Leo Baeck Institute, 129 E. 73rd St., New York, NY 10021.
Lesbian Studies (See Lesbian Feminist)
Lesbian Feminist, 243 W. 20th St., New York, NY 10011.
Leviathan, Redwood Bldg., Univ. of California, Santa Cruz, CA 95063.
Library Chronicle, Univ. of Texas, Humanities Research Center, Box 7219, Austin, TX 78712.
Lilith Magazine, 250 West 57th St., New York, NY 10019.
London Jewish Chronicle, 25 Furnival St., London, EC 4, U.K.
Melton Journal, 3080 Broadway, New York, NY 10027.
Mizrachi Woman, 817 Broadway, New York, NY 10011.
Midstream Magazine, 515 Park Ave., New York, NY 10022.
Modern Hebrew Literature (See Institute for Translation of Hebrew Lit.)
Modern Judaism, Johns Hopkins University, 701 W. 40th St., Ste. 275, Baltimore, MD 21211.
Moment Magazine, 462 Boylston St., Boston, MA 02116.
Mosaic, 1 Endleigh St., London, WC 1, U.K.
Na'Amat USA Women's Labor Zionist Org. of America (formerly Pioneer Women), 200 Madison Ave., New York, NY 10021.
National Jewish Monthly (see Jewish Monthly)
National Jewish Resource Center, 421 Seventh Ave., New York, NY 10001.
National Women's Studies Newsletter (See Women's Studies Quarterly)
Nefesh, 226 Sussex Ave., Morristown, NJ 07960.
New Glide Publications, 330 Ellis St., San Francisco, CA 94102.
New Menorah (formerly Menorah) Bnai Or Religious Fellowship, 6723 Emlen St., Philadelphia, PA 19119.
New Outlook, Americans for Progressive Israel, 150 Fifth Ave., New York, NY 10011.
New Traditions Magazine, 270 W. 89th St., New York, NY 10024.
Off Our Backs, 1724 20th St. NW, Washington, DC 20036.
ORT (See Women's American ORT Reporter)
Outlook (see Women's Outlook or Jewish Women's Outlook of Women's League for Conservative Judaism)
Pedagogic Reporter, JESNA, 730 Broadway, New York, NY 10003.
Pioneer Woman, 200 Madison Ave., New York, NY 10016. (See also Na'Amat USA)
Present Tense Magazine, 165 E. 56th St., New York, NY 10022.
Reconstructionist, 270 West 89th St., New York, NY 10024.
Reform Judaism, 838 Fifth Ave., New York, NY 10021.
Religious Education, 409 Prospect St., New Haven, CT 06511.

Response, 523 W. 113th St., New York, NY 10021.
Sex Roles, Plenum Publishing Co., 233 Spring St., New York, NY 10013.
Shdemot, Kibbutz Aliya Federation, 27 W. 20th St., New York, NY 10011.
Sh'Ma, Box 567, Port Washington, NY 11050.
Shmate Magazine, Box 4228, Berkeley, CA 94704.
Shofar, 222 Recitation Bldg., Purdue Univ., West Lafayette, IN 47907.
Signs, University of Chicago, 5801 Ellis Ave., Chicago, IL 60637.
Sinister Wisdom, POB 1308, Montpelier, VT 05602.
Sociological Review, New Series, University of Keele, Staffordshire, ST5, 5BG, U.K.
Sojourner, 143 Albany St., Cambridge, MA 02139.
Student Struggle for Soviet Jewry, 200 W. 72nd St., New York, NY 10023.
Studies in Judaism (See European Judaism)
Tikkun Magazine, 5100 Leona St., Oakland, CA 94619.
Tradition, 220 Park Ave. So., New York, NY 10003.
United Synagogue Review, 3080 Broadway, New York, NY 10027.
Village Voice, 842 Broadway, New York, NY 10010.
Weiss-Rosmarin, Trude (See Jewish Spectator)
Western States Jewish Historical Quarterly, 2429 23rd St., Santa Monica, CA 90405.
Westwood Press, 5500 Central Ave., Boulder, CO 80301.
WomanSpirit, 2000 King Mountain, Wolf Creek, OR 97497.
Women's American ORT Reporter, 315 Park Ave. So., New York, NY 10003.
Women's Caucus, Religious Studies Newsletter, Graduate Theological Union, 2465 LaConte, Berkeley, CA 94709.
Women's Center, Mercaz Ha-Carmel, Haifa, Israel.
Women's League for Israel, 515 Park Ave., New York, NY 10022.
Women's Studies International Forum, Pergamon Press, Maxwell House, Fairview Park, Elmsford, NY 10523.
Women's Studies Newsletter (See Women's Studies Quarterly)
Women's Studies Quarterly, Feminist Press at CUNY, 311 E. 94th St., New York, NY 10128.
Women's Tefillah Network, POB 236, Brooklyn, NY 11230.
Women's World, Bnai Brith Women, 1640 Rhode Island Ave., NW, Washington, DC 20036.
World Jewish Bible Society, 18 Arbarbanel St., Jerusalem, Israel.
World Zionist Organization, POBox 92, Jerusalem, Israel.
Yiddish (See American Assn. of Professors of Yiddish)
Young Judaean Magazine, 50 W. 58th St., New York, NY 10021.
Youth & Nation, 150 Fifth Ave., New York, NY 10011.

INDEX

Abrams, Jeanne 29
Abzug, Bella 29
Ackelsberg, Martha 177
Adelman, Penina V. 108, 172
Adelsberg, Sandra 169
Adelson, Dorothy 145
Adler, Celia 127
Adler, Marjorie Duhan 46
Adler, Polly 23
Adler, Rachel 12, 108
Adler, Ruth 1,4,88
Aguilar, Grace 8
Agus, Arlene 113
Aharoni, Andree Ada 55, 98, 145, 161
Ain, Stewart 29
Albert, Alexa A. 18
Alexander, Lynn 161
Alkalay-Gut, Karen 172
Allen-Shore, Lena 73
Aloni, Shulamit 55, 56
Alpert, Rebecca 29, 108
Alstat, Philip R. 68
Amichai, Yehuda 153
Amir, Aliza 147
Andrews, Grace 8
Angoff, Charles 23
Antin, Mary 1, 119, 172
Antonovsky, Aaron 53
Appelfeld, Aharon 159
Araten, Rachel Sarna 94
Arendt, Hannah 1
Arich, Aliza 127
Arich, Hannah 127
Aronson, Leonard J. 108
Arzt, Aliza 177
Asch, Sholem 46
Aschkenasy, Nehama 108, 172
Ashkenasy, H. 96
Atkinson, Linda 155
Auerbach, Marilyn Iris 109
Averbuch, Gloria 56
Avery, Evelyn M. 29, 88, 177
Axelrod, Albert 4
Azaryahu, Sara 145

Back, T.T. 109
Badt-Strauss, Bertha 23,88
Baer, M.F. 127
Baetz, Ruth 119
Bakan, David 1
Balka, Christie 147
Balser, Ruth 29
Bandler, Michael J. 68
Bankier, Joanna 72
Banks, Lynne Reid 91, 101
Barach, J. 147
Barag, Gerda G. 29
Bar-David, Molly Lyons 53
Bargad, Warren F. 172

Baron, Dvora 8
Baron, Sheryl 29
Barringer, Felicity 138
Bar-Yosef, Rivka 56, 145
Bart, Pauline B. 30, 119
Bass, Ellen 72
Bat-Ada, Judith 147
Baum, Camille 47
Baum, Charlotte 23
Bauman, Batya 30
Bauman, Janina 155
Baumgold, Julie 30
Bayer, Ellen 32
Beck, Evelyn Torton 23,119,127,165
Becker, Robin 119, 128
Bedford, Sybille 8
Beizer-Bohrer, Ruth 147
Bell, R. 56
Bell, Roselyn 12
Belli, Donna 84
Bellman, Samuel Irving 90
Bender, Esther 30
Benkler, Rafi 68
Ben, Yaakov I. 63
Ben-Shaul, D'Vora 148
Ben-Yosef, Avraham C. 56
Ben-Zvi, Rachel Yanait 53
Berg, Mary 65
Bergelson, David 97
Berger, B. 30
Berger, Dena 70
Berger-Sofer, Rhoda 165
Bergman, Helene Audrey 109
Berkenfield, Janet 177
Berkman, Ted 23
Berkovits, Eliezer 12
Berman, Hannah 8
Berman, Louis A. 30
Berman, Saul 12,10,9
Berman, Susan 30
Bermant, Chaim 161
Bernstein, D. 147
Bernstein, Michal 12
Bershadskaya, Liuba 63
Betsky, Sarah Zweig 72
Biale, Rachel 101
Bilik, Dorothy Seidman 65
Bird, Phyllis 12
Birenbaum, Halina 65
Birman, Abraham 72
Birman, Tzippora 68
Birnbaum, Martha Rock 12
Birstein, Ann 47
Bissell, Sherry 30
Bitton-Jackson, Livia 94,156
Black, J. 128
Blair, Leona 153
Blank, Amy K. 73
Blau, Zena Smith 30

Bleich, David J. 12
Bletter, Diana Katcher 128
Blicksilver, Edith 89,165
Bloch, Alice 119
Block, Chana 73, 163
Bloch, Irvin 23
Bloom, Clair 119
Bluestone, Naomi 30
Blumengarten, Louis H. 30
Blumenthal, A.H. 56
Bob, Ellen Sharon 12
Bocage, Angela 109
Bogarin, Jonathan 128
Bondy, Ruth 56
Borenstein, Emily 74, 163
Borts, B. 109
Boucher, Sandy 31
Braginsky, Judy 128
Brand, Sandra 65, 98
Brandow, Selma Koss 80
Brandstadter, Evan D. 80
Braude, Ann 109
Brayer, Menachem 172
Breitberg, S. 56
Brenner, Marie 47
Breslauer, I.H. 148
Breslauer, S.D. 109
Brettel, Caroline B. 176
Brewer, Joan Scherer 168
Bristow, Edward J. 94, 96
Brodbar-Nemzer, Jay Y. 177
Broder, Bill 98
Broder, Kurian 98
Brodkey, Harold 138
Broner, Esther 10,47,62,101,138,
   148,153
Bronznick, Shifra 31
Brooten, Bernadette J. 94, 165
Brown, Laura 31
Brown, Pryde 31
Brown, Rosellen 47
Brownmiller, Susan 4
Brozan, Nadine 31
Bruce, Laurie 23
Bruce Pratt, Minnie 120
Bubis, Gerald 128
Buchwald, Lynne S. 165
Bulka, Reuven 172
Bulkin, Elly 73,120,139,162
Burch, Claire 74
Burnstein, Patricia 139
Busch, Frederick 139
Bush, Lawrence 139
Byer, Etta 23
Bytensky, Bella 120

Cantor, Aviva 4,5,13,31,68,101,109, 128,177
Cantor, D. 110
Chiswick, Barry R. 120
Christ, Carol P. 10
Chyet, Stanley F. 172
Clamar, Aphrodite 13
Clar, R. 128
Clayton, John 129
Cohen, Arthur A. 139
Cohen, Esther 129, 139
Cohen, Geula 53, 91
Cohen, Ida Selavan 13
Cohen, Rose 23
Cohen, Sarah Blacher 90, 120
Cohen, Shaye, J.D. 110
Cohen, Steven Martin 31, 129
Cohn, Judy Birnbaum 31
Cohn-Sherbok, D. 129
Cohn-Sherbok, L. 110
Condon, Richard 159
Cook, Blanche Weisen 32
Coombs, A. 129
Cooperman, Jehiel 72
Cooperman, Sarah 72
Corcoran, Martha 13
Coughlin, M.D. 161
Courter, Gay 139
Cowan, Evelyn 63
Cowen, Ida G. 64, 145, 161
Craven, Toni 101
Christ, Carol P. 10

D'Alpuget, Blanche 172
Dame, Enid 74, 163, 173
Danab, Mint 129
Darel, Sylvia 64
Dash, Joan 24, 53
Datan, Nancy 32, 53, 145
Daum, Annette 18, 32, 129
David, Janina 65, 155
David, Jay 5
Davidman, Lynn 148, 165
Davidovich, David 101
Davidowicz, Lucy 13
Davidson, Gusta 68
Davidson, Margaret 53
Davidson, Sara 24, 139
Davidson, Sue 27, 123
Davis, Barbara Hillyer 130
Davis, Elizabeth Gould 1
Davis, Esther 56
Davis, Hanna B. 129
Dayan, Yael 53, 56, 62, 145
de Beauvoir, Simone 57
Del Fatlore, Joan 120
Demetz, Hana 65, 159

DeNola, David 69
Dick, Judah 110
Dobrin, Arnold 53
Dresner, Ruth Rapp 96, 130
Drexler, Rosalyn 47
Drew, Jill 130
Dribben, Judith Strick 65
Drinnon, Anna Maria 24
Drinnon, Richard 24
Dryfoos, Susan W. 120
Dubrovsky, Gertrude 130
Duckat, Walter 5, 96
Dulzin, Annette 57
Durka, G. 110
Durrell, Lawrence 8
Dworkin, Susan 32
Dye, Nancy Schram 120
Dykewomon, Elana 121, 163

Edelheit, Abraham J. 169
Edelheit, Hershel 169
Edelhert, Martha 32
Edelman, Gary Edward 121
Edinger, Dora 1
Eider, Shimon D. 101
Eisen, Naava 53
Eisenpreis, Bl 110, 130
Eisenstein, Ira 110
Elazar, Daniel J. 110
Eliav, Arie L. 65
Elizur, Judith Neulander 57
Elkin, Lillian 57
Ellis, Julie 98, 139
Elwell, Sue Levi 101, 165, 169
Engel, Barbara Alpern 5
Engel, Sophie B. 165
England-Schaffer, Naomi Y. 110
Ephron, Nora 57
Epstein, Helen 32, 65
Epstein, I. 5
Epstein, Leslie 139
Epstein, Perle 24, 57
Epstein, Raymond 165
Epstein, Seymour 47
Erens, Patricia 121
Ettinger, Elzbieta 70, 121, 173
Evanier, David 140
Evans, Jane 32
Ewen, Elizabeth 121
Faessler, Shirley 140
Fainaru, Edna 148
Falk, Candace 121
Falk, Marcia 110, 162, 163
Falk, Ze'ev 10
Farber, Norma 74
Farstendiger-(Navon), Sylvia 68
Fein, H. 130
Feinstein, Elaine 159

Feinstein, Sarah 32, 130
Feld, Merilla 65
Feldbrand, S. 102
Feldman, David M. 10, 13
Feldman, Marla J. 121
Feldman, Yael S. 148
Feldstein, Donald 32
Felix, Cathy 166
Fell Yellin, Sarah 74
Fenelon, Fania 65
Ferber, Edna 24
Ferber, Nat J. 24
Ferderber-Salz, Bertha
Feron, James 130
Filsenberg, Rosa 33
Field, Carole 68
Field, Herman 70
Findly, Ellison Banks 103
Fine, Irene 102, 166, 169
Fineman, Irving 24
Fink, Greta 2
Finkel, Gilberta 166
Fisch, Linda Yellin 166
Fisher, Florence 24
Fishman, Leora 33
Flexner, Eleanor 33
Florence, Ronald 5
Fogel, Ruby 74
Foldes, Susan B. 69
Ford, Gertrude 140
Forse, Chana 33
Fox, Karen L. 110
Frank, Anne 159
Frank, Blanche 80,111
Frank, S.S. 130
Frank, Shirley, 33
Frankel, G. 96
Frankel, N. 96
Frankel, William 64
Frankfort, Ellen 121
Freed, Lynn 173
Freedman, Marcia 57, 91, 148
Freedman, Nina 14
Freeman, Cynthia 47, 140
Freeman, Lucy 2
Freespirit, Judy 122
Fridkis, Ari Lloyd 130
Friedenson, Joseph 155
Friedfertig, Raizel Schnall 102
Friedland, Charlotte 96
Friedlander, Albert H. 92
Friedlander, Dov 57
Friedman, Bruce Jay 47
Friedman, David 57
Friedman, Joan S. 166
Friedman, Joni 5
Friedman, Melvin J. 90
Friedman, Mordecai A.
Friedman, Nathalie 130

Friedman, Reena Sigman 14
Friedman, Rosemary 140, 161
Frye, Thelma Ruby 57
Frymer, Hanita Blumfield 80
Fuchs, Esther 102,111,148,149,173
Furstenberg, Rochelle 14,58,111,131

Gabor, Georgia M. 155
Gantz, Paula 131
Ganz, Marie 24
Ganz-Ribner, Mindy 14
Garb, March 111
Garson, Sascha 33
Gary, Romain 2
Geller, Laura 14, 178
Geller, Ruth 140
Gellis, Audrey 14
Gendler, Everett 111
Gendler, Mary 14, 111
Gershon, Karen 74
Gertel, Elliot 33
Ghatan, Hedidah H.E. 173
Gidding, Joshua 47
Gilad, Lisa 149
Gilson, Estelle 33
Ginor, Fanny 53
Ginzburg, Eugenia 94
Girgus, Sam B. 122
Gittelsohn, Ronald B. 14, 102
Gittleman, Sol 2
Gittleson, Natalie 33
Gladstone, Frances 140
Glanville, Brian 64
Glanz, Rudolph 24
Glass, Sharon
Glazer, Myra (Schotz) 58, 72
Gluckl (of Hameln) 2
Goitein, S.D. 5,64,94
Golan, Aviezer 145
Gold, Doris B. 33,34,74,131,170
Goldberg, Doris 34
Goldberg, Leah 74
Goldberg, Steven 24
Goldenberg, Naomi R. 10
Goldhammer, Paul 43
Goldin, Grace 10
Goldkorn, Dorka 69
Goldman, Alex J. 173
Goldman, Ari L. 111
Goldman, Avia Dayan 131
Goldman, Emma 24, 122
Goldman, Rachel 34
Golomb, Deborah G. 131
Goldreich, Gloria 47, 140
Goldscheider, Calvin 34, 122
Goldsmith, E. 131
Goldstein, Alvin H. 24
Goldstein, Elyse M. 178

Goldstein, Rebecca 140
Goldstein, Ruth Tessler 47
Goldworth, Bella 8
Goodblatt, Robert 33
Goodhill, R.M. 149
Gordimer, Nadine 63
Gordis, Robert 14, 96, 111
Gordon, Barbara 25
Gordon, Eric 178
Gordon, Maralee 34
Gordon, Martin L. 15
Gordon, Susan 69
Gornick, Vivan 25
Goshen-Gottstein, Esther 54
Gotlieb, Phyllis 75
Gottlieb, Freema 102
Gottlieb, Lynn 15, 112
Gould, Lois 47
Gould, Mary Jane 47
Gould, Shirley 15
Grade, Chaim 8, 173
Grant, Annette 5
Grant, Myrna 63
Gratz, Rebecca 88
Gray, Bettyanne 2
Green, Hannah 48
Green, Kathy 106
Green, Leona S. 178
Green, Tova 131
Greenberg, Blu 15, 23, 102, 112
Greenberg, Dan 25
Greenberg, Eliezer 73
Greenberg, Irving 15, 112
Greenberg, Joanna 48
Greene, Diana 34
Greenspahn, F.E. 112
Greenspan, E. 34
Grinstein, Alexander 35
Grosman, Ladislav 70
Gross, David C. 2, 71
Gross, Joel 9, 99, 153
Gross, Rita M. 15, 112
Grossman, Chaika 69
Grossman, Cissy 97
Grossman, Dvora 112
Grossman, Edward 178
Grossman, Roz 15
Grossman, S. 112
Gruber, Ruth 54, 62
Gruen, Louise M. 10
Grunfeld, Frederic V. 35
Guber, Rivka 65
Guggenheim, Peggy 2, 122
Gurdus, Luba Krugman 66, 92
Gussow, Don 140
Guttman, A. 112

Haber, Barbara 84
Hadas, Pamela White 75
Hadas, Rachel 75
Haddad, Yvonne Yazbeck 103
Halporn, Louise 9
Hamelsdorf, Ora 80, 169
Handelman, Shanah Sara 16
Handleman, S. 80
Hanna, Evelyn 95
Hansen, Lilian Leah 95
Hapgood, Hutchins 35
Harris, Alice Kessler 48
Harris, Kevin 103
Harris, Lis 103
Harris, Marylou 35
Harrison, J.H. 131
Hart, Kitty 66, 155
Harvey, Warren Zev 112
Hasanovitz, Elizabeth 25
Hauptman, Judith 16
Haut, Irwin H. 16, 103
Hay, Peter 173
Hazelton, Lesley 54,146,174,
Heller, Celia S. 2
Hellman, Aviva 140
Hellman, John 95
Hellman, Lillian 25
Henig, Suzanne 75
Henry, Sondra 2, 96
Herbstrith, Waltraud 155
Herman, Ilana 64
Hersh, Gizelle 156
Herzberger, Magda 156
Heschel, Susannah 103, 112
Heyman, Eva 66
High, Monique Raphael 9, 15
Hilf, Mary Asia 25
Hill, Melvyn A. 6
Hillesum, Etty 156
Hirschhorn, Barbara 131
Hobhouse, Janet 25
Hobson, Laura Z. 48, 122
Hoffman, Elaine
Hoffman, Michael J. 25
Hoffman, Roy 122
Hofstein, Saul 35
Holder, Maryse 66
Holender, Barbara D. 163
Holtzman, Will 122
Hornik, Edith Lynn 35
Horowitz, Eugene 48
Horowitz, Sima 84
Howard, Doris 174
Howard, Margo 122
Howe, Florence 72
Howe, Irving 73, 123
Humphries, Ami 132
Husbands-Hankin, Shonna 11
Hyman, Frieda Clark 179
Hyman, Paula 16,12,35,113,

Ibn Ezra, Yakkov 16
Ingber, Judith Brin 91
Insdorf, Annette 169
Inwald, Doris 35
Isaacman, Clara 174
Isaacs, Susan 141
Israel, Richard 35
Jackson, Bernard S. 103
Jacob, H.E. 25
Jacobs, Nancy L. 36
Jacoby, Susan 36
James, Janel Wilson 10
Janowitz, Naomi 16
Jastrow, Marie 25
Jayanti, Miriam 166
Jensen, Cheryl 113
Jensen, Joan M. 123
Jochnowitz, Carol 36, 113, 132, 179
Johnson, George E. 16
Jolles, Andree 113
Jong, Erica 48
Jordan, Ruth 146
Joseloff, Samuel Hart 73
Joseph, Joan 99
Joseph, Shirley 149
Julianelli, Jane 36
Jungreis, Esther 103

Kanigel, R. 132
Kaplan, Arlene M. 16
Kaplan, Johanna 48
Kaplan, Joseph C. 16
Kaplan, Marian A. 3,6,88,97,156
Kaplan, Sharon 16
Kapp, Yvonne 2
Karmel, Ilona 174
Karmel-Wolfe, Henia 70
Karp, Lila 49
Kashner, Ritz 153
Kats, Elizabeth 66
Kahan, Rhea 141
Kahanoff, Jacqueline 58
Kalechofsky, Roberta 48, 89
Kamen, Marcia 16
Kaminska, Ida 2
Kaminska, Ruth Turkow 2
Kaminskaya, Dina 95
Katz, Esther 156
Katz, Judith 132
Katz, Sanford N. 25
Ka-Tzetnik 159
Katzenelson-Rubashow (Shazar),Rachel
Kaufelt, David A. 49, 160
Kaufman, A. 58
Kaufman, D.R. 113

Kaufman, Myron S. 141
Kaufman, Shirley 75
Kateb, George 123
Kaye/Kantrowitz, Melanie 123,132,163
Keats, John 25
Kellen, Konrad 36
Keller, Mollie 146
Kelly, Myra 49
Kerdeman, Deborah 174
Keren, Thea 146
Kessler-Harris, Alice 36
Kessner, Carol S. 132, 179
Kimball, Gussie 25
Kirk, Robert 66
Kirschenbaum, Carol 179
Klagsbrun, Francine 10, 113, 132
Klarsfeld, Beate 64
Klein, Carole 3, 123
Klein, Elizabeth 163
Klein, Gerda Weissman 66, 123
Klein, Judith Weinstein 132
Klemesrud, Judy 36
Klepfisz, Irena 75, 132, 163
Klibanski, Bronya 69
Kluger, Ruth 66
Kobler, Franz 3
Koehler, Joan 17
Koehn, Ilse 66
Koevary, Hanna 69
Kohak, Efrayim 66
Kohan, Rhea 49
Kohut, Rebecca 26
Kolmar, Gertrud 75
Kolt, Frances 179
Koltun, Elizabeth 17, 88
Koltuv, Barbara Black 113, 174
Konheim, J. 113
Koppelman, Susan 141
Korczak, Ruzka 69
Korn, Rachel 164
Kossover, Toni 49
Kotlar, Helen 156
Kovaly, Heda Margolius 66, 174
Kramer, Sydelle 16
Krantz, Judith 141
Krause, Corinne Azen 36
Krausz, Judy 58, 133, 149
Kranzler, David 155
Kreitman, Esther Singer 141
Kremer, G.H. 133
Kronenthal, Rena 149
Kruger, Mollee 75, 164
Krummel, Regine P. 133
Kuchler-Silberman, Lena 66
Kur, Carol 36
Kurtz, Irma 49
Kushner, Lawrence
Kushner, Rose 36
Kukoff, Lydia 103
Kuzmack, Linda Gordon 170

Lacks, Roslyn 104
Lahav, Pnina 58, 59
Laiman, Leah 17
Lamm, Bob 37
Lamm, Maurice 104
Lang, Lucy Robins 26
Langer, M.E. 133
Langus, Anna 66
Larkin, Joan 73
Laska, Vera 157
Latham, Judy 11
Lauterstein, Ingeborg 70, 160
Lavender, Abraham D. 37
Lazarus, Emma 75
LaZebnik, Edith 3
Leahy, Syrelle Rogovin 49, 160
Lebeson, Anita 26
Leftwich, Joseph 73
Leibler, D. 59
Leifer, Daniel L. 17
Leitner, Isabella 67,157
Lelchuk, Alan 49
Lengyel, Olga 157
Lerman, Pamela Faith 114
Lerner, Anne Lapidus 17,79,133
Lerner, Diana 59
Lerner, Elinor 133
Lerner, Gerda 37
Lester, Elenore 37, 97, 133
Lev, Yehuda 133
Levavi, Lea 150
Leven, Schneir 64
Levenberg, Diane 75, 114, 133
Levenberg, S. 59
Levenson, Edward R. 166, 169
Levertov, Denise 92, 164
Levett, Jay 114
Levin, Alexandra Lee 88
Levin, Bonnie 175
Levin, M. 133
Levin, Meyer 70
Levin, Nora 3
Levine, Faye 49, 99, 141
Levine, Jacqueline 44
Levine, Louis 37
Levine, Ruth 80
Levine, Sheila 141
Levinson, Norma 141, 161
Levinthal, I.H. 17
Levner, Lily Gluck 71
Levy, Harriet Lane 26, 88
Levy-Hass, Hanna 157
Lewis, Helen S. 37
Lieberman, Betty 37
Libo, Kenneth 123
Lieberman, Betty 37
Lieberman, Sharon 37
Lieblich, Amia 146
Lifshin, Lyn 92
Lindheim, Irma L. 54

Lipman, Eugene 17
Liptzin, Sol 6, 104
List, Shelley Steinman 49
Litman, Jane (aka Litwomon) 99, 114
Litvinoff, Barnet 126
"Liza" 37
Livingston, Nancy 37
Livneh, Neri 150
Loeb, Garry Allan 166
Loewe, Louis 95
London, Lauri 150
Louvish, Misha 59
Lowenstein, Andrea Freud 123
Lowenthal, Marvin 3, 123
Lowenthal, Rita 134
Lubelsky, Masha 150
Lubert, Steven 79
Lubetkin, Zivia 157
Lukas, Susan 49
Lustig, Arnost 71, 160
Luxemburg, Rosa 95
Lytle, Elizabeth Edith 54

Magida, Arthur J. 179
Mailer, Norman 37
Maimon, Ada 54
Makouska, Irina 37
Malcolm, Sarah 37
Malina, Judith 123
Maller, Allen 37, 38
Mallon, J.V. 134
Malus, Elinor 150
Mandelkern, Nick 134
Mann, Denise Berg 11
Mann, Gertrude 67
Mann, Peggy 54, 66, 69, 155
Maoz, Benjamin 53
Marcus, Jacob Rader 6, 124
Margolis, Daniel 17
Margolis, Patty 17
Margolis, Vera S. 38
Markus, Julia 141
Marsella, Joan F. 80
Mason, Ruth 38
Masor, Jenny 26
Masters, Anthony 67
Marx, Anne 75
Mathews, Carole 166
May, Antoinette 6
Mayer, Barbara 38
Maynard, Fredelle Bruser 26
Mazey, Robert 73
Mazow, Julia Wolf 26, 124
Mazur, C. 84
Mednick, Martha
Meed, Vladka 67

Meir, Golda 54
Meir, Menahem 146
Mehren, E. 114
Meiselman, Moshe 11, 17
Melamed, Aliza 69
Mendels, Pamela 114
Merkin, Daphne 175
Merriam, Eve 26, 38
Meyer, Annie Nathan 26
Meyer, Michael 6
Meyers, Carol 89, 97
Meyers, Janet 38
Myerhoff, Barbara 26
Meyerson, Robert 80, 166
Michel, Jean 63
Michel, Sonya 23, 38
Michelson, Frida 157
Miedzyrzecka, Vladka (Meed) 69
Mierzenski, Stanislaw 70
Miller, Alvin S. 38
Miller, J.D. 38, 134
Miller, Yisroel 104
Milton, Sybil 157
Mintz, Ruth Finer 73, 76
Miriam, Selma 134
Mirsky, Norman 38
Mitovsky, Dina 62, 153
Moise, Penina 76
Monson, Rela Geffen 39, 167
Moore, Abigail S. 134
Moore, Deborah Dash 134
Morales, Rosario 134
Morgan, Carole 49
Morgan, Moshe 104
Morgan, Robin 76
Moriel, Liora 150, 179
Morton, Leah 27, 175
Morton, Nelle 104
Morrell, Samuel 114
Morris, Benny 134, 150
Mort, Jo-Ann 134
Moskin, Marietta D. 11
Mosco, Maisie 141
Moskowitz, Faye 95, 135
Mozeson, Isaac 162

McCarthy, Mary 26
McFarland, Dorothy Tuck 95
McLaughlin, Eleanor 12

Nachman, Elana 89
Namztlas, Judith 95
Nardi, Shulamit S. 59
Narell, Irena Penzik 39
Nathan, Maud 27, 89

Nave-Levinson, P. 114
Negh, Claudine 157
Neidle, Cecyle S. 27
Nesvisky, Matthew 59
Neu, Dianne 175
Neuberger, J. 114, 161
Neuda, Fanny 89
Neudel, Marian 17
Neusner, Jacob 11, 17, 89
New, Elisa 180
Newhouse, Nancy R. 175
Newman, Leslea 175
Newman, Mordecai 39
Neumark, Yosef 115
Nimrod, Naomi 10
Nissinson, Marilyn 39
Noble, Shlomo 6
Nomberg-Przytyk, Sara 158
Nordquist, Joan 170
Novak, William 39
Novick, Marian 142
Novitch, Miriam 67
Nulman, Macy 97
Nunnally-Cox, Janice 104

Oberski, Jane 158
O'Brien, Patricia H.
Obukhova, Lydia 105
Ochs, Carol 105
Ofseyer, Jordan 17
Oliver, Rose 39
Olsen, Tillie 50
Olshaker, Ed 97
Opfell, Olga 175
Ostow, Mortimer 18
Oyserman, Erika 59
Oz, Amos 62
Ozick, Cynthia 50, 142, 180

Padan-Eisenstark, Dorit 59
Paley, Grace 50, 90, 175
Palgi, Michal 146, 150
Parent, Gail 50
Parker, H. 150
Parker, S. 150
Pastan, Linda 164
Patai, Raphael 11
Patz, Naomi 105
Peck, Arlene G. 27
Peli, Pinchas 115
"Penny" 37
Pepper, S. 84
Perman, Jane 105
Pesetsky, Bette 142
Pesotta, Rose 3, 27

Petesch, Natalie L.M. 50
Pfeffer, Leo 18
Philipson, David 27
Phillips, Melanie 18
Picon, Molly 27
Pibkas, Danny 145
Piercy, Marge 50
Pilcer, Sonia 142
Pincus, Chasya 54
Plain, Belva 142, 175
Plaskow, Judith 10, 18, 39, 40, 115, 180
Pogrebin, Letty Cottin 18, 40, 59, 135
Polikoff, Nancy 135
Polner, Murray 40
Polt, Harriet 6
Pomerantz, Marsha 151
Porter, Jack Nusan 6, 69
Porter, Judith R. 18
Posner, Marcia 170
Postal, Bernard 40
Potok, Chaim 142
Potter, Clare 170
Poupko, Chana K. 18
Poverman, C.E. 99
Powers, Anne 9
Powers, James L. 80
Pratt, Norma Fain 40, 135
Precker, Michael 59
Prell-Foldes, Riv-Ellen 18
Pressma, D.C. 135
Priesand, Sally 11, 40
Prose, Francine 99

Rabb, Christine 59
Rabikowitz (Ravikovitch) Dalia 54, 60, 76
Rabin, Roni 180
Rabinowicz, Harry M. 7
Rabinowicz, Rachel 105
Rabinowitz, Dorothy 158
Rabinsky, Beatrice 67
Rabson, Diane 162
Rackman, Emanuel 19
Raday, F. 151
Rakowski, Puah 7
Rapaport, Lynne 79
Raphael, Marc Lee 105, 135
Rapoport, Nessa 50, 89, 142
Raskin, Barbara 50
Ratok, Lily 151
Rayner, Claire 99
Raynes, Rose 40
Read, Constance 115
Rechtman, Janet 50
Reguer, Sara 40, 136
Reibel, Paula 99

Reifman, Toby Fishman 11
Rein, Natalie 54
Reinharz, Shulamit 151
Reisman, D. 60
Reisman, R.F. 136
Reisman, Y. 115
Remy, Nahida 3
Rennert, Maggie 55
Resnick, Elaine 19
Ribalow, Harold U. 7, 124
Rice, Sherri L. 170
Rich, Adrienne 164, 175
Richardson, Joanna 3
Richter, Ida 50
Riesman, D. 7
Ringelheim, Joan Miriam 156
Ritterband, Paul 124
Rivlin, Lily 7, 9
Roazen, Paul 124
Roberts, Hyman 19
Rochlin, Fred 124
Rochlin, Harriet 124, 142
Rockland, Mae Shafter 40
Rogan, Barbara 62, 153

Rohrlich, Ruby 95
Roiphe, Anne 41, 51, 90, 124, 180
Romain, S.S. 115
Rose, Leesha 67
Rose, Louise Blecher 51
Rose, Ernestine L. 41
Rosen, Donia 67
Rosen, Gladys 41, 136
Rosen, Norma 7, 142
Rosen, Ruth 27
Rosen, Sherry 151
Rosenak, Michael 151
Rosenbach, A.S.W. 171
Rosenbaum, Irving J. 67
Rosenberg, Janet 7
Rosenberg, Leah 124
Rosenberg, M.J. 41
Rosenberg, R. 161
Rosenbluth, Margie 41
Rosenbluth, Sally 51, 142
Rosenfeld, Lulla 63
Rosenstein, Harriet 9
Rosenthal, Clifford N. 5
Roskies, David G. 88
Rosner, Menachem 60
Ross, Bette M. 11, 105
Ross, Elaine 7
Rosshandler, Felicia 99
Rossman-Mallow, Adar 41
Rossner, Judith 51, 142
Rosten, Leo 64
Rotenberg, Mark 19

Roth, Cecil 3
Roth, Joel 11
Roth, Philip 51
Rothbard, Dvorah 60
Rothchild, Janice 41
Rothschild, Sylvia 51, 67
Roumani, Eve 79
Routtenberg, Max 19
Rozycka, Eugenia 69
Rubenstein, Erna F. 158
Rubenstein, Sandra 166
Rubin, Gary 115
Rubin, Jane 19
Rubin, N. 151
Rubin, Ruth 3, 167
Rubin, Sheila 115
Ruby, Walter 136
Rudolf, Anthony 73, 162
Ruether, Rosemary Radford 12, 105
Rusinek, Alla 63
Ruskay, Sophie 63
Russell, Diana E.H. 60
Russell, Letty M. 105

Sachs, Nelly 76
Sacks, Bracha 19
Safir, Marilyn 146
Saidel, Rochelle 116
Salaman, Nina 76
Salkin, Jeffrey 136
Salomon, Charlotte 158
Salomon, George 170
Sampter, Jessie E. 27, 75
Samuels, Gertrude 55
Sandberg, Martin I. 116
Sandberg, Sara 27
Santera, Victor D. 84
Sartre, Jean-Paul 89
Sasso, Sandy Eisenberg 19
Scarf, Mimi 167
Schaeffer, Susan Fromberg 51, 71, 143
Schapiro, Freyda 102
Schappes, Morris U. 27, 41, 73, 92
Scharansky, Avital 4
Schatz, Julius 171
Scheier, Paula 41
Schenker, Jonathan 64
Scheppes, David 4
Scherer, Rebecca 97
Scherer Brewer, Joan 176
Schlachter, Gail 84
Schneerson (Lubavitcher Rebbe)

Schneider, Ilene 19
Schneider, Nina 9, 143

Schneider, Susan Weidman 41, 42, 116, 125, 151
Schneiderman, Rose 27
Schneier, Sarah 7
Schnek, F. 19
Schnur, Susan 116
Schoen, Elin 42
Schreiber, Regina 136
Schuler, Else Lasker 76, 164
Schulman, Sarah 143, 176
Schulweis, H.M. 116
Schwartz, G. 28
Schwartz, Helene E. 19
Schwartz, Howard 73, 116, 162
Schwartz, M. 116
Schwartz, S.H. 116
Schwartz, Mary Cahn 7, 42
Schwarzbaum, Lisa 116
Scliar, Moacyr 176
Scott, Beverly 60
Segal, Brenda Lesley 9
Segal, Edith 76
Segal, J.B. 90
Segal, Sheila F. 42
Segal, Shulamit 151
Selavan, Ida C. 42, 95, 125
Selden, Ruth R. 20
Seligman, Ruth 151
Seller, Maxine S. 7
Senesh, Hannah 67
Servan-Schreiber, Claire 64
Setel, T. Drorah 106, 116
Shadar, R. 152
Shafransky, Renee 180
Shalom, Sabine 125
Shamir, Ruth 153
Shapiro, C. 97
Shapiro, Dee 42
Shapiro, Haim 181
Shapiro, Manheim S. 43
Shapiro, Miriam 43
Shapiro, Rhonda Rieser 99
Sharger-Handelman 176
Sharma, Arvind 176
Sharon, L. 60
Sharon, Lynn 60
Sheklow, Edna 28
Shelach, Ilana 56
Shelley, Martha 92
Shiels, Barbara 161
Shifrin, T. 152
Shimoff, Melanie B. 136
Shokeid, Moshe 91
Shoro, Rima 136
Shoub, Myra Nelson 97, 167
Shulman, Alix Kates 28, 125
Shulman, Gail B. 20

Siegal, Aranka 158, 160
Siegel, Beatrice 95
Siegel, Rachel 20
Siegel, Richard 96
Siegel-Itzkovich, Judy
Sigler, B. 60
Silberman, Charles 125
Silk, Mark 116
Silman, Roberta 90
Silver, Eve 69
Silver, Helen S. 43
Silver, George A. 43
Silver, Roslyn 43
Silver, Vivian 43, 152
Simon, Kate 125, 176
Simon, Rita J. 176
Sinclair, Jo 51, 90
Singer, Betty 43
Singer, Isaac B. 9
Singer, June Flaum 176
Singer, Sholom 20
Sklarew, Myra 43, 75, 164
Slater, Robert 55, 146
Slesinger, Tess 51
Slobin, Mark 162
Small, Rona 43
Smith, Barbara 120
Smith, Betsy Covington 20
Smith, Beverly 136
Smith, Robert Kimmel 51, 143
Smolar, Boris 43
Snitow, Virginia 44
Sochen, June 44, 125
Soferr, Barbara 60
Sokoloff, J.A. 60
Solender, Elsa 44
Solomon, Flora 126
Solomon, Hannah G. 28
Spero, Moshe Halevi 20
Spiegel, Marcia Cohn 73, 98, 117, 134, 137, 181
Spiegel, Penina 143
Spiegler, S. 117, 137, 152
Spiro, Melford E. 55, 147
Spitzer, Julie R. 106
Starkman, Elaine Marcus 77, 164
Steel, Danielle 51, 143
Stein, Leon 28, 126
Stein, Toby 143
Steinberg, Ruth 152
Steinsaltz, Adin 106
Stember, Sol Judith 143
Stern, Elizabeth G. 28
Stern, Geraldine 55
Stern, Sol 60
Stiller, Nikki 44, 60, 61
Stillman, Roberta 51

Stokes, Rose Pastor 44, 137
Stone, Ellen 137
Stone, Sylvia 126
Stone, Amy 21, 44, 61
Strassfeld, Michael 96
Strassfeld, Sharon 44, 106
Straus, Dorothea 126
Stuart, Sandra Lee 71
Suhl, Yuri 28, 67
Swerdlow, Paul 167
Swerdlow, Tess 44
Swidler, Leonard 8, 12
Swirsky, Michael 79
Symon, Pamela 152
Syrkin, Marie 28, 45, 55, 61, 69, 70, 77, 126, 1

Tabory, E. 152
Tagliacozzo, Rhoda 52
Taitz, Emily 2, 96, 97, 181
Talbot, Toby 126
Talmon, Yonina 55
Tannenbaum, Judith 77, 164
Tauber, Rhea 176
Tax, Meredith 137, 143
Tec, Nechama 158
Temerlin, Maurice 45
Tenenbaum, Sylvia 52, 90, 99
Teubal, Savina J. 106
Thistlethwaite, S. 117
Thomas, D.M. 160
Tiger, Lionel 55
Tilchen, Maida 137
Tillion, Germaine 68
Timberg, Judy 45
Tindall, Gillian 63
Tishman, Peggy 137
Toder, Nancy 126
Toll, W. 138
Tolley, Jacquelyn 106
Tonner, Leslie 28, 143
Topol, Allan 62, 154
Tornabene, Lyn 28, 45
Torres, Tereska 28
Traub, Barbara Fishman 68
Trenchard, Warren C. 106
Trible, Phyllis 21, 89, 106
Trupin, Sophie 177
Tshelebi, Evliya 147
Tucker, G. 21
Turitz, Leo E. 138
Turk, Deborah 45
Tussman, Malka Heifetz 77
Tzur, Jacob 61

Ullian, Florence 61, 152
Ullrich, Fred 126
Umansky, Ellen 21, 107, 117, 181
Untermeyer, Jean Starr 92

Van der Haag, Ernest 45
Van de Ven, Nicole 60
Varon, Miriam Laserson 71
Viertel, Joseph 62
Villenchik (Williams) Penina 117
 (aka Penina V. Adelman)
Viorst, Judith 45

Wachtel, Nili 138
Wagenknecht, Edward 126
Wald, Lillian 28
Walden, Daniel 126
Waldman, Bess 143
Wall, Susan 8
Waskow, Arthur 114
Water, Pearl 45
Waxman, Chaim 45
Weatherford, Doris 177
Webb, Liliane 100
Wechter, Vivienne Thaul 77
Weil, Greta 160
Weinberg, Sydney Stahl 138
Weiner, Greta 21, 117
Weiner, Nella Fermi 117
Weingarten, Violet 52
Weinreich, Alisa 70
Weinstein, Frida Scheps 160
Weinzweig, Helen 52, 143
Weiss, A. 117
Weissler, Chava 107
Weissman, Debbie 21, 61, 91
Weiss-Rosmarin, Trude 3, 21, 46, 118, 138
Welch, Susan 126
Wengerhoff, Pauline 98
Wenig, Maggie 16
Werner, Alfred 64
Wexler, Alice 126
Wheeler, B.C. 118
Whelton, Clark 46
White, Barbara 46
Whitman, Karen 91
Whitman, Ruth 77, 158, 164
Wiest, S. 118
Wigoder, Deborah 28
Wilentz, Gay 181
Willis, Ellen 46, 127
Wilner, Eleanor 164
Wilson, James Janet 107
Winslow, Thyra Samter 52

Wischnitzer, Mark 4
Wisse, R. 118
Wohlgelernter, Devora L. 18
Wolf, Jacqueline 118, 158
Wolf, Laura B. 167
Wolf, Thea 145
Wolfenstein, Martha 9, 46, 100
Wolff, Charlotte 159
Wolff, Lieselotte 98
Wolk, Rochelle Saidel 46
Wolpin, Nissan 21, 118
Worthen, Helen Harlow 52, 144
Wouk, Herman 52
Wyden, B. 28
Wyschogrod, Edith 22

Yaffe, Richard 22
Yanina 138
Yates, G.G. 118
Yelin, Shulamis 77
Yellen, Richard M. 22
Yezierska, Anzia 4, 29, 46, 52, 144
Yglesias, Helen 52
Yochelson, Mindy 61
Young-Bruehl, Elisabeth 127
Young, Elise 164
Young, Leila Rosen 182
Yuval, Annabelle 61
Yuval-David, Nira 152

Zakon, Miriam Stark 107
Zar, Rose 160
Zassenhaus, Hiltgunt 68
Zbrowski, Mark 4
Zdrojewicz, Malka 70
Zeitlin, Marianne L. 144
Zeldis, Chayym 73, 154
Ziemer, Susan 138
Zohar, Danah 29
Zola, G.P. 118
Zones, Jane Sprague 107
Zuckerman, Alan S. 122
Zunser, Miriam Shomer 4
Zwi, Aza 152

MAR 0 2 1990